A STONE FOR EVERY JOURNEY

A STONE FOR EVERY JOURNEY

Traveling the Life of Elinor Gregg, R.N.
by

Edwina McConnell and Teddy Jones

SUNSTONE PRESS
SANTA FE

Photographs of Elinor D. Gregg
Collection Santa Fe, NM.
Used with permission of Mrs. Nancy Meem Wirth.

Sunstone books may be purchased for educational, business, or sales promotional use. For information please write: Special Markets Department, Sunstone Press, P.O. Box 2321, Santa Fe, New Mexico 87504-2321.

Library of Congress Cataloging-in-Publication Data

McConnell, Edwina A.
A stone for every journey : traveling the life of Elinor Gregg, R.N., / by Edwina McConnell and Teddy Jones.
p. ; cm.
Includes bibliographical references.
ISBN 0-86534-444-2 (hardcover)—ISBN: 0-86534454-X (softcover)
1. Gregg, Elinor D. 2. United States. Indian Health Service. 3. Nurses—United States—Biography. 4. Indians of North America—Medical care. 5. Nursing—United States—History—20th century.
I. Jones, Teddy, 1943- II. Title.
[DNLM: 1. Gregg, Elinor D. 2. United States. Indian Health Service. 3. Nurses—United States—Biography. 4. History of Medicine, 20th Cent.—United States. 5. History of Nursing—United States. WZ 100 G819m 2004]

RT37.G74M336 2004
610.73'092—dc22
[B]

2004022920

Published in Santa Fe

WWW.SUNSTONEPRESS.COM
SUNSTONE PRESS / POST OFFICE BOX 2321 / SANTA FE, NM 87504-2321 /USA
(505) 988-4418 / *ORDERS ONLY* (800) 243-5644 / FAX (505) 988-1025

ACKNOWLEDGMENTS

"YOU CAN'T DO RESEARCH IN YOUR BASEMENT," a friend told me. This book is testament to that statement. This book is the result of, as my mother would say, "Being seen and seeing." The number of people who made this book possible is astounding. My gratitude to:

ARCHIVISTS AND LIBRARIANS:

Frances Overcash, Archivist, Children's Hospital Archives, Boston, MA; Paula Stewart, Archivist/Records Manager, Amon Carter Museum, Fort Worth, TX; Alice Ewing, Archivist, Sangre de Cristo Girl Scout Council, Las Vegas, NM; Claire Goodwin, College Archivist, Simmons College, The College Archives, Boston, MA; Barbara Dey, Reference Librarian, Colorado Historical Society, The Colorado History Museum, Denver, CO; Judy Dodge, Local History and Genealogy Department, The Berkshire Athenaeum, Pittsfield, MA; Tana Lundahl, Coordinator, Human Resources Staffing and Employee Relations, American Red Cross, National Headquarters, Falls Church, VA; Brian A. Sullivan, Reference Archivist, Harvard University Archives, Pusey Library, Cambridge, MA; Stephanie Chontos, Primary Source Network Research Specialist, Henry Ford Museum & Greenfield Village, Dearborn, MI; Reference Librarians, Microtext Department, Boston Public Library, Boston, MA; Elizabeth C. Tunis and Stephen J. Greenberg, Reference Librarians, History of Medicine Division, National Library of Medicine, Bethesda, MD; Jessica Steytler, Archivist, Congregational Library, Boston, MA; Charmayne Young, Director, Buechel

Memorial Lakota Museum, St. Francis, SD; Marcella Cash, Sicangu Heritage Center, Archivist/Director, Sinte Gleska University, Mission, SD; Deborah Greene, Archive Staff, Hampton University Archives, Hampton, VA; Donzella Maupin, Assistant to the Archivist, Hampton University Archives, Hampton, VA; Michelle Ortwein, Curator, Waltham Historical Society, Waltham, MA; Jack Eckert, Reference Librarian, Rare Books and Special Collections, Francis A. Countway Library of Medicine, Boston, MA; Janice Zwicker, Archivist & Reference Librarian, Waltham Public Library, Waltham, MA; Alex Rankin, Assistant Director for Manuscripts, Boston University, Special Collections, Boston, MA; Jean Waldman, RN, Volunteer, Historical Resources Department, American Red Cross Museum, National Headquarters, Washington, DC; Robert A. McCown, Manuscripts Librarian, The University of Iowa, The University Libraries, Special Collections, Iowa City, IA; Alfreda L. Irwin, Historian, Chautauqua Institution, Chautauqua, NY; Robert Koehler, Chief Librarian, Meriter Hospital, Madison, WI; Valerie Porter-Hanson, Research Room Administrator, South Dakota State Historical Society, State Archives, Pierre, SD; R.W.A. Suddaby, Keeper of the Department of Documents, Imperial War Museum, London, England; Dianne O'Malia, Archivist, The MetroHealth System Archives, Cleveland, OH; Mary Davis, Pikes Peak Library District, Penrose Library Complex, Colorado Springs, CO; Ginny Kiefer, Curator of Special Collections/Archivist, Tutt Library, Colorado College, Colorado Springs, CO; Leah Davis Witherow, Archivist, Colorado Springs Pioneers Museum, Colorado Springs, CO; Deborah Martin, District Registrar, Student Records, Colorado Springs School District Number Eleven, Planning, Research and Evaluation, Colorado Springs, CO; Kathleen Ferris, Head Archivist, University of New Mexico, Zimmerman Library, Center for Southwest Research, Albuquerque, NM; Research Staff, State Historical Society of Wisconsin, Madison, WI; Staff, National Archives I, Washington, D.C.; Staff, National Archives II, College Park, MD; Marilyn R. Finke, Reference/Preservation Staff, National Archives-Central Plains Region, Kansas City, MO; Staff, Gorham Public Library, Gorham, ME; Frear Simons, Grace Episcopal Church, Colorado Springs, CO.

PROFESSIONAL INDIVIDUALS

Violet Catches, Pierre, SD; Martina Ladeaux, Rosebud, SD; Webster Two Hawk, Tribal Government Relations Office, Pierre, SD; Kathy Fleury, Tribal Government Relations Office, Pierre, SD; Christina M. Graf, Newton, MA; Harry S. McClarran, Wooster, OH; Kathryn H. Kavanagh, Bel Air, MD; Lettie Gavin, Seattle, WA; Rob Gregg, Medfield, MA; Herbert Hoover, PhD, Beresford, SD; Lenore Poulson, Colorado Springs, CO; William D. Clyde, Jr., San Antonio, TX; Joan E. Lynaugh, PhD, FAAN; Ray Pulsifer, Limington, ME; Wendell Oderkirk, RN, PhD, Las Cruces, NM.

PERSONAL INDIVIDUALS:

Sherry Brenner, Christine Ludwig, Hedi Weiler, Yvonne Munn, Mary Sue Kern, Colleen Gullickson, Ellen K. Murphy, Robert Koehler, Sharon Snyder, Louise Juliani, Patricia Downing, Judith Manning, Jill Hilbig, Veronica Broughton, Sybil McCulloch, Juliet Horrocks, Robert Horowitz, Jerry Eggen, Cathy R. Woodburne, Teddy Jones, Paul Fetherstone and Sandy, William and Marta Barkell, Joyce Perkins.

—E.A.M.

Because I became a part of this book's development after the major research was complete, I did not meet most of the people mentioned by Edwina in the acknowledgment file that I found in her computer (printed above). Perhaps she was not finished with that list. I know she wanted also to acknowledge the help of each person listed under Interviews in the Resource Section. Their contribution was important. I regret any omissions and I echo her thanks to all mentioned above. Thanks go also to those who read various draft versions of the manuscript and provided valuable criticism to me—Doctor Luther Christman, Karen Dadich, Rob Gregg, Barbara Meem, Ellen Murphy, Yvonne Munn, Darlene Norton, Brenda Patterson, Bobby Stone, Victoria Thompson, Nancy Meem Wirth and Richard Wood. And thanks to you too, Mr. Jones.

—T. L. J.

Copyright by Laura Gilpin, 1979 Amon Carter Museum, Fort Worth, Texas, #P 1979.230.1064, Bequest of the artist.

INTRODUCTION

Elinor Gregg, R.N. became the first Supervisor of Nurses for the Indian Service in 1924. She held a pioneering position in a vast agency that affected the lives of Native Americans all across the United States. She had no predecessor. In the fourteen years of her tenure in that position she was instrumental in the development of both the health service and the nurses within it. Surely that accomplishment would have earned her a place in the history of American Nursing. Yet, when undergraduate nursing student Edwina McConnell was introduced to Gregg through her papers in the Nursing Archive at Boston University, she realized that Miss Gregg's story was not widely known among nurses. Throughout her career as a nurse from the late 1960s until her death in 2002, Dr. McConnell remained interested in Elinor Gregg. In the 1990s she focused that interest and began to collect extensive additional data, intending to write Gregg's biography.

As she gathered stories and documents about "Aunt El's" life, she came to know her as a person, to the extent it is possible to know a person without ever meeting her. The information she collected convinced her that the importance of Elinor Gregg's story was not to be found simply in an analysis of her professional career, but in her life and how she lived it.

A promise I made to Edwina that I would complete her work if something prevented her from doing so resulted in my receiving after her death a vast amount of research material, most of ten chapters written as if they were a memoir by Elinor Gregg, and no outline. After several months' immersion in the data, I could only agree that Miss Gregg's importance was broader than her professional accomplishments. It was in her way of being—a person whose greatest accomplishments were in her effects on others.

Elinor Gregg's relationship with Melody and Alice, the University of New Mexico nursing students she meets in 1966, is fiction. It was created to demonstrate the ways this wise, caring woman affected those she knew. The reminiscences she shares with them are drawn from the primary and secondary research materials. Those memories describe the rich, full life of an independent woman; a nurse whose experiences take her from Boston through the Great War, from the Rosebud Reservation in South Dakota to the farthest reaches of Alaska; a family stalwart; a community volunteer; and a mentor and friend to many. Much of her conversation in the book is in her own words, taken from letters to family and friends.

The first ten reminiscence chapters were written almost entirely by Edwina McConnell. I believe that she would be pleased that "Aunt El" affected two additional lives through this story as it is now told. Melody and Alice were certainly better for having had the experience. And I hope that this story will entertain and interest each reader and perhaps provide a bit of guidance in the process.

—Teddy Jones
August 2004

I SAID I WOULD GO

WHEN I SAID I WOULD GO, THE DIE WAS CAST, and I've never been sorry. I wired them on October 19, 1922, that I would go, and I left Boston on the 26th in my open Ford runabout. Today, November 15th, I'm at the Winner Hotel, Winner, South Dakota. I've just finished my breakfast and am waiting for the stage to Rosebud.

We struck wet weather in Saint Paul and it got wetter and wetter until we were going through such fierce mud the last 40 miles that I put up the car at Bridgewater, South Dakota and came the remaining 200 miles by train and stage. It cost quite a lot but has been worth it in seeing the country and riding with the natives.

This is the life! The prairies are lovely white with a thin layer of snow and yellow grass sticking up through. The hay is piled up and shivering cows and horses are grazing or have rubbed the snow off the hay and are clustered on the lee side of the pile. Wisps of white clouds float high in the blue sky and I can see the whole big bowl of it instead of just a strip. The buttes and the sky blend in the distance. I'm not quite sure whether I'm looking at clouds or mountains. I like the looks of this country so well that I think I'll take up a homestead claim and live out here three years. I haven't seen the Indians yet, just a few of their shacks and tents when we were driving in.

My companion last night in Winner was a woman who cooked in White River, South Dakota for six years while she was proving her homestead claim. Of French or rather Luxemburg parentage, Miss Didier speaks French, German, English, and some Indian. She weighs 279 pounds and knows everybody she sees on the road. She lives with her "maw" down in Nebraska.

When we got into this hotel the desk clerk asked us whether we would like a room with a double bed or two three-quarter beds. I voted 3/4 so fast that Miss Didier never got a chance to express an opinion. I know I'm heavy myself but I couldn't see the poetry (as Alan calls it) of having a 279 pound stranger in my bunk. I perhaps should explain that the clerk said he hadn't enough rooms for us each to have one.

The land I see from the stage en route from Winner to Rosebud is fenced, mostly by being planted with kafir and corn, and windbreak trees around the houses and barns. It looks like a typical "hard scrabble" economy laid out north and south and east and west, in checkerboard parallel dirt roads. The main traveled roads are graveled and scraped. Although more wind-swept and with longer treks between gas stations, the country reminds me of the Colorado of my childhood.

My first view of Rosebud is from the top of the hill where the Sioux chief, Sinte Gleska (Spotted Tail) is buried. A neat, simple layout of red brick and white frame buildings with outlying corrals and log huts sits in a sheltered natural bowl. The low hills surrounding The Agency or reservation headquarters fold gently into one another, eventually rising and giving way to rolling plains. Delicate wild pink roses will carpet these hills in June. Eight inches of snow fell yesterday. So today they're a study in white, dotted with evergreen yuccas whose brown flower stalks mark their position.

It's nearly eleven a.m. when the stage pulls up at the hotel, a big, two story white clapboard square with a wide wrap-around front porch and a lean-to addition. My first order of business is to find Agency

Superintendent James H. McGregor. A desk clerk directs me to The Office, a two story, red brick veneer building that, like the hotel, helps form the quadrangle.

Turning left in front of the hotel, I walk along the shoveled cement sidewalk to the far end of the rectangular snow-covered lawn with its flagpole and irrigation ditches. Someone has expended considerable effort for summer greenery and shade trees. In less than five minutes I'm standing in front of The Office. A square narrow tower protrudes from the left side of the building. The cupola on top of this wing houses a bell. Like my own recent journey, the cupola's weather vane points steadily westward. For a moment I wonder what I've gotten myself into. But it doesn't matter. I'm here.

Taking a deep breath, I step up onto the porch. I open the front door onto a narrow hallway lined with benches filled with Indians. The men are dressed in blue denim jeans, shirts, jackets, boots, and broad-brimmed, high-crowned felt hats. The women wear Mother Hubbard dresses and are wrapped in heavy shawls.

Like a jam-packed physician's office, the hallway holds humanity in all stages—toddlers, school age children, parents, grandparents, young men and women, old men and women—not talking much. Many of the old men are smoking carved pipes decorated with feathers. The smoke smells not quite like tobacco. The aromatic fragrance of dried red willow mixed with Bull Durham nearly covers up all other odors, including skunk, which the old timers are not above eating.

I carefully navigate around several cuspidors as I edge my way to Superintendent McGregor's office. He's expecting me today. I telephoned yesterday from Winner, not knowing that in South Dakota Indian country promptness doesn't have the sacred value that it has in Massachusetts.

As soon as Superintendent McGregor sees me he smiles. He pushes back from his paper-strewn desk and walks over to greet me. "I've been looking forward to meeting you," he says warmly. "I hope the trip from Bridgewater wasn't too tiring. Please, sit down."

No sooner do we exchange pleasantries than the noon dinner bell sounds. On our way back to the hotel where I'll be eating my meals, Mr.

McGregor explains that the Rosebud Reservation was created 33 years ago in 1889. But the Rosebud Agency was established 44 years ago in 1878 for the Brulé Sioux under Chief Spotted Tail. The US Army was responsible for administering the agency. The stockade that surrounded the agency in 1878 is now gone.

Communities or districts sprouted up all over the reservation. Without formal boundaries, they were named for tribal leaders such as Two Strike and He Dog, or for physical features such as Little White River and Oak Creek. Eventually these districts became the sites of issue stations, "boss" or district farmers' residences, schools, and field matrons' stations.

As we climb the hotel steps, Mr. McGregor tells an Indian man to take my bags to my room in the employee's quarters. Opening the front door of the hotel, we step into the reception area, which gives way to a corridor. We pass a line of black coat hooks sticking out from the wall and squeeze by a narrow table with a kitchen chair at each end. We come first to a small parlor furnished with rocking chairs and a pump organ, and then finally to the dining room.

Almost immediately Mrs. Brown, the hotel manager, emerges from the lean-to kitchen, wiping her flushed, sweaty face with her apron. "This is Miss Elinor Gregg, the nurse the Red Cross has sent us," Mr. McGregor explains.

"I'm very pleased to meet you, Nurse Gregg. Will you be having lunch?" asks Mrs. Brown. Twenty-eight cents, I learn, will also be the price of each meal ticket.

When Mr. McGregor spies Mrs. Cross, a clerk who does stenographic work for him, he asks her to show me over to my room in employee's quarters after I eat. Turning to me he says, "I'm going home to dinner. When you get settled, come back to the office. I'll introduce you to the office force and then we'll talk."

Now I'm on my own. Mrs. Brown leads me past occupied tables for two, four, and eight, to an empty table for four. She then hurries back to the kitchen. Sitting in elegant solitude, I notice the iron pipes holding up the crossbeams of the ceiling. Two men come late for dinner. One is Mrs. Cross's husband.

The diners look me over furtively. None of them speaks, not even Mrs. Cross, and I must admit, neither do I. I do smile at them though when I can catch their eye.

I wonder what I look like to them. I'm 36 years old and 5 feet 7 1/ 2 inches, with blue eyes (sparkling I'm told) and a florid complexion. My reddish hair is parted in the middle and pulled loosely back away from my face. In my gray chambray overseas Red Cross uniform, I feel like neither fish nor fowl. I certainly don't feel Bostonian, and I don't think that I talk like a New Englander. I don't know why I think my dining room companions would think this, especially since none of us is saying anything, but I do.

About one thing I'm certain. Many of the diners know why I'm here and some know who I am. President Harding appointed Charles H. Burke Commissioner of Indian Affairs in March 1921. When he visited the reservation approximately a month ago, he spoke about a variety of issues, including health care. He told the Rosebud Indians that he hoped to see a good hospital on every reservation, and enough physicians and nurses to take care of all the sick. He would also like to replace the field matrons with trained nurses. Then he explained about the survey and demonstration work that three graduate nurses on loan from the American Red Cross would be doing. He told the gathering that one of the nurses would be assigned here.

Even if no one heard Commissioner Burke, my coming would not have been a surprise. A letter from him to Superintendent McGregor in late October announced my arrival, and news travels fast among agency personnel.

Pa Brown soon serves my dinner of gray boiled beef and yellow cabbage. While eating, I decide that tomorrow I'll try to get acquainted with the other diners. For breakfast I'll choose the big table and then can venture to say, "May I trouble you to pass the butter?"

After I finish my coffee and crumb pie, a sort of custard fortified with bread crumbs, I wait in the entry hall for Mrs. Cross. She introduces me to her husband; he's a financial clerk at The Agency. They live in three rooms on the ground floor of the red brick employee's quarters near The Office. Walking up the stairs to my room, Mrs. Cross tells me that no one else is on this floor, so I'll have the standard bathroom all to myself.

I don't know what I'm expecting when I open the door to my room, but it isn't black and tan striped wallpaper with very large pink roses! In only a few minutes I find all kinds of faces in these flowers. As soon as the wallpaper recedes from my vision, I see a fair-sized room with two windows, one facing east, one facing south, and a round black stove. A double bed, a rocking chair, and a kitchen table with two straight-backed chairs are more than adequate. I doubt that I'll be spending much time in my room anyway. The wall calendar has only a semblance of a picture, which given the design of the wallpaper is enough.

I unpack my toothbrush and night things and then turn my attention to the bedding. All seven blankets are olive drab army surplus and heavy as lead. At least I can look forward to my own bedding, if and when my trunk arrives, and in the meantime I won't be cold. I check the wood and coal box and stoke the soft coal stove before I leave.

Several Indians are standing outside The Office. I smile and say "Hello" as I pass. Walking into the narrow crowded hallway for the second time today, I now see that The Office has no reception room. Indians waiting for attention sit on the benches in the hallway. When the hallway becomes too crowded, the Indians move outside. They must get very cold this time of year.

Superintendent McGregor wants me to meet the agency staff—15 clerks, a telephone operator, a farmer, a lawyer—and more. We begin with Chief Clerk F.A. Coe. Superintendent McGregor's second in command is responsible for the general administration of the reservation, including maintenance of the physical plant. As the Special Disbursing Agent, he makes all the payments associated with running the reservation as well as those from individual Indian accounts. He supervises the interpreters, the Indian police, and the general clerical and accounting forces. Not surprisingly, this thin, little gray man looks worried.

To one and all Mr. McGregor proudly introduces the public health nurse on loan from the American Red Cross. "She'll be here and at Pine Ridge a year," he says. "As part of her work she'll probably visit each Indian home under my jurisdiction, providing care in many cases. Her nursing assistance will directly benefit the agency's health program. And, the results of her work may help convince Congress of the need for expert health workers among the Indians."

Each employee smiles when we're introduced and they're all politely interested in my work. I smile, too, and tell them I look forward to getting acquainted.

Mr. McGregor wants me to meet one other person. We walk to the opposite end of the quadrangle, cross the road to the left of the general store, and go around the corner. Standing in front of the garage, wiping his greasy hands on a rag, is George Andrus. "This man can fix anything," says Mr. McGregor. "He's an expert mechanic. He does all the intricate mechanical work and car repairing at the agency. He keeps our cars going despite their age and our limited funds."

"How was your trip?" George asks, his eyes twinkling. "I hear you had to leave your car in Bridgewater because of the mud."

"You heard right, George. I did. I hadn't seen mud like that for quite a while. But up until then the roads had been pretty good and I didn't have any car trouble. It rained a few days, but most of the time it was warm and sunny."

George is too polite to ask, but is wondering, I'm sure, if I made the trip alone. I don't mention that Richard and I traveled together from Chicago to Sioux Falls. He didn't drive, but I surely appreciated his company. As I watched him board the train for Chicago, I felt both sad and excited. I'd miss him and his companionship, but I was eager to be on my own in Indian country.

Sensing that I've finished, Mr. McGregor pushes his glasses up on his nose. "Take good care of her, George." He says he will and I believe him.

During the short walk back to The Office, Mr. McGregor points out the Indian Day School and the county public school. "Between fourteen and twenty pupils go to each of these schools," he explains.

With introductions over, at least for now, Superintendent McGregor assures me of all possible assistance in carrying out my work. "I'll give you the medical supplies and surgical dressings you need," he says, "and I'll also provide you with stenographic services. Commissioner Burke has authorized me to provide gasoline and oil for your car free of charge from the Government supply. George Andrus will make minor repairs."

I'll make reports to Superintendent McGregor and also send two copies of my monthly reports, both narrative and statistical, directly to Elizabeth G. Fox in Washington, D.C. She'll forward a copy to the Commissioner of Indian Affairs. Miss Fox, National Director of the Public Health Nursing Service at the American National Red Cross, and Commissioner Burke cooperated closely to arrange this project.

Comfortably seated in his office, Superintendent McGregor asks me about my plan of work. "Getting to know Rosebud is my first priority," I explain.

I know that the health of Indians on reservations has long been a problem. Tuberculosis and trachoma, a contagious eye disease, are most prevalent. Unsanitary living conditions contribute to both. Lack of funding restricts medical care largely to hospitals. Preventive work is practically nonexistent. I've heard all of this, but I want to observe the conditions at Rosebud firsthand. I'll learn about the people, their way of life, and their health problems by inspecting the day and boarding schools, getting to know the field matrons and their work, meeting more of the agency personnel, touring the agency hospital, conferring with the physician, and visiting the Indians in their homes.

Mr. McGregor thinks my plan sound. In keeping with it, he invites me to a conference on Friday with the various district farmers and field matrons. No sooner do I accept this invitation than he asks me to spend a week with him in his office as he takes care of agency business. "We'll have a chance to get better acquainted and you'll learn how the work at the agency is conducted," he says. I'm pleased that Mr. McGregor suggests this because I've done no reading about the Indian Service. I want to form my own opinions.

A bald man limping into the office follows a knock at the door. My guess is that the limp is the result of a repaired clubfoot. Superintendent McGregor introduces William R. Eddleman. He doesn't seem very cordial as he joins us.

Superintendent McGregor explains that as the agency physician, Doctor Eddleman has charge of all activities relating to health and sanitation, including the work of the field matrons. In addition to being in charge of the agency hospital, he looks after the general health of the Indians on the reservation. He visits the boarding schools and the day schools and makes sure that the children are inoculated against smallpox and other contagious diseases. He reports directly to the agency superintendent.

Doctor Eddleman apologizes as he stifles a yawn. "It's been a long day already," he says. "After seeing patients at the agency hospital early this morning, I drove fifteen miles to the Boarding School in Mission, came back to Rosebud, drove thirty miles to Black Pipe, and then came here."

"Is this a typical day?" I ask.

"More or less."

"Do you ever meet yourself coming and going?"

"Sometimes."

Superintendent McGregor smiles and tells me that for the past six years Doctor Eddleman's been doing the work of two doctors. Realizing that I don't know about medical care for the Indians, Superintendent McGregor explains. The reservation has positions for two full-time physicians, a hospital service physician and a home or field service physician. The field service position's been vacant for six years. So Doctor Eddleman's been providing both hospital and home care for nearly 6,000 Sioux. Assistant doctors come and go. One left six weeks ago, and his replacement won't be here for at least another three weeks.

A contract physician in Hamill, 90 miles northeast of The Agency, makes calls at the extreme eastern end of the reservation. This physician, who's in private practice, has an agreement with the Indian Service. He'll make a specific number of professional visits to the Indians and will also perform other medical services for them.

As I listen to Superintendent McGregor describe my proposed plan of work, I'm sure that Doctor Eddleman is wondering what I'll be able to do to improve the health of the Indians. Because I'm a Red Cross nurse on loan to the Indian Service, and not a nurse of the Indian Service, Doctor Eddleman is not responsible for the success of my work. Nevertheless, he begins to warm. We discuss my need for standing orders that will let me care for patients with certain medical conditions without contacting him.

"If you're going to be making home visits, I think you'd better fill your public health nursing bag with an ample supply of aspirin for rheumatism and headache; sulphur ointment for scabies and other skin diseases; Argyol (mild silver protein) for inflamed eyes; and oil of wintergreen for rheumatism. You'd also better carry green soap and corrosive sublimate, a disinfectant; wild cherry cough syrup; and Epsom salts, a laxative." I write the orders and he signs them.

Doctor Eddleman is eager to have me visit the agency hospital and suggests that we go now. But it's late, and I prefer going tomorrow morning. He acquiesces, but seems none too pleased.

Soon the five o'clock bell rings and everyone in The Office files out, including Superintendent McGregor and myself. The typical working hours are eight a.m. until five p.m., six days a week, with an hour off between 12 and 1 for dinner. Mr. McGregor has invited me to meet his family before I go to the hotel for supper. The superintendent's red brick home with its white post and cross-rail fence helps form the quadrangle. The wing on the left front corner of the house balances the tower rooms on the right front corner. A porch shelters the front door and the three large windows of the downstairs tower room.

Mr. McGregor introduces me to his wife Nella and their children, John, Jean, and Virginia. The children's eagerness and conversation, combined with their mother's warm greeting, make me feel welcome immediately. In contrast to Mr. Mac, who is short and rotund, Nella is thin and wiry. Now devoted to her home and family, she taught school for three years in the Philippines shortly after they were married. Mr. McGregor visited the schools in a supervisory capacity.

In 1898 when the United States declared war with Spain, Mr. McGregor withdrew from the teacher's college he was attending in Indiana to enlist with the American forces. He served throughout the war and then worked at the Congressional Library in Washington, D.C. before he and Nella went to the Philippines. When they returned, he transferred to the Indian Service.

I look forward to getting to know the McGregors, but keep my visit brief because their supper is on the stove. Mine of homemade bread, beans, squash, raisin pie, fresh milk, and coffee waits at the hotel. But if I want my room to be warm, I'll have to stoke the stove before I eat.

It's dark when I leave the hotel. I stop on the way to my room to watch the stars twinkling in a cloudless sapphire sky that seems never ending. I'm glad to be here and working again.

Usually I'm a night owl, but not tonight. The Agency has electricity only until ten-thirty p.m. and I have neither candles nor lamp. Oh well, an early night is probably good. Today's been busy and all learning. Somehow I'm sure this will be the rule, not the exception.

THE CLOSER WE GET, THE MORE IMPOSING IT becomes. The large rectangle perched on a black hillside transforms into a two-story, red brick building. Wings project from the back and each side. At the front stands a row of columns. These and the triangular area above them remind me of a Greek revival style house.

A longish flight of stairs brings us to a landing. We catch our breath before starting up a second shorter flight to the double size front door. Turning around and looking southwest we see agency headquarters a mile away.

While we're enjoying the crisp early morning air and looking at a distant cottonwood-lined ravine, Doctor Eddleman tells me that the agency hospital was completed eight and a half years ago in 1914. Reputed to be one of the finest in the Indian Service, the hospital was closed for nearly a year in 1919. That November the soft coal, which comes by wagon freighter from the railroad in Crookston, Nebraska, didn't arrive, and the thermometer in the hospital's main hall stood at zero. Because the water wasn't shut off, the pipes froze. The plumbing and the building were so badly damaged that it was mid-August of the next year before the repair was completed and the building was reopened. As if reading my mind, Doctor Eddleman reassures me that quite a few freighters made the 25-mile trip from Crookston last week with coal for the agency. I feel warmer—and curious.

"Why didn't the coal arrive that year?" I ask.

"The contract for the coal is made at the Purchase Division in Washington, D.C., not at the agency," Doctor Eddleman explains. "The Division didn't forward the contract promptly, so the coal wasn't delivered."

Responding to the puzzled look on my face, he continues. "The Purchase Division buys and transports the supplies that the Indian Service needs. Its activities cover life from cradle to grave. So you can imagine the quantities and varieties of items required. Every year field officers like Superintendent McGregor estimate the supplies they'll need for the coming year. They send these estimates to the Purchase Division. It revises them, obtains bids, and awards the contracts. The contractors ship nearly all supplies to central warehouses in Chicago, St. Louis, and San Francisco. The supplies are inspected and then distributed in small lots to the agencies and the schools. Bulk shipments, such as coal, are an exception. They're sent to the agencies directly."

Thanking Doctor Eddleman for my lesson in supply procurement at the Office of Indian Affairs, I wonder if the people in the Purchase Division have ever been cold. This system of getting supplies seems very cumbersome. I hope I don't need anything in a hurry.

Turning our backs on the view, we're soon standing in the hospital's main hall. Just a few more steps take us to the two patient wards on this floor. Doctor Eddleman introduces me to the head nurse, a practical or undergraduate nurse with six months training. She works only in the hospital and gets considerable professional support from her husband, Doctor Eddleman. I accompany him as he examines the patients. Three have fractures, five are recovering from accidents, four have wounds that required minor surgery, and three have had babies. Another two, who are old and have no one to care for them, are here for shelter and food. They and other ambulatory patients eat with the employees in the dining room.

Doctor Eddleman's bedside manner impresses me. He smiles and speaks quietly and respectfully. Sometimes he puts his hand on a patient's shoulder. That the patients like him is obvious.

The obstetric care at the hospital is good and more Indians are coming here to give birth. At home a new mother and her baby might be parked in a tent behind the log hut for a month with only a pallet, regardless of the season. This custom must make two weeks of socialization, rest, and plenty of food in a warm hospital very appealing.

My tour of the first floor continues with a visit to the operating room. It's equipped with one operating room table; the usual surgical instruments; a temperamental, ineffective autoclave for sterilizing the instruments and dressings; and a recently purchased Sorenson suction apparatus. "With that suction device I can now perform tonsil and adenoid operations here," Doctor Eddleman enthusiastically tells me. "That should result in a large saving. The Indians won't have to travel long distances to larger places at great expense for these procedures." Since the apparatus arrived about ten days ago, Doctor Eddleman and his staff have performed tonsillectomies on seven children. Last week's patients were Hilda Ironwing, Cornelia Stead, Levi Bordeaux, and John Jordan. All went home the day after surgery. None had any ill effects.

Unlike the suction apparatus, the other service equipment is a handicap. Laboratory instruments are practically non-existent. There is no X-ray machine and no laundry equipment. Two hospital personnel usually take the wash the 15 miles to the boarding school every Saturday. When the hospital is full, they go almost daily. They use the school laundry from four p.m. until nine p.m. and then drive back. Electricity at the hospital is available from The Agency until ten-thirty p.m. only. After that, the staff must use kerosene lamps for light.

Thanks to the housekeeper the hospital is relatively clean. The upkeep of the property, however, is poor. There are three bath and toilet rooms on the first floor, but the slop-hoppers haven't worked for a year. You have to flush with a pail of water every time you empty anything into them. The Indian laborer at the hospital fires the furnace, keeps the grounds in order, milks the cows that belong to the hospital, and pumps water into the storage tanks. Unfortunately, neither he nor the general mechanic at the agency is a plumber.

Although the hospital's capacity is 30 patients, it can accommodate only 17. The two large wards upstairs can't be used. Intended for tubercular patients, these unheated wards have many windows. Most are cracked, so the rain beats in and the snow sifts through. I'm surprised not to see drifts on the floor from the season's first snowstorm earlier in the week.

Plans are afoot to heat these two wards. Superintendent McGregor is going to have the flue made about six feet higher. The resulting draft will increase the efficiency of the heating plant considerably, and covering the boiler with asbestos will save heat. Mr. McGregor is also taking steps to have radiators installed in the wards. These changes should increase the hospital's maximum capacity during the winter. How the meager staff will be able to care for more patients I don't know. They have all they can handle now. If the number of patients didn't decrease some weeks, I doubt that the staff could get the work done as well as they do.

Mrs. Eddleman has two young Indian assistants, who are hands and feet, but no head, under her tutelage. These three women do the nursing, day and night, give out medications in the dispensary, and do what they can when the doctor is out on a call. They also make all the hospital linen, all the sterile goods, and all the patients' clothes. I'm exhausted just thinking about all that they do, and for such munificent sums. Mrs. Eddleman earns $740 a year, the attendants $300 each, plus their board, and the cook about $500. Doctor Eddleman's annual salary is $1,400 a year, plus living quarters, heat, and electricity.

Thinking about what I've just heard, I wonder. "Since the two wards upstairs aren't used for tubercular patients, where do they get care?" I ask Doctor Eddleman.

"The policy of the Office of Indian Affairs is to leave adults with active tuberculosis in their homes and to send school-age children with active disease to sanatorium schools," he explains. "But we have no means here of caring for Indians with tuberculosis. Dealing with the disease is nearly impossible."

"Only last week," he says, "I was called out to see an Indian woman. She had a lung hemorrhage because of tuberculosis. There was nothing I could do for her." Almost as if talking to himself he muses, "I seem to make many long drives to see hopeless tubercular cases." The discouragement in his voice makes me wonder what I'll be able to accomplish.

"The Indians don't understand the need for isolation and their unsanitary home conditions spread the disease," Doctor Eddleman explains. "I've talked with Superintendent McGregor about the problem. Tomorrow we're going to meet with the field matrons about improving conditions in the homes. I don't know if it will make any difference, but at least we can try."

As we walk in silence to Doctor Eddleman's government Ford, my mind reels with all that I've seen and heard this morning. I'd like to know what Doctor Eddleman thinks about the field matrons, those white female field workers hired as advisors to the Indian women, particularly since he has charge of their work. I have no idea how much he'll be willing to divulge. After all, I'm an unknown quantity, an outsider from the Red Cross. The privacy of the car seems an ideal place to broach the topic, so I plunge in. "What do you think about the work the field matrons do?" I ask.

After a few moments, Doctor Eddleman replies thoughtfully. "The field matrons are well-intentioned. They try to teach the Indian women about housekeeping and other household duties. But field matrons are not graduate nurses. They're simply not trained to do the kind of health work we need in the field." As he talks, I suddenly realize I'm the only graduate nurse for nearly 6,000 Sioux.

Doctor Eddleman stops the car in front of the general store at the agency. I thank him for the tour and for the information he's given me. Assuring me that he'll be at tomorrow's conference, he discloses that he's looking forward to it. "It's the first one we've had." Watching him drive toward St. Francis, I wonder, what prompted the conference and who is "we"?

Since I'm a bit early for dinner, I'll buy candles and a kerosene lamp. At least I'll have light tonight if the electricity fails. It frequently does, I'm told. The general store with its well-worn wood floor, pressed tin ceiling, and glass-fronted display cases carries almost everything imaginable—dry goods, tools, fascinating gadgets, and food. Fresh fruit, including apples and oranges, is available in winter. Unfortunately, a head of lettuce is more than 40 miles away.

Crossing the quadrangle on my way to the hotel, I meet H.P. Davis. The farmer for the agency district is nice-looking in an outdoor way. He seems shy. Yet only a week or so ago, this young man and Stock Detective Frank C. Rogers raided a home in Carter, about 45 miles northwest of Rosebud. They made quite a haul— three jugs, three half gallons, and several small bottles of very fine moonshine. The still was one of the most up-to-date Detective Rogers had ever found, but the telltale mash was missing.

Unlike yesterday, I do not sit in elegant solitude at dinner. Mr. and Mrs. Cross invite me to join them. I smile at the few diners I've met and the Crosses introduce me to several others. We're nearly ready for dessert when greetings of "Hello, Harry!" announce the very late arrival of Harry Presho. He's been the mailman only a few months. As soon as he won the contract in June for carrying the mail from Crookston, Nebraska, to Mission, South Dakota, he bought a new International Speed Wagon so that he could transport passengers, as well as mail. He delivers the agency mail to the general store about half-past noon every day except Sunday. Maybe next week I'll have a letter from Marjorie or Mother.

By one o'clock I'm ready to spend the afternoon with Superintendent McGregor learning how the agency runs. I've stoked the stove in my room and taken care of the essentials. Yesterday I learned that The Office has no toilets. In fact, the only proper toilet facilities anywhere around the agency are in private homes. The edict of mothers from time immemorial rings in my ears. "Go before you leave home or you'll regret it."

Before delving into the afternoon's work, Superintendent McGregor asks me if I'm getting settled in. "Yes, thank you," I reply. "My room's very comfortable. I spent this morning with Doctor Eddleman at the hospital.

He showed me the new suction apparatus and explained the plans for heating the second floor." (I don't mention the faces in the wallpaper roses.)

Superintendent McGregor reveals that Commissioner Burke prompted these changes. Examination of reports on file in the Indian Office convinced him that Rosebud Hospital should be more useful. Desirably located, it could serve a large territory. Yet the number of patients was sometimes too low for its economic operation. With the hospital's full corps of employees, overhead expenses were nearly the same for a few patients as for a hospital filled to capacity. So the Commissioner asked Superintendent McGregor to increase the hospital's patronage.

Commissioner Burke also intends to correct conditions that detract from the popularity of the hospital. He plans to hire experienced personnel as soon as possible, preferably those without small children who must be quartered there. The world war ravaged the Indian Service's field force; nearly half of the physicians and nurses transferred to war work. The temporary employees hired to fill the vacancies had no medical experience. Not surprisingly, the quality of care declined and the patients became dissatisfied. This is one reason the Indians prefer treatment in "outside" or non-agency hospitals.

"About the conference tomorrow," says Mr. McGregor adjusting his glasses. "I asked the district farmers and field matrons to come to the agency because I want to hear more about conditions in the field. And I know that the field workers have concerns. I asked them to bring notes of questions that puzzle them so that we can discuss them and reach a common understanding."

I'm pleased to have the opportunity to meet the field workers, especially the field matrons. Their work is the closest thing to public health nursing on the reservation, and I want to know what they do. I plan to spend time with each of them in their districts. This conference will give me a chance to get to know a bit about them. How pleased they'll be to meet me is questionable. It's no secret Commissioner Burke would like to replace field matrons with trained nurses. The field matrons, I'm sure, see me as promoting this change and ultimately eliminating their positions. I doubt that I'll be very popular with them.

"The field workers know that you'll be at the conference," says Superintendent McGregor. "And I've already told the field matrons to cooperate with you in your work."

I'm grateful for Superintendent McGregor's support and tell him so. He hands me a circular. It's called "Qualifications, Responsibilities and Duties of Field Matrons." Smiling, he says, "I thought you might like a copy of the field matron's official guide and manual." While I'm looking at the first page, he hands me a sheaf of paper. "I thought you'd want the monthly reports of the field matrons. So I took the liberty of getting last year's reports for you." As I watch my stack of reading material grow I know that I'm going to need those candles and lamp.

In preparation for tomorrow's conference, I'd like to know what the district farmers do. Before I can ask, Superintendent McGregor explains. "A district or boss farmer is an agricultural instructor. He's supposed to teach the Indians in his district how to farm and how to raise livestock. He's to give them advice about buying cattle, seeds, and farming equipment, and about planting crops and taking care of animals. He's also supposed to visit the Indians on their farms. But things here at Rosebud are different."

"How are they different?" I ask.

"Most of the land is allotted and the reservation area is extensive," he continues. "A district farmer here is more like a subagent or a field agent. He lives in his district and looks after the Indians who live there. To them he's their personal agency representative because the agency is anywhere from twelve to ninety miles away."

Being on unfamiliar territory, I ask, "On what type of matters would the district farmer represent the agency?"

"Mostly land issues. White ranchers and farmers lease a great deal of land from the Indians. The district farmer makes the leases, collects the rentals, settles disputes, and surveys allotments. The land lease and land purchase business keeps him so busy that he has little time to teach the Indians how to cultivate their idle acres."

Suddenly Chief Clerk Coe is standing in the doorway. He needs to speak with Superintendent McGregor and has some forms that need his attention. Several Indians have requested purchase orders for groceries.

As agency superintendent, Mr. McGregor must review and pass on all requests for purchase orders, whether for groceries, clothing, chickens, building materials, or milk cows. I'm sure I'll need to know more about purchase orders. For the moment, however, I'm content to know that I need to know more.

As Mr. Coe leaves, I see many Indians waiting in the hallway to meet with Superintendent McGregor. "They're here to talk about their pensions," he tells me. "Some are here at my request; others have come on their own."

One Indian wants to file a pension claim and several want information about pending claims. These Indians enlisted in the United States military service and served as scouts in Indian wars. A Congressional act of March 1917 provides for pensioning them. Mr. McGregor, as the agency superintendent, helps them prepare their claims and corresponds with the Indian Office about them. I can only imagine the amount of correspondence involved.

Today Superintendent McGregor tells a widow whose husband was a scout that she'll get his pension. Superintendent McGregor seems as pleased to give her this news as she is to hear it. His reputation for being courteous is well deserved.

After these Indians leave, Mr. McGregor thumbs through the mountain of correspondence on his desk. While reading a letter he bursts out laughing, and then shakes his head in disgust. "You know," he says, "if this weren't so sad, it would be funny. A white man from Wisconsin wants an Indian wife. He's asked me please to recommend a suitable mate. What this man really wants is land and he sees marrying an Indian woman with an allotment as a way of getting it."

There it is again, the word allotment. I'll have to learn a new language if I'm to really understand the work of the agency. The Office of Indian Affairs is just like any other organization. It has its own rules and vocabulary. Which reminds me. I want to get a Sioux dictionary and a grammar book. Then I can perhaps learn some common words as well as some medical terms.

Introducing me to the last caller of the day, Superintendent McGregor says, "May I present Miss Elinor Gregg, our Red Cross nurse. She arrived only yesterday."

"Welcome to Rosebud. I'm pleased to meet you," replies Edward J. Peacore warmly. "When Superintendent McGregor learned that you were coming to the agency, he said that you'd probably want to visit the boarding school. You're welcome anytime." I thank him for his hospitality.

As principal, Mr. Peacore is directly in charge of the Rosebud Boarding School, under the superintendent's supervision. He's here to talk with Mr. McGregor about the remodeling and building activities at the school. During the last 18 months, the government has spent $100,000 to improve it. New buildings have been added, existing buildings modernized. Only one project is unfinished.

"We need to complete the well and the water plant. Then we'll have water service to the new buildings and water for fire protection," explains Superintendent McGregor. "But we need eight hundred dollars to complete the project." I must look puzzled because he begins to elaborate.

"The school's main water supply is Antelope Creek, but the water's contaminated. It's unfit for domestic use without being boiled, so we use it for everything except drinking. Drinking water comes from a small well. We had hoped that the new well would give us all the water we need. It doesn't. The flow is seventeen thousand gallons a day, half the amount that the school needs. Even when this well is finished, we'll still have to pump water from the creek. We'd like to use electric motors to pump the water. Because the electricity comes from the school's power plant, they're much less expensive than the gasoline engine we have been using. We need and have two motors, but one is broken. The cost of repairing that motor and installing both of them is about eight hundred dollars."

Recalling Doctor Eddleman's explanation of supply procurement in the Office of Indian Affairs, I ask Superintendent McGregor if it will be difficult to get the money.

"I don't know. There's a fund called Indian School Buildings, Sioux reservations, North and South Dakota. I wrote Commissioner Burke two weeks ago asking for an allotment from it."

"What will you do if the Commissioner says no?"

"Continue as we have and not use the larger well."

I find myself wondering if this expensive economy is typical of the Office of Indian Affairs. Time will tell.

I soon hear the five o'clock bell ring. In some respects it seems that I've been here forever, but in others, it seems as if I just stepped off the stage.

In my room after supper, I glance at this week's *Todd County Tribune.* According to "The Only Newspaper Published in Todd County, South Dakota" I have arrived. On the front page under the heading of Locals, I read that "Miss Gregg the Red Cross nurse of Boston, Mass., passed through Mission Wednesday to take charge of the Red Cross work on the Rosebud and Pine Ridge reservations. She is a nurse of long experience and has been identified with the American Red Cross for years having served in France during the war."

The field matrons will have one question after reading this—"How long will she last?"

JUNE 14, 1966—ALBUQUERQUE, NEW MEXICO

"THIS IS REALLY HELPFUL—THE TAPES, I MEAN. I know we'll still be going to visit Miss Gregg several times, but the tapes will make it so much easier to write the paper at the end of the course. And making the tapes was actually her idea, so I don't feel bad about imposing on her since she actually seemed to want to do them. I probably shouldn't admit this, but I was hoping this gerontology course might be an easy way to get an A and collect credits for graduation all at the same time. Look's like I might've been wrong. The reading probably won't be so bad, but this project could take a lot of time and work and even more if we didn't have the tapes she's making for us," Melody said as she adjusted her maternity skirt and checked her watch. "Guess it means I'll be doing my usual ten p.m. to midnight studying routine after Brice and the baby are in bed."

"What're you going to call the baby when this new one's born? I've never heard you mention his name," Alice asked, hurrying to keep up with her classmate as they approached the library entrance.

Melody halted, her usually pleasant features clouded. She pulled her long dark hair away from her collar, distracted for a few seconds. Turning to Alice, she said, "You're right. I guess I've been concentrating on too many other things. But he still seems like a baby to me. It's hardly fair for him to have to be big brother Brice Johnson, Junior when he won't even be two when this one comes." She shook her head and recomposed her typically sunny smile.

As they seated themselves in one of the small-group study rooms, Alice took a tape recorder from her bag. "I'm glad we got assigned a nurse as our interview subject. You know, I'm amazed at how clear her memory is at eighty years old. I'm thinking maybe we could use some of what she tells us about nursing later for the nursing history class. I mean, I know this whole reminiscing or life review thing is supposed to be good for her as an elderly person. But still, some of the things she's done—she's not just a nurse. Can you believe we only have two more semesters of nursing after this summer, then State Board exams, then . . ." She trailed off as she concentrated on plugging the recorder into an outlet and inserting a tape.

"After we went up to Santa Fe and met her and she was so interested in us and so full of life and fun to be around, I started thinking this might be pretty interesting after all—not just some old person rambling about how things used to be. And then when we listened to that first tape she made for us, I was looking forward to this second one. And she's doing exactly what she promised she would—making one tape a week and mailing it to us. I got the book she wrote, *The Indians and the Nurse*. I've already read it and she's telling us lots more than she wrote in there. I also like the way she showed us how she remembers things in such detail. You know, how she just closes her eyes and imagines she's there and tells it as if she's reliving it. I wonder if she forgets current things like I read some older people do." Alice stopped her rapid-fire monologue. She looked up at Melody, who'd again lost her smile and was staring out the window. "Are you okay?" Alice asked.

"Oh, sure. I was just thinking about all the things at the house I need to get done before Brice gets in from work. If it's messy or if supper's not on when he gets there, he gets in a bad mood. It would be a lot easier if he got off in time to pick up the baby at the sitter on his way home.

Anyway, I've got three hours before I have to leave here. I was listening to what you said, though. Can I have Miss Gregg's book since you've already read it? I can read it tonight after they're asleep. Knock on wood, I've been really lucky the baby hasn't been sick lately and has been sleeping all night. If I can go to sleep by midnight and get up at six, I'm fine and can do everything I need to. Listen to me, off the track again. Let's get to work." Melody took a pen and paper from her tote bag. "I'll make notes on what we want to ask Miss Gregg more about when we see her."

Melody put a hand out to stop Alice before she could start the tape. "Oh, wait, I wanted to ask you. Do you think it's okay that we're getting the tapes and doing the visits, too? I hate to ask Professor Orr because I don't want her to tell us not to use the tapes. But, I read the assignment for the project again and with what I read about reminiscing, I think maybe the assignment is supposed to all be done face-to-face. What do you think?"

Alice gave her an appraising look, "What I think is, there's no sense worrying about it right now. Miss Gregg seemed really pleased that we wanted the tapes. So, if we use them for what we write up, fine. If not, that's fine, too. And, my pregnant friend, I think you could wear yourself out trying to do all you do—be a mother, be a wife, learn to be a good nurse, and make perfect grades."

"Oh, please don't say that. Brice harps about my priorities like that. He says I should put him, the baby, and the things that need doing at the house first and then everything else only if there's time. I don't argue with him about it any more. But, I notice that he doesn't mind me getting a paycheck when I work as a nurse's aide. I just make sure I take care of all those things so he doesn't have anything to gripe about. It's not that he's wrong, really. He just wants what's best for the family. But, I know I can manage that and still do well in school. I have so far, anyway." Melody nodded, jaw tightening as she echoed herself, "I have so far."

With a raised eyebrow and a smile she mimicked Alice's earlier tone, "And you, my skinny red-haired friend, haven't exactly been sliding through school yourself. Dean's list, Nursing Students' Association officer, volunteer at the Veterans Hospital, engaged to a handsome guy—all that doesn't describe a dolt."

"Who's skinny?" Alice asked.

Melody shook her head, "Certainly not me. Five months pregnant and already I've gained sixteen pounds. I'd nearly gotten back to my pre-baby weight when I turned up pregnant again. Now I have that extra five plus these new sixteen. I've got to stop gaining or I'll be a blimp. And a blimp with no clothes that fit!"

"You didn't intend to get pregnant?" Alice asked.

"No, well, not so soon anyway. I was pretty upset—crying in the doctor's office and feeling sorry for myself. But, now I've felt the baby move and it's a real person to me so I've pretty much gotten used to the idea," Melody said. "That's how it was the first time, too."

"You didn't plan the first pregnancy either?" Alice looked surprised. As her friend shook her head, Alice muttered, "I'm worried that may happen to me too. I don't want children for quite a while, if ever. I'm beginning to wonder why I'm engaged."

Both were silent for a couple of minutes. "The only thing I'm sure about is that we have work to do. Better get to it."

Alice diverted them both back to the business at hand. "I was thinking about how she took the Red Cross job on the reservation without knowing anyone out there or even what to expect. Just got in her car and drove all the way from the East Coast out to South Dakota. Seems rather brave or at least adventurous, to me. Do you think you'd do something like that even with conditions as they are today?" Alice asked. "In school they've talked about how we should consider what the job description is, how we will fit in the work setting, whether it will offer advancement and some job security and whether there will be a good orientation. No one ever suggests taking a job for the adventure. For that matter, I don't recall hearing anything about being of help to the less fortunate."

"You're right, there's a lot of encouragement to find success and security. But to be fair, I think that helping those in need isn't mentioned because it's an underlying assumption. That's pretty basic to all nursing," Melody said. "To answer your question, I doubt, even if I wasn't married, a mother, and pregnant, that I'd be bold enough. I do think it's easier for a woman to take risks if she's single."

"I wonder if it's that way or the reverse, a woman stays single because it's important to her to be able to take risks or to make choices without having to consider husband or children. Or maybe it's different for each person, but I know it has to do with making choices rather than having them made for you," Alice said.

"Here's the note she included with this tape," Alice, handing the sheet to Melody, wrinkled her brow in thought.

You might find that you've opened a spigot that can't be shut. Doing as you asked me to—just telling what I remember—has made me verbose, I'm afraid. When one lives with family or sees only old friends, it's easy to stop telling your stories for fear of being boring—"Oh, Aunt El, you've told that one before," I can imagine them thinking, although most are too polite to say so. For that reason, I find myself entertaining the past only in silence. While that is often enjoyable, it is so much nicer to have a fresh audience who, for whatever reasons, are interested in the tales. Because you assured me that you are interested in my whole life, not just my Indian Affairs experiences, I allowed myself to go a bit farther afield in the stories on this tape. I look forward to your visit because I have found some photographs to show you.

Elinor Gregg

"Maybe we'll learn something about making choices from Miss Gregg before the summer's over," Alice said as she switched on the tape.

IN HIS MIND'S EYE

"WE'D VERY MUCH LIKE YOU TO UNDERTAKE A health demonstration project in South Dakota. Will you do it?"

That was a month ago. I was in Washington, D.C. at the headquarters of the American National Red Cross. Elizabeth G. Fox, National Director of the Public Health Nursing Service at the American Red Cross, had invited me to come from Boston.

"Commissioner of Indian Affairs Charles H. Burke has asked the Red Cross for help in getting a higher level of health care worker in the Indian Service on the reservations," Miss Fox began. "As far as he's concerned, the health care of the Indians is far from adequate. Most of the reservations have hospitals and of course these have doctors and some graduate nurses. But the doctors have no public health experience. Field matrons provide any health care in the homes. But with few exceptions, these women are absolutely untrained and are very ordinary individuals."

Commissioner Burke blamed the lack of adequate and trained personnel on Congressional ignorance. Congress didn't know about the conditions on the reservations. The commissioner's predecessor hadn't brought the conditions to its attention.

"Personally," offered Miss Fox, "I think that in his mind's eye the commissioner has a vision of public health work on the reservations under the direction of competent doctors and public health nurses."

While living in South Dakota, Charles H. Burke had been Chairman of a Red Cross Chapter. There he witnessed what county public health nurses could accomplish. As the Commissioner of Indian Affairs, he'd been greatly impressed by the work of a public health nurse who had made a comprehensive health survey on an Indian reservation in Montana.

"The Commissioner believes," Miss Fox continued, "that if he can describe the deplorable health conditions of the Indians, Congress will see the need for a much higher grade of health service. And, if he can demonstrate the benefits of having public health nurses on reservations, he can then persuade Congress to appropriate the funds necessary to pay their salaries. He believes that the Red Cross can help the Indian Service make a case that will appeal to Congress."

"What kind of help does he want?" I asked, my interest aroused.

"He's asked the American Red Cross to make a health survey and to demonstrate public health nursing on several of the poorer reservations. We've agreed to provide three expert public health nurses. Miss Florence M. Patterson is to survey health work among the Indians in the Southwest. Miss Augustine Stoll will provide public health nursing service on the Jicarilla Reservation in New Mexico. And we'd very much like you to go to the Rosebud and Pine Ridge Reservations in South Dakota to do similar work."

The appointment was for a year. The pay was $2200 per year, plus $600 for traveling expenses to the reservation, and $200 for miscellaneous expenses. The Red Cross would pay this. For its part, the Indian Service would provide my transportation on the reservation and give me a place to live. In some ways I'd be like all workers on the reservation. I'd be responsible to the superintendent and under his direction. In addition, I'd be guided and supervised by the Central Division of the Red Cross. Rosebud and Pine Ridge were in its territory.

“Please think it over and let me hear from you, tentatively at least, within the next few days,” Miss Fox said.

Even as I thanked her for offering me the position, I knew. This pioneering job appealed to me.

As I left her office, Miss Fox said, “See what you can do to give the Indians better health care and education.” That was four weeks ago. Now at the Rosebud Agency, I’ll see what I can do.

The clock strikes ten. Superintendent McGregor glances around the room. This morning he sees the four field matrons and seven of the district farmers. The only field worker missing is J.A. Rennick, the district farmer from Herrick.

“I want to thank everyone for coming,” Superintendent McGregor says. “I am extremely pleased to present Miss Elinor Gregg. She’s a public health nurse on loan to us from the American Red Cross. For the next year, she’ll be here at Rosebud and over at Pine Ridge. Her duties will be similar to those of a visiting or county health nurse in an average white community.” Hearing this, I smile. What average white community has nearly 6,000 Sioux Indians living in an area slightly larger than the state of Rhode Island?

“Miss Gregg wants to learn about health conditions on the reservation,” he continues. “She’s already met with Doctor Eddleman and toured the hospital. Soon she’ll be spending time with Mrs. Gardner, Mrs. McDonald, Miss Rasch, and Miss Moran.”

No doubt these field matrons are thrilled to hear I’ll be visiting each of them and observing their work. I interpret their smiles as tolerance and thinly disguised indifference.

“I want a better understanding between the field and this office,” says Superintendent McGregor getting down to business. “That’s why I asked you all here today. Although this is my first opportunity as superintendent to meet with you, I’m very well aware of your work.” Is it my imagination or does he look at the field matrons when he says that? “From now on, we’ll meet every month to discuss health subjects and conditions in general,” he announces. “I’d like us to talk candidly about problems that you see either in the field or in the hospital.”

His statement reminds me of lines from *Through the Looking Glass.* "The time has come to talk of many things," the Walrus says to the Carpenter as they walk along the beach.

Several farmers have received complaints of Indians gambling. All the Indians like to gamble, the women even more than the men. Superintendent McGregor and the farmers agree; successfully prosecuting such cases is difficult. By the time the officers get to the house, the Indians, warned by their sentries, have stopped. The officers find the Indians engaged in a peaceable and legal pastime.

The farmer from Okreek is concerned about some young Indian men in his district. They refuse to work and they spend their time and energy hunting moonshine. Farmers from other districts also voice this concern.

"Liquor traffic on the reservation is on the increase," Superintendent McGregor says. "Most of the traffic seems to be carried out by lawless white persons. They often get Indians to peddle the liquor for them."

"Do we ever catch any of these moonshiners?" Miss Rasch asks.

"We did catch one white man selling liquor from his Buick," Superintendent McGregor replies. "He pled guilty in federal court. Unfortunately, the indictment didn't mention that he was using his car to peddle the liquor. So the judge fined him a hundred dollars and gave him back his car."

"More severe penalties might help suppress the liquor traffic," one of the farmers suggested. Everyone agrees. Superintendent McGregor says that he'll pass this suggestion on to Commissioner Burke.

The reservation has special officers for the suppression of liquor traffic among the Indians. The stock detective and the regularly appointed government farmers are deputies. "Why not deputize the Indian police as well?" someone asks. Several other field workers nod in agreement.

"I don't think that's advisable," Superintendent McGregor answers. "After all, the Indian police aren't exempt from temptation. And rarely do the Indians make the liquor; they just sell it for the white moonshiners."

No one has any more comments about liquor traffic so Superintendent McGregor moves on to the next item.

"Several of you have asked me about buying horses for the Indians at this time of the year. My opinion is that all Indians should raise and sell their own horses and break them to work. No country is better adapted to horse raising than this reservation. So it seems very poor business for the Indians to pay their white neighbors anywhere from one hundred fifty to three hundred dollars for a team of horses that they could raise themselves."

"More than a year ago," he continues, "the Indian Office asked each superintendent to adopt a five-year policy for his agency. Rosebud has had three superintendents in the last year. Because of these changes we're a year behind. But a definite part of my five-year policy is that the Indians will raise and break their own horses. Now is the time for them to begin." He asks if the farmers have questions about this. None of them does.

Superintendent McGregor wants to talk about one more thing before we go to dinner—the cattle industry that Rosebud doesn't have. Eight years ago the superintendent started a cattle industry for the Indians. It now amounts to nothing. The cattle that the Indians didn't sell or butcher died in snowstorms.

As I listen to plans for rekindling the industry, I think about the conference. For me it's an education that's bound to pay off. I'm learning about some of the ways of the Sioux, the social and administrative aspects of Indian work, general politics, and district personnel. I'm pleased that Superintendent McGregor included me.

"Come early next spring," he says, "I plan to buy a considerable number of livestock. So please study the Indians in your districts. Identify those who have the ability to become successful stockmen and talk with each of them personally."

Superintendent McGregor hopes that each farmer can find several Indians who have the desire and the funds to buy between ten and 25 young cows. The cattle will be a source of food for them and will certainly encourage them to stay at home.

"Many Indians on this reservation have money that they should invest in cattle," he explains. "Soon their money will be gone. They'll have no stock and no experience raising stock. They'll have to depend solely on manual labor for their subsistence. I can see no reason why the Rosebud

Sioux must continue to be cattle consumers. With close supervision, they can once again become cattle owners."

Some of the district farmers exchange questioning glances. I gather that at least a few of them have doubts about something. But what? I'm sure they don't doubt that cattle are a good source of food. So perhaps they doubt that the cattle will encourage the Indians to stay at home and become cattle owners. Indeed, this proves to be the case.

Only last year each farmer bought many chickens and milk cows on behalf of the Indians in his district. When winter and spring weather was stormy and cold and the roads nearly impassable, the Indians were interested in the animals and even in planting crops. But as soon as the weather and the road conditions improved, most Indians lost interest. They traveled to visit friends and to attend Indian Dances and celebrations. Often, they stayed away for days at a time. Shut up in a barn or a hen house, the chickens died for want of food and water. The milk cows wandered off.

The whites value eggs and milk as food. The Indians don't. To the Indians staying home to care for hens and cattle is not part of their cultural heritage. Traveling, visiting family, and attending Indian Dances and celebrations are. It's not surprising. After all, the Sioux are traditionally a nomadic people. Until the late 1800s, skilled horsemen wandered the vast northern plains and beyond. The Indians have a great pride in their race. Most don't want to mimic the whites.

It's nearly noon, so Superintendent McGregor suggests that we go to dinner. We'll reconvene at one p.m.

I'm not sure if the field matrons feel obligated to ask me to join them for dinner, but they do. Walking purposefully to the dining room, we all agree that we're hungry and that it feels good to stretch our legs.

The district farmers sit at one table in the dining room. We sit at another, talking about the weather and food preservation. Each of the field matrons has put up at least 500 jars of fruits, vegetables, and jellies for the winter.

Taking advantage of a lull in the conversation, Mrs. Flora Gardner says, "I don't know why I didn't think of this before, but it's just occurred to me. A year ago August we had a man named Gregg call at the agency. I know it was August, because it was the same time that Lew Haukaas got bitten by a rattlesnake. He threw a hammer at the snake and stunned it. Then he picked up the hammer and tried to hit the snake on the head with it. I don't know what ever possessed Mr. Haukaas to do that," she says shaking her head in disbelief.

"He probably didn't want the snake to get away," Miss Rasch says.

"Yes, I'm sure that's right. Anyway, the snake was too fast for him." (And probably very angry, I think to myself.) "It bit him on the finger. Poor Mr. Haukaas had to go to the hospital."

"What about Mr. Gregg, Flora?" Miss Moran asks.

"Oh yes, thank you, Margaret. I don't recall his first name. But I do remember that he was the principal of the Hampton Institute. That school in Virginia with a program for Indians. Would he be any relation to you, Miss Gregg?"

"Yes. He's my brother, James."

"Oh, I see."

I'm not sure what she sees, and I'm not going to ask.

"Flora, you always know what's going on at the agency," Mrs. McDonald says, her blue eyes twinkling. "I think it's because you live in Parmelee." Mrs. Gardner smiles knowingly.

"Parmelee is fifteen miles northwest of here, Miss Gregg," explains Mrs. McDonald. "The rest of us live about thirty miles away in various directions. Lottie's up in Norris, Margaret's in White River, and I'm over in Wood."

Cutting short my geography lesson Miss Rasch asks, "Do you come from a large family?"

"Yes. I have six brothers and sisters."

"Are they older or younger?"

"Five are older. One is younger and James is the eldest."

While we're waiting for dessert Mrs. McDonald asks me if this is my first time in the west. "I read in this week's paper that you're from Boston."

"I was born in Colorado Springs and spent the first twenty years of my life there."

"How long have you been at Rosebud, Mrs. McDonald?" I ask.

"About thirteen years. I came to South Dakota in nineteen hundred five to work at Fort Thompson on the Crow Creek Reservation. I was an assistant matron in the Indian Day School there for about four years. Then, in nineteen hundred nine, I was promoted to field matron and came here."

As soon as I finish my dessert I excuse myself. The field matrons will want some time alone, to talk about me, perhaps even to dissect me. I'm sure I've left them with more questions than answers.

At one p.m. Superintendent McGregor begins by announcing, "We're going to conduct a progressive health campaign on this reservation. As field workers you have intimate knowledge of the Indian families in your districts. You know who's sick and needs care. So it's important that you cooperate with the doctor. He may decide to send an Indian to the hospital or to the dispensary. Or, he may decide that an Indian can be cared for at home. Commissioner Burke suggests that when Indians are cared for at home the field matrons systematically follow up. I expect that his wishes will be carried out."

And just in case someone doesn't understand, Superintendent McGregor adds, "I also expect everyone's most earnest cooperation in connection with the hospital and follow-up work in the homes."

As I listen to Superintendent McGregor I think about the field matrons. Last night I skimmed the official guide and manual that he'd given me. According to the circular, the position of field matron is more than a job. It's an opportunity to serve others and to sacrifice oneself in the interest of humanity.

To be a field matron a woman must have the desire and aptitude to teach the Indians how to better themselves and improve their lives. A field matron needs physical, moral, and mental strength, as well as a real missionary spirit and a genuine spirit of helpfulness. She must be self-reliant and self-directing. A field matron is personally interested in the Indians, promotes their general welfare, and never offends them.

Doctor Eddleman had said that the field matrons were not graduate nurses. Yet, according to the official guide and manual they were to assist the physician, advise expectant women, help confined women, save babies, prevent tuberculosis, combat trachoma, and teach Indian women about nursing and child care. That was in addition to teaching about heating the home, airing bedding, preparing and serving food, keeping and caring for domestic animals, disposing of human waste, rubbish, and garbage, and organizing societies for social and intellectual improvement.

The duties of the field matron depend on agency location and local conditions, among other things. Too varied and extensive to list in the circular, the duties related to ten specific areas: home, premises, health and sanitation, saving of babies, practices and customs, domestic instruction, school cooperation, industrial cooperation, employment limitations, and special classes. The manual read more like a sermon than a blueprint. The message was that any good woman can teach all good women what every good woman should know.

The field matron program had been established in 1890. The Religious Society of Friends funded the first field matron position for eight months. Then in its Indian Appropriation Act for Fiscal Year 1891, Congress authorized the Office of Indian Affairs to hire one field matron. Although the field matron program had grown, its primary objective remained advancement of the Indian people. Some whites saw Indian women as the last to yield to modern trends. If these "standpatters" could just see the value of modern ways and customs, the Indians would progress much faster down the road to civilization. Only women could reach women and so the field matron program was born.

I don't realize how deep in thought I am until I hear Superintendent McGregor say, "health survey." What have I missed? Not much, he's just started talking about the health survey that he and Doctor Eddleman will be making. Together they'll visit all the Indian homes and prepare a health record for each person. Eventually they'll have information about the health condition of every Indian on the reservation.

"Commissioner Burke has directed all agency superintendents to conduct a health survey," Superintendent McGregor explains. "He thinks that these visits will fit in nicely with our progressive health campaign here at Rosebud. Doctor Eddleman and I agree."

We spend the rest of the meeting working on a plan to improve sanitary conditions in the Indian homes. "Home and living conditions are important factors in general health," Superintendent McGregor begins. "When you see unsatisfactory conditions, correct them. The process will be slow in some cases," he admits, "but persistence will produce very noticeable results." Doctor Eddleman nods in agreement. He then speaks at length about tuberculosis and how home and living conditions can contribute to its spread.

I know that tuberculosis is the major cause of death among the Indians. For some reason though I'm surprised to hear that nearly a third of the 6000 Indians at Rosebud have the disease.

When Doctor Eddleman asks for ideas that would help prevent the spread of tuberculosis, someone says, "Tell them not to spit on the floor." Not a bad starting point, I think, and say so.

"Tell them to stay away from each other," someone else says.

Thanking the field workers for their suggestions, Doctor Eddleman says, "Well, we may not be able to convince them that isolation is important. But maybe we can teach them not to spit on the floor."

By three p.m. the field workers and Superintendent McGregor have reached agreement on many issues. Equally important, we have a plan for improving conditions in the Indian homes. Its effectiveness, I suspect, will depend on how it is presented and to whom.

"Thank you all for coming," Superintendent McGregor says, "and for talking openly about your concerns. I look forward to our meeting next month."

I spend what's left of the afternoon with Mr. McGregor in his office learning more about the workings of the agency. Before he begins meeting with the Indians he says, "You perhaps wondered what prompted some of my comments at the conference." Actually, I had. But I knew he must have a reason. Reputed to be impartial and firm, he made decisions only after carefully weighing the merits of a situation. Moreover, he was no stranger to the Rosebud Reservation or to the Indian Service.

Mr. McGregor had come to Rosebud the first time in 1914. As Principal, he'd turned a disorganized and run-down boarding school into one of the best. He'd accomplished the same feat earlier in Oklahoma at the Rainy Mountain Indian School. As a reward, Commissioner of Indian Affairs Cato Sells made him Superintendent of the Cheyenne River Reservation and School in South Dakota. After that Mr. McGregor became the Supervisor of Indian Schools with headquarters at Helena, Montana.

"Almost as soon as I returned here four months ago, Doctor Eddleman began telling me about the field matrons. He has to rely on their judgment in order to help the Indians. But some of the field matrons seem to hide behind their ignorance. They take the position that they're not trained nurses and therefore aren't supposed to know about health matters. Only one of the four field matrons was cooperating with Doctor Eddleman. And at least one was almost openly hostile toward him."

Who was cooperative and who was hostile? Mr. McGregor doesn't say and I don't ask.

"In September," he continues, "I notified Commissioner Burke of the situation. "I told him that if I couldn't fix it, I'd advise him. By return mail he suggested that I hold monthly meetings with the field workers and hospital employees. I'd get intimate knowledge about the field and hospital conditions, and I'd have an opportunity to check more closely on the work of the field matrons."

"I didn't mince any words when I asked the field matrons to attend the conference," Superintendent McGregor admits. "I told them that the Indian Office had received information that the team work among the field matrons and hospital here wasn't very good. As a result, the commissioner had written me personally that I was to look into the matter and take steps to remedy it."

I thank Superintendent McGregor for his candor. I'm pleased that he trusts me. I also appreciate this information because I'll be visiting the field matrons. Sooner rather than later seems advisable. Mr. McGregor agrees. Who to visit first? To help me decide, he tells me a bit about each of them.

"Mrs. Gardner is married to the district farmer in Cut Meat, a two hundred square mile area with an Indian population of eight hundred. The Gardners have been in the Indian Service many, many years and know a great deal about it. You'd never to know it to look at them, but they're both in their late sixties. They're nearly ready for their pensions."

No wonder Mrs. Gardner is so poised.

"The Gardners live in Parmelee," Mr. McGregor continues, "a town of less than fifty people. Being only fifteen miles from the agency, the Gardners can easily conduct any business that needs my approval. Also, with the hospital so near, they don't get very involved in too many health problems. They refer the Indians to the hospital."

"What about Lottie Rasch?"

"She lives in the Black Pipe district. It's near the cluster of stores that the white settlers call Norris. She's been there at least ten years and in the Indian Service much longer. People in the community really like her."

"What about her involvement in health care?"

"That seems limited to giving out aspirin, castor oil, and sulphur ointment to Indians who come to her. A top buggy and a pair of spotted ponies were her transportation for years. They're gone now, so most of the time she has to depend on either the district farmer or day-school teacher to visit the five hundred Indians who live in her three hundred square mile district."

"I know that Mrs. McDonald lives in Wood and is married to the district farmer for Butte Creek. What else should I know?" I ask.

"Well, Wood is a town of two hundred people about thirty miles northeast of Rosebud. Since Mrs. McDonald is married to the district farmer, she, like Mrs. Gardner, has access to transportation to visit the eight hundred Indians living in her three hundred square mile district. Also Mrs. McDonald has some practical nursing experience. If I'm not mistaken, she worked for a country doctor in Minnesota."

"And finally," I prompt, "we come to Miss Moran."

"She's stationed at the three hundred square mile Little White River district, which is home to around five hundred Indians. She lives in White River, a smallish community about thirty miles north of the agency. I wouldn't be surprised if she resigned soon. She may well be gone by the first of the year."

By the time we finish, I have valuable information about the field matrons. I also understand the importance of having a car. Without one or some way to commandeer one, a field matron is sunk. She can't hope to visit the Indians in their homes. Most of them live in one room log cabins in the outlying districts.

I'm glad to have my own transportation. I can go where I want when I want. But if getting to the agency was any indication, my Ford won't always get me there. Mr. McGregor tells me who to see about getting a horse.

Toward the end of the afternoon Mr. Coursey steps in to talk briefly with Superintendent McGregor. He introduces me to the lawyer who's responsible for the land inheritance work. "You were at the Gardners in Parmelee on business when she arrived on Wednesday," Mr. McGregor explains.

After Mr. Coursey leaves, Mr. McGregor asks me if I'm getting acquainted with the people who live at the agency. The population totals about 120. "I've met quite a few," I answer. "Next week I'm going to call on the Episcopal Missionary."

The Catholic, Protestant Episcopal, Congregational, and Presbyterian denominations look after the religious welfare of the Indians on the reservation. But the Catholic and Episcopal Churches have the most membership and the most religious activity. The many Catholic and Episcopal Churches scattered over the reservation make it convenient for the Indians to attend church services.

Mr. McGregor advises me that in addition to meeting with Reverend Mr. John B. Clark, I must be sure to call on the Reverend Father Buechel and the Mother Superior at St. Francis.

The most effective Indian Service employee lives without religion. Or if he can't live without it, at least he doesn't attend church. The Indians are not ecumenical. Episcopalian Indians won't welcome an employee who attends a Presbyterian service. Likewise, Catholic Indians won't accept the teachings of an employee who worships with the Protestants. I'm grateful for Mr. McGregor's advice. I'd like to commit as few faux pas as possible.

I can easily live without organized religion. I'd had my fill of it. My father was a Congregational minister, and I attended enough church functions as a child. I'd gone to Sunday school and church every week. Unlike my elder sister Marjorie, I was never allowed to stay home. She'd put up such a fuss about going that my parents would relent.

Funnily enough, Marjorie got religion at the ripe old age of 37. And she got it hard. She entered a novitiate in the Episcopal Church. She loved all the symbolism and dramaturgy. Father said she would last, but she didn't. She left the convent after a few months, but she never lost her religious convictions. I've always wondered if her experiences in France during the War had anything to do with her staunch religious beliefs.

WITH TIME TO SPARE

I've been here only three days, and already I'm leaving. My fellow passengers and I ride contentedly in silence. As the miles slip away, the open space of the reservation runs to the horizon. My mind drifts to nothingness until we reach Mission. A young man, probably in his early twenties, dressed neatly in a suit, overcoat, and broad smile boards the stage. He pulls out a small black notebook and begins writing. After about half an hour, he returns the notebook to his pocket. A few more minutes pass and he asks me what I think about the countryside. "I like it," I reply smiling. "It seems to go on forever."

"Have you ever seen any Indians?" he asks.

"A few on the Rosebud Sioux Reservation," I answer, not quite sure where this conversation is headed.

"I spent a couple weeks there about two months ago," he volunteers eagerly. "Actually, I've spent the last six months learning about the Indians of the northern Plains. My newspaper wants me to write a series of articles about them. I myself am really interested in how the government treats them. Consider this. In eighteen sixty-eight, a treaty created the Great Sioux Reservation. This territory included parts of present day Nebraska, Wyoming, Montana, and all of what's now South Dakota west of the Missouri River. But after gold was discovered in the Black Hills of South Dakota in eighteen seventy-four, the government removed the hills from the Great Sioux Reservation."

"Wasn't that a treaty violation?"

"And more. To the Sioux and several other tribes, the Black Hills are the sacred heart of the Great Plains."

"So removing the Black Hills from the Sioux homeland was like pouring salt into a wound."

"Yes, and unfortunately for the Indians, that's continued. Thirteen years later, in eighteen eighty-nine, the government carved six smaller reservations out of the Great Sioux Reservation. One of these was the Rosebud Sioux Reservation. But even after these six reservations were removed from the Sioux homeland, eleven million acres remained."

"What happened to all that land?"

"The government offered the Indians fifty cents an acre for it. When they refused, the government went to a dollar fifty. That offer came with a thinly veiled threat. Accept it or we'll take the land."

The journalist anticipates my curiosity. The government returned the land to the public domain of the United States.

"Are you really interested in all of this?" he asks.

"Most definitely," I reply, smiling.

"Shall I continue?" he asks, hoping that I'll say yes.

He smiles. Perhaps he can't believe his good fortune. He has a captive audience who's interested in what he has to say.

"Once created," he continues, "these smaller reservations were subject to Congress' General Allotment or Dawes Severalty Act of eighteen eighty-seven."

By this time, the other passengers are no longer pretending to ignore our conversation. They're openly listening to it. Maybe they know about the General Allotment Act. But I don't, so I ask him what its purpose was.

"To assimilate the Indians," he responds. "The act assaulted tribalism. It divided a reservation into parcels. Although single people got at least forty acres, married women got nothing. Heads of families got one hundred sixty acres. That's one quarter of a section," he explains. "But the idea of someone actually owning the land was completely foreign to the Indians. They believed that the land, like them, belonged to the Creator. Individual land ownership and the right to private property are principles of the white man. And, the Indians really didn't get the land anyway."

"What do you mean the Indians didn't really get the land?" I ask.

"The government didn't think they were competent to manage their own affairs. So it held the titles in trust, sometimes as long as twenty-five years."

"And what do you think Congress did with the surplus after each Indian had received his allotment?" he asks with a slight edge to his voice.

I'm not sure that he either expects or wants me to respond, but I'd been brought up to answer questions honestly. Evasive answers were considered the same as lying, and most assuredly a sin. So I tell him that I don't know what Congress did.

"Sold the surplus land at bargain prices to white homesteaders and land-speculators," he says.

What happened to the money from the land sales?"

"The proceeds were earmarked for Indian needs and put in a tribal fund. That way the government didn't have to pay as much to support them."

"What was the effect of all this on the Rosebud Reservation?" I ask.

"I know this would mean more if I had a map to show you," he says apologetically. "But in eighteen eighty-nine the boundaries of the Rosebud Sioux Reservation were the Nebraska State line on the south, the Missouri River on the east, the Big White River on the north, and the Bennett County line on the west. Two years ago the Rosebud Sioux Reservation was around five and a half million acres. Thanks to the General Allotment Act and the opening of counties to white settlers, the Indians lost about ninety million acres. That's about two-thirds of the entire reservation land base."

Funny, sometimes the more I know, the more I know I don't know. I find myself asking my learned companion what an Indian does with his allotment.

"Depends on whether he has a fee patent or not," he begins. "You see, a fee patent is like a deed. An Indian gets a fee patent only when the Secretary of the Interior judges him to be competent. If an Indian has a fee patent, he can do what he wants with his land. But if he doesn't have one, all he can do is farm the land. If he wants to sell, lease, or mortgage it, he needs either the permission or the supervision of the Interior Department.

The young newsman checks his watch as if deciding how much more he can tell me before we reach the end of the line. Having decided, he proceeds. "The trust status is really quite interesting."

The inflection in his voice seems to ask if I want to hear more. I do, and simply say, "Really?" This is all the encouragement he needs.

"The government says that the trust status is for the Indians' own good," he continues. "That it protects them from unscrupulous whites and from themselves. The government says it doesn't want the Indians to fritter away their resources. So if an Indian who doesn't have a fee patent leases or sells his allotment, this 'unearned' income goes into his individual Indian money account. The Office of Indian Affairs determines how the proceeds are doled out to him at the agency. Usually the Indians have to use a purchase order to access the money in their account. Rarely does the government give them cash."

Only yesterday Superintendent McGregor told me that he was responsible for about 5,000 separate Indian accounts totaling 1.1 million dollars. Now I know where some of that money comes from. And I fully understand his appreciation for the machine bookkeeping system that was introduced two years ago.

"There's another aspect to this trust status," my companion reveals. His increased sense of urgency is palpable as he talks more rapidly and moves to the edge of his seat. "The government's forcing the Rosebud

Sioux to become self-sufficient yeoman farmers. But they're not farmers, never have been. In fact, 'scratching the ground' is a dishonorable way of life."

"But tradition aside," he continues, "it's hard for the Indians to earn their living by farming. A single allotment isn't enough for commercial activity and a family's allotments are rarely contiguous. The Indians would rather lease their land and they could earn much more money doing so. But the Office of Indian Affairs says that unearned income from trust property isn't really income. According to them it produces idleness, not self-sufficiency. The Indians must 'earn' their money. And, they're to do it by becoming farmers."

Finally, the young man sits back in his seat and draws a deep breath. "There you have allotments in a nutshell. Well, maybe not a nutshell," he laughs. I smile. Then, as if suddenly grasping the implications of what he's told me, he softly laments. "Just think. Only one hundred years ago the Sioux and other Indian tribes were independent sovereign nations. Now they're dependent wards of the United States government."

Moments later, the stage pulls into Winner. My head is spinning. I certainly have a great deal to think about. Only a few days ago I had said I needed to learn more about the Office of Indian Affairs. Now I have started.

As we part company, I thank my traveling companion for enlightening me. "Thank you for listening," he replies. "Telling you how the government controls the lives of the Indians has helped me organize my thoughts. It's also given me ideas for my articles."

I reach the train with time to spare. Finding my seat, I relax. The sound of the wheels on the tracks soon mesmerizes me. The next thing I know I'm waking up. The train whistle announces our arrival in Bridgewater. My Ford awaits and the road beckons.

JUNE 16, 1966—ALBUQUERQUE

"YOU MOVE AWFULLY FAST FOR A PREGNANT woman," Alice said, laughing as she caught up with Melody near the library. "I've been following you for two blocks and you never slowed down to enjoy this beautiful day for a second."

"If I walk fast enough, maybe I'll outrun the weight that's chasing me. Everything I eat turns to fat, I think." Melody stopped and turned, "Just look at me! No, from behind, I mean. That's me, not baby that's gaining." After a couple of seconds looking intently at Alice's flushed face, she said, "I can tell from looking, you're excited. Something good happening?"

"Let's go in, and I'll show you."

Passing into the library, Melody was thankful for the cool and quiet, a welcome contrast to the bright warm day on campus. Her brisk walk had made her long hair damp against her neck. She lifted the dark curls and fanned herself as they walked to the study room. As she and Alice passed them, two young men stopped their conversation and smiled and nodded in greeting. Alice elbowed Melody and whispered, "See, even pregnant you turn heads."

“Are you kidding? It’s you and that red hair. I’m just lucky to be walking with you. Besides, you know married women are invisible,” Melody said, elbowing Alice in return. Holding the door open, she urged, “Get in here and tell me what’s going on. I can’t remember when I’ve seen you as excited.”

“Look at these brochures. The Peace Corps has recruiters on campus today. I stopped at their table and talked with the two people there. They’re not much older than we are, and they’ve already served one assignment. Al was in Ghana and Eileen was in Uruguay. They both loved what they did. He worked on agricultural projects, helping people grow improved seed for their crops and teaching about irrigation. She worked helping establish an elementary school in a rural village. I could tell they were both so committed to helping people and to making the world a better place. They really felt they had done some good. Eileen said she learned so much more than she taught. Her eyes just lit up when she was telling me about her village. The pay isn’t much besides living expenses and travel, but think of the experience. Eileen told me she came back a different person—that now she has a whole different idea of what’s important in life.”

“What about the language? Were they sent to countries that they already knew the language of or did they have some special training? I’d think a person would have to be fluent if they were going out to work in some rural area.”

“Part of the training before they were sent to their assignments was intensive language and cultural education about the country they were going into. Oh Melody, it sounds like such an adventure. Al said that nurses are needed in lots of the countries that have invited the Peace Corps. Did you know that there are fifteen thousand Peace Corps volunteers right now, in countries all over the world?” Alice closed her eye. “Imagine it, me in a village in South America helping start a clinic to improve child health. It’s hot, I’m wearing shorts and a big shirt and native sandals and a big straw hat. Little children are holding onto my legs and their mothers are asking me questions about infant diarrhea in some Indian dialect—

and I understand. I'm giving health advice in their language. Can you see it?"

"Yes, and mosquitoes and snakes and your pale gringa skin has burned and you have new freckles, lots of them," Melody said, laughing. "Very romantic."

"Oh, it isn't romantic but it's adventurous and it's worthwhile. Except maybe the sunburn and the freckles. That's why I had on the hat. Seriously, what do you think?"

Melody paused before answering. "I think it sound very exciting. Are you seriously considering it?"

"I don't know. But, I'm seriously intrigued. I remember when President Kennedy first started the Peace Corps. I was about fourteen and in high school. The idea was appealing to me even then—for as long as anything can appeal to you at fourteen. It made a big impression on me when he asked how many of us would be willing to serve their country and the cause of peace by living and working in developing countries. I wanted to answer—to say I would. And then today, there were Al and Eileen, asking the same question, but directly to me. I wanted to sign up on the spot. The idea of being of some real use in the world just pulls at me." After a moment she said quietly, "Realistically, I know I've made other plans and that Carlos would have a hemorrhage if he knew I even stopped to talk to the recruiters. Especially Al—he was so handsome."

"Aha, so that's their method. Send out a couple of poster-pretty recruiters to get people to stop and talk. Guess it doesn't hurt to get people's attention."

"Got mine!" Alice smiled and her blue eyes twinkled. "Melody, promise me you won't mention this to anyone. I don't even know what I'll think or how I'll feel about this in the morning. So, I'd rather no one knew."

"Don't worry. I know how it is to have a dream and have someone put a damper on it. Did you promise to talk to the recruiters again?"

"They'll be back next month and I told them I might stop in to see them. I didn't even sign my name on their 'more info' sheet because I was concerned about having mail from them lying around." Alice hesitated,

"Listen to me—talking about adventure in some remote part of the world and being afraid to make waves at home in Albuquerque." As she took a tape from her bag, Alice said, "The Peace Corps sounds like something Miss Gregg would have done doesn't it?"

Melody nodded. "Exactly."

"After we listened to that last tape, I could just see her driving around the wilds in her little Ford, daydreaming about her new job and being on her own to figure out what needed to be done. I think it wasn't just being in a primitive area that she enjoyed, but also having the challenge of doing something that was innovative as well as useful. I'd like to know that when I'm her age I could look back and remember doing at least one thing like that in my life." As she spoke, Alice's intensity was evident in her erect posture and her serious expression. Suddenly she relaxed into the chair, held up both hands as if surrendering, "Okay, I'm through talking about me. Ready for this next tape?"

WE CARRIED ON

I'M GLAD TO BE BEHIND THE WHEEL OF MY FORD again. Thankfully the roads are dry. The mud earlier this week reminded me of France during the Great War. Some things you never forget. You may not think about them often, but they're there, waiting only for a smell, a sound, or a sight to bring them to life.

I stepped onto French soil on May thirtieth, nineteen seventeen, as a member of Base Hospital Number 5, also known as the Second Harvard Unit. We had crossed the English Channel from Folkestone, England earlier in the afternoon. Our packet ship the "Princess Victoria" was loaded to the gunwales. In addition to the 250 members of Base Hospital Number 5, she carried groups of nurses and officers of every description and nationality. A transport alongside was packed with soldiers. The destroyers that surrounded us for protection were invisible in the dense, soupy fog. Throughout the two-hour crossing they had blown their horns incessantly. Everyone breathed a sigh of relief when we were safely in the quay at Boulogne-sur-Mer. The 64 other nurses of Base Hospital Number

5 and I gladly took off our cork life belts and emerged from our lower deck cabins.

After disembarking we boarded the big auto buses that were waiting for us. From our seats we watched the cargo of three transport ships pass. English, French, Portuguese, Australian, and Russian soldiers formed a seemingly endless stream. Finally we spotted our boys. Watching them march to a frail and unique version of the Star Spangled Banner played by a scrub orchestra of convalescent patients from one of the hospitals brought tears to our eyes and lumps to our throats.

Finally the drivers put the buses in gear. Then we jounced over cobblestone streets amid cheers of soldiers, women, and small boys. The French people cried *Les Américains* and *Vive l'Amerique,* pleased that America had at last joined against the Germans. I had taken French in high school and wondered if I'd remember anything. At least I could understand what the people were saying.

We drove through beautiful rolling countryside, replete with gardens, trees and stone cottages. Some had tiled roofs, others thatched. After about 15 miles we passed a big encampment. Soldiers scrambled to the fences as we passed.

About 9:30 p.m. we entered a city of tents and huts. "Welcome to Number 11 British General Hospital, Camiers," the driver said. As the buses made their way slowly through the camp the nurses chatted excitedly. I'd gotten to know them, some better than others, since leaving Boston on May 8th. Doctor Harvey Cushing, the director of Base Hospital Number 5, had organized the unit at Peter Bent Brigham Hospital, Boston and at Harvard Medical School, Cambridge, Massachusetts. So sometimes the unit was referred to as the Peter Bent Brigham Unit. With the exception of a few others and myself the nurses came from the Brigham.

Nearly all of the nurses were in their early to mid-twenties. At least five years younger than I, many were only a few years older than my sister Faith's eldest child. Four years ago when he was 13, I had taken him on the train from Boston to school in California.

Being among the first women to be called to active duty with the U.S. Army was for most of the nurses the greatest opportunity of their lives. Moreover, regardless of our personal thoughts about war, we knew that we were doing the right thing. Despite our confidence, however, I suspect that each of us was wondering what our lives would be like here. Base Hospital Number 5 was on loan to the British Expeditionary Forces for a year and Number 11 would be our home.

No sooner had we stepped down from the buses than we were escorted to the "Sisters" mess. Large wicker chairs, window seats, a piano, and flowers made the cozy living room all the more inviting. We hadn't had anything to eat since leaving London at twelve-thirty p.m. so we were glad that supper was soon served. The cold meat, potato and green salads, fruit, bread, butter, and coffee tasted the best of any fare we'd had since sailing from New York on May 11th.

After supper we all dug into the mountain of suitcases outside the nurses' mess. The glow of a single flashlight aided our excavation. We were ordered to report for breakfast the next morning at seven and then we followed a sergeant up and down the paths as she assigned us to our huts. They reminded me of the cabins at a rustic summer camp in New England. Each cabin had five to seven rooms. Each room boasted a low homemade table and two beds that were made up on boards about six inches from the floor. Numerous nails, a row of strong clothes hooks, and a storage box protruded from the wall. As soon as I unpacked my towel and toothbrush I walked up the dirt road, affectionately called the Avenue, to the bathroom.

Back in my room sleep didn't come easily. Trains chuffed all night and I couldn't curl myself into a ball small enough to keep warm. At last the dawn of my 31st birthday broke sunny and clear. After a breakfast of cold meat, tea, bread, and jam, I walked through the sea of tents to the surgical ward where I was to be the head nurse. What a change, I thought, from last month when I'd been the Superintendent of Infants Hospital in Boston.

British General Hospital Number 11 was primarily a tented camp. With exception of the nurses and those patients housed in one of three hut wards, everyone else lived in tents. Patients and enlisted men occupied crowded rows of canvas marquees; the officers took up quarters in a cluster of bell tents.

The hospital's usual capacity was 1,850 beds. But in an emergency this number was increased to 2,000 by using bed-sacks. During the Somme offensive, which had begun about seven weeks ago, 8,000 severely wounded soldiers had passed through General Hospital Number 11. Only 600 were still here. All the others had been evacuated. This was fortunate because Base Hospital Number 5 had personnel and equipment to care for only 1,040 patients at any one time. And our equipment still had not arrived from Boston. Many soldiers who remained were seriously injured and their wounds badly infected. I met some of these men when I made rounds in my ward with the medical officer.

It seemed as if I'd been on duty only a few minutes when we heard firing from the direction of Boulogne. Soon the guns on the hill just over our camp came to life with devastating commotion. Even though the German plane was far above their reach, all the anti-aircraft guns in the area fired.

We ran out of the tent to see the little silver fish sailing over. They looked about two inches long in the bright sunshine. When our anti-aircraft bullets came raining back down we beat it back into the tent only to find that the bullets came though the canvas with considerable force. Nobody was hit, but we plucked several shells out of mattresses. One bullet fell between a doctor and a patient whose wound he was dressing.

I finished the first half of my shift at 1:30 p.m. and didn't have to be back on duty until four p.m. So a couple of other nurses from Base Hospital Number 5 and I walked with some British nurses to the hills. They would have surrounded the camp had the sea not been on one side. Even from a mile away they were so clearly outlined against the cloudless blue sky that we could see several people walking on top of them. The hills were a treeless canvas in various shades of green splashed with brilliant yellow and blue. As we got closer those splashes became fields of flowers. In only a few weeks orange-red poppies would dominate.

"We're lucky," said one of the British nurses. "This is the first glorious weather that we've had since last year." The British nurses, or sisters as they're called, told us that they came to the hills as often as they could. It was easy to understand why. The war seemed far away despite the huge war hospital camp stretching below.

The hospitals of the Dannes-Camiers group were located east of the railway line that ran between the twin townships of Dannes and Camiers. The British had designated this tract, which was about a mile long and half a mile wide, as a hospital camp. They subdivided it into six sections and allotted one, 2,000-bed general hospital to each. The 12,000-bed hospital complex was only one part of the much larger Camiers-Ètaples group along the main Boulogne-Amiens Railway line. This huge area was primarily a training ground for troops. But the hospitals on this ten-mile stretch from Dannes in the north to Ètaples in the south could care for 70,000 sick and wounded soldiers. British General Hospital Number 11 was the most northerly in this series of hospitals.

Picking out the location of British General Hospital Number 11 from the hills was easy. The huge Portland Cement works at its northern boundary was clearly visible. In operation constantly, the cement factory was often lighted at night. A large ammunition dump was close. Enclosed in barbed wire a camp of Kaffirs of the South African Labor Corps lay to the south of the hospital. A railway embankment formed its western boundary. I felt sure that the Jerries would hit the hospital if they tried to bomb any of the prime targets.

Working in a military hospital was new to all members of Base Hospital 5. As soon as I was called to active duty last month on May 6th, I began to learn a new language, that of the U.S. Army. Two phrases that we all learned immediately upon arriving at General Hospital Number 11 were "Convoy" and "Evacuation." "Convoy" meant that we'd be receiving wounded from the Casualty Clearing Stations. These advanced surgical units were located as close to the front as possible and were highly mobile. They could be moved at a moment's notice. Battlefield medical officers sent men to a Casualty Clearing Station who needed emergency surgery and subsequent removal to a stationary rear area hospital such as ours.

"Evacuation" meant sending those who were wounded or sick to a place farther from the front, after treatment at one of the stationary hospitals. Often evacuation was back to England or "Blighty" as many fondly called their homeland. So, we received patients by convoy and sent them away by evacuation.

Being able to handle large numbers of casualties was critical especially during an offensive. So the army had established a system of general hospitals along the main lines of communication on the British front. Like General Hospital Number 11 these hospitals were the last link in the chain of care for wounded and sick soldiers. In the language of the Army "wounded" indicated a battle casualty, "sick" did not. So a soldier who had a compound fracture of the bone was "wounded" only if the enemy had caused the injury. Otherwise he was classified as "sick." Capacities of the base hospitals varied from 500 to 2,000 patients.

The convoys usually arrived either in the early evening or before six a.m. Automobile ambulances met the ambulance trains at the siding and rushed the wounded to the hospital. We had about half an hour's notice before patients began arriving. Usually the walking wounded appeared first. With help of a wounded comrade or an orderly, they hobbled out of the dusty-gray ambulances. Before the war these old sight-seeing cars had populated city streets and sent pedestrians scurrying.

The walking wounded went first to a receiving tent and then to the bath house. All their clothing, most of it mud-caked, was sent to the disinfection tent. After receiving clean clothes the patients went to their assigned quarters and had their wounds dressed.

Next in the stream of patients came the stretcher cases. As soon as they passed through the reception tent the bearers carried them to their assigned wards and carefully placed them on mattress-covered iron cots. For the first time in weeks or even months, the soldiers lay in clean, comfortable beds. Most of the soldiers were exhausted after long hours of sleepless travel and we had to wake them up to give them hot soup.

Nurses often cut away dressings applied in the field so that the medical staff could examine the wounds. Some of them were horrific. Arms, legs, and parts of faces had been blow away and large areas of muscle and flesh were missing because of shrapnel, shell, and grenade fragments. Shreds of dirty clothing were almost always imbedded in the wounds. By the time some of the patients got to us maggots were feasting on the dead tissue. Often patients had lain for hours or even days in water-filled shell holes without medical attention. For centuries Northern France had been cultivated and lavishly fertilized with manure. So the pervasive mud and dirt teemed with disease-causing organisms, including those that produced gas gangrene.

We might keep soldiers at General Hospital Number 11 to recuperate or send them across the Channel to Blighty. The severity of their wounds or illness determined their fate. We evacuated patients about twice a week unless a push was going on at the front. Then we might send an evacuation group out every day. The number of patients admitted and discharged varied according to the need for vacant beds, patients' conditions, and available transportation. Closing the Channel to clear it of mines often delayed the transfer of patients to England. Even though patients were leaving, the work didn't stop. Each soldier got clean linen, had his dressing changed, and was fed before leaving.

Although the workload tended to be irregular, we were very busy most of the summer. But we never worked at a fever pitch like they did at the Casualty Clearing Stations. Our work ran on an even keel. Each nurse had a pass from one p.m. until nine p.m. once a week. We might lose other time off, but only the operating room nurses had their night's sleep interrupted.

In June we cared for between 800 and 1,000 soldiers every day. The weather was accommodating and exceptionally fine for Picardy. The days were so hot and the nights so cold that we were glad not to have a thermometer.

On July 1st, 1,876 sick and wounded crowded our marquees. Each housed from 48 to 60 patients. Although severely understaffed, we carried on. We were able to do so only because 225 British personnel, including 40 Volunteer Aid Detachments (V.A.D.s) who worked as nursing assistants, bolstered our numbers.

In mid-July we received the first casualties from mustard gas. When the Germans first used it in large amounts the night of July 13-14, 3,000 soldiers suffered from gas poisoning. Blisters covered their faces. Red, and weeping pus, their eyes were shut tightly against the light. The full effects of this colorless and comparatively odorless gas became apparent hours after an attack. Then began a terribly painful, jagged cough; lips cracked and noses ran buckets. In four or five days gassed victims got very short of breath and could only cough, gasp, and drink water. Being able to do so little for them made us feel helpless.

At the end of July the reinforcements that we had cabled home for two months earlier arrived. Of the 80 enlisted men and 20 nurses that we'd requested, the War Department authorized 40 enlisted men, five officers, and 15 nurses. The nurses came from Connecticut, New Jersey, Maryland, and Virginia, adding to the diversity of our group.

We hadn't requested more rats because the place was infested. But this wasn't all bad because it created entertainment. Saturday afternoon British soldiers came from a nearby machine-gun encampment. Armed with ferrets and a motley collection of dogs, these Tommies surrounded a building and hunted for rats.

Offensive and defensive operations in Flanders flooded all the base hospitals with wounded in August. Ours was no exception. On August 1st alone, we had 964 admissions. These casualties heralded the Third Battle of Ypres that had begun the day before. The objective was German-held ports on the Belgian coast. The Allies, including British, Canadian, and Australian troops fought this long and bitter battle on waterlogged earth in the driving rain.

By the end of August, 5,000 patients had passed through the hospital. Because Base Hospital Number 5 was assigned to active duty with the British Expeditionary Forces, our patients were primarily Tommies until the end of the month although we had a few Australians and New Zealanders. Then we began to get a lot of Canadians. By the end of the battle in November, 1917, the Allies had advanced five miles and incurred more than 300,000 casualties.

Although the first three months flew, feelings of unrest prevailed among all members of the unit. Ever since we arrived in May rumors that we'd soon be moving began to circulate. General Hospital Number 11 had been operating for two years. It showed definite signs of wear and tear, had no laboratory, and was in a badly drained area full of old sump-pits. Unrelenting rains the last few days of June and early July confirmed that the hospital was, indeed, in an undesirable area. Wet weather made some patient areas uninhabitable.

Despite continuing rumors about moving, being here was exciting. Everything was new and different. I wanted to capture some of what I was seeing on film. So in late August I asked my youngest brother Alan to get me a vest pocket Eastman Kodak film developing tank that didn't need the absolute darkroom. I also asked him to send me some mild Russian cigarettes. I didn't know any special names so left the brand to his judgment. In order to escape the censor I asked someone to mail my letter. That way I could tell Alan that I was in Camiers.

Earlier I had sent money for a bicycle. It might seem like an extravagance, I told him. But really, it wasn't. I felt that I was getting very stale with what went on off duty. Tennis matches appealed to some; the lectures, concerts, and dramatic performances held for Sisters and officers in the Y.M.C.A. hut to others. But I was interested in seeing the environs. It would be great to have some means of locomotion other than shanks mare.

Since we'd arrived, General Hospital Number 11 had been exempt from bombings. This changed the night of September 4th. Around 10:45 p.m. I was getting ready for bed. This was the second of two strenuous days and I was looking forward to turning in. While I was brushing my hair the electric lights flashed twice and suddenly the entire camp went black. This plunge into darkness, which was controlled by a central switch, signaled a pending air raid. About ten minutes later the lights came on again and we all breathed a sigh of relief. Then just as quickly as they had come on, they went out. We rushed into the bright moonlight. Almost as soon as the air raid siren at the cement factory began to wail we heard the distant whir of the airplane. Immediately the swish and deafening explosion of bombs enveloped us.

A lone German Gotha dropped seven bombs or aerial torpedoes in our area. The first tore a deep hole in the athletic field of the hospital to our south. The second torpedo fell on the hospital next to us. Luckily the bomb was a dud.

The five remaining bombs hit us directly. Two fell among the officers' tents located at the southern section of our area. The low-flying fragments of these daisy-cutter bombs scattered far and wide. One fragment pierced the bed cradle on a patient's cot. After exiting this frame that keeps bed linens off a patient's body, the fragment lodged in the good leg of a patient two beds away. The patient in the middle bed escaped unscathed. The next day we found fragments of these bombs in the officers' wooden mess hut 160 feet away.

The third and fourth bombs struck one of the five marquee wards. One bomb exploded at the near end of the patient-filled ward, the other directly on a tent. These bombs also damaged the adjacent ward.

The fifth bomb flattened the reception tent. Fortunately the unit wasn't "taking in" at the time. Had it been, the number of causalities would have been unfathomable because the reception tent is the most congested spot in the hospital camp when a convoy arrives.

As soon as the attack was over, we began picking up the pieces and simply carried on. An officer and three enlisted men had been killed instantly, the first mortalities for Americans at Camiers. Three officers, 28 enlisted men, and a nurse were wounded, five severely. We were accustomed to dealing with a lot of urgent cases when a convoy arrived. But the casualties of this air raid were thrust upon us without warning. Moreover, we had no electricity. So all activities that night, including surgery, were performed by candle and lantern light. Everyone pitched in because there was so much to do. But being busy was a blessing; we didn't have time to think about what had just happened.

The next day we were eager to hear Miss Eva Jean Parmelee's story of the raid. She was the nurse on duty in the ward that was bombed. "My orderly, Oscar Tugo, came running from his supper," she said. "I met him in the road in front of our two tents. Suddenly we heard the hum of the planes and saw a sputtering streak of sparks drop from the sky. The orderly cried out, 'Why, they're here!'"

"After a deafening report, I found myself in the ditch. The choking, sulphurous smell and the noise made me feel as if I were being stirred up in a great bowl of reeking gunpowder. Four more reports followed and I said to myself: 'We're done for—they're wiping us out!'"

"Then I heard the calls of the wounded: 'Sister-Sister!' I jumped up and with flashlight in hand ran to the tent door. The man nearest to me was bleeding badly. Doctors, nurses and men with stretchers were arriving, so I crossed over to the other tent. The whole front section had been blown up, beds, lockers, floor and all. Not a patient was in sight. Although wounded, they were all alive and had been moved to other wards."

Miss Parmelee's orderly was killed, but she suffered only two tiny face wounds and a black eye. She remained on duty the rest of the night and only the next day discovered that she had been wounded. When she went to the operating room to have a small shell fragment removed from her eyelid she was surprised to find at least six large holes in her sweater and heavy outer coat. Shrapnel had torn away her skirt and apron and severed her watch. Only the strap from which it had hung from her apron remained. She never found the watch.

A few days later we had a military funeral for three privates and the officer who'd been killed in the raid. The service was held at the English military cemetery about three miles away. Thousands of officers, enlisted men, and nurses attended. Bow-legged-bantam Highlanders led the procession, playing a dirge on their bagpipes. Finally the bodies were laid to rest in the sand dunes between Camiers and Ètaples.

Nearly every clear night after the attack brought air raid signals. So we began to look forward to cloudy and rainy nights because Fritz didn't come then. The air raid signals were silent and the arc of the searchlights absent. We could go to bed and sleep peacefully.

In mid-September I'd had a note from Alan. He would be here November 1st. I could hardly believe it. It would be swell to see him!

Alan had wanted to volunteer for war service when the German cavalry entered neutral Belgium on its way to invade France in August 1914. But he was a third year medical student at Harvard University and was advised to finish his medical education and internship. It was

September 1917, when he joined the First Harvard Medical Unit. The unit had been organized to serve with No. 22 British Expeditionary Forces, a neighbor of Number 11 British General Hospital, Camiers. Doctor Hugh Cabot was in charge.

I was night supervisor all of October and the workload was tremendous. A daily hospital census of from 1,533 to 1,677 was not uncommon. Being night supervisor was a pleasant change from teaching Harvard graduates how to sweep and mop, and wash a basin. Unfortunately I didn't see as much of the boys as I did when I was a head nurse and I missed the fun of giving them pleasant surprises and nice teas. They adored a 'salmon tea' which was bread and butter, tea, and canned salmon. Very tasty! I was finally getting to understand their accent. I even understood when one man said, "I sat on the hedge of the bed, and my 'ed haked 'alf han 'our."

The convoys when they came were a sight, 150 or more tired boys and on the whole so uncomplaining. It certainly bucked up my respect for the human creature about 75 per cent. Of course, as night supervisor I was now seeing everything in all the wards and I had much more of an idea of the whole. The jaw cases, for instance, were in a place by themselves. New faces took weeks to make, but the results were quite beyond the imagination.

The weather during most of October was devilish again. Hailstorms and thunder and lightning combined with the nearly continuous cold heavy rain meant trench feet and no more advance. Much of the soil here and to the north was clay, which made matters even worse. And such mud! I had no idea of what mud could be until I saw a suit of it with a pair of eyes, a mouth, a steel helmet, and a bloody white sling walk into my ward.

Faith sent me hand-knit socks for the boys. And we had already received plenty of pillows, cushions, wristlets, and mufflers to pack the boys off to Blighty with on cold nights. I hoped that our supply of warm clothing would last. I envisaged everyone at home doing some type of war work. A few folks predicted that the war would be over by Christmas. But most thought we'd be here until October next year. Either way, I'd very soon have use for my nice hot water bags.

I'd worn woolen underclothes, stockings, spencer, and sweater, plus a coat and a raincoat for the month. Only one night was I almost too hot. The fiendish dampness and the fact that I never got into a dry spot kept me cold. I'd bought a very nice Jaeger blanket and the nurses had been given Jaeger sleeping bags that would be wonderful in winter.

From seven-thirty p.m. until seven-thirty a.m., I tramped about in rubber boots with my skirts pinned up. It took about two and a half hours for me to make complete rounds. I went around once before midnight, once again to the sickest patients, and then once again in the morning for the report. How the patients slept was astonishing. In a civilian hospital a nurse would be on the clean jump every minute of the time with 50 patients. But here everyone was often either comfortable or asleep for 30 minutes at a time.

After nearly five months, I had come to know the Tommy thoroughly. And of course the Tommy was now every class of society except the very highest. I had an autograph book that got filled up very fast. Some of the sentiments were most amusing. I sent father some letters that I'd received from the boys when they got to Blighty.

I received a bunch of mail in October. The mails had been awfully slow lately, taking at least a full month to arrive from home. Now I had a great many letters to answer and only wished that I could show my friends and family the nice fat rats that played tag on, in, and under the tents during the night. An orderly said, "I don't mind them running down the tent with a cigarette in their mouth, but their chewing tobacco is such a dirty habit!" The nights were amusing and dreadful at the same time.

The undercurrent of unrest about moving came to a sudden halt on Monday, October 29th. We were to take over Number 13 General Hospital at the Casino in Boulogne on November 1st. So much for being promised at least ten days notice before moving. Thirty nurses went the morning of November 1st. Some other nurses and I who'd been on night duty went a few days later. The rumor mill had both old units Number 11 and Number 13 going to Italy for duty with the British Army. The Hun invasion in Italy and the revolution in Russia made these dark days for the Allies.

Before we'd received orders to move, Miss Carrie H. Hall, our chief nurse, had been arranging for a sheet and pillow case party with all the Halloween stunts. We had had dances before, but the V.A.D.s weren't permitted to dance. So Miss Hall decided to have a party that they could attend without criticism. The American officers participated merrily as did our English friends. Miss Hall and another nurse draped officers in sheets and tied cotton masks on their faces. They had real pumpkin jack-o-lanterns and doughnuts made of real flour, though goodness knows where the flour came from.

By Saturday, Base Hospital Number 5 was at Number 13 General with 900 patients. The hospital's usual capacity in winter was 631 beds, in summer around 800. Patients were housed not only in the Casino, but also in four huts on the Casino grounds.

Patient rooms in the Casino were adorned with huge mirrors, ornate stucco, gold arches, and a multitude of once-white wall decorations. The white building was built almost entirely of glass and the large windows provided magnificent views of the beach, the harbor, and the sea. As a head nurse I was responsible for two 50-bed huts filled with soldiers who had been burned or gassed.

Because of its accessibility to hospital ships in the port, Number 13 had been regarded as an evacuation hospital. However, because of the shelter that the Casino offered and because of our expert Corps of surgeons and medical staff, Number 13 was reclassified as a heavy surgical hospital. We were also to care for as many non-surgical cases as possible. The Casino, in terms of space, was well adapted to being a hospital. Some parts even had steam heat. However, in other ways the Casino, which the English had taken over at the beginning of the war, was less than ideal. For example, several improvised ward kitchens had no running water. In spite of inconveniences we soon settled at the Casino with a new feeling of *esprit de Corps*.

Although not a very large city in peace time, Boulogne now teemed with troops and officers of every description all the time—English, Canadian, Australia, New Zealand, American, French, Portuguese and every now and then a Hindustani, South African both white and black, and Chinese. The latter were here as workmen.

November seemed to be bound together by food. Early in the month Alan and I were able to have supper together. He was wearing the English uniform because he'd been given an honorary, temporary commission in the Royal Army Medical Corps when he arrived in London in September. I was glad that he was in the English uniform. The "Shave Tails" of the American uniform looked rather dowdy when compared with the much more tailored outfit of the British. Moreover, I could speak to him more freely. Socially we nurses were classed with the enlisted men. So we were forbidden to go out with the officers. Because Alan was my brother I could have supper with him, but I had to be careful not to make it too often.

Later in the month all members of the unit celebrated our first Thanksgiving in France with a turkey dinner. Our French cook at the nurses' mess in The Hotel de la Marine outdid herself. She prepared soup; roast turkey, fresh raised in Boulogne; mashed potatoes; stuffing; onions; celery; squash pie; cheese; nuts; raisins; fruit; coffee, and bread. The butter tasted so much better than oleo.

The British system gave us a great deal of freedom in administering our own quarters and mess. We provided our own food. The British government gave the U.S Army a board allowance for us. From this our Chief Nurse was responsible for buying rations from the British government at a definite rate. The balance of the money we spent in open French markets. There were, to be sure, some restrictions as to hours when we could purchase and prices that we could pay. Certain articles we couldn't buy at all. But we had a fairly varied and entirely nourishing diet.

Despite this sumptuous meal on a festive occasion, no one regretted having come for the duration. Yet, thoughts of our families were never far. Some nurses recounted humorous events of past Thanksgivings at home. I could envision the table at my sister Faith's at 40 Old Orchard Road in Chestnut Hill, Massachusetts groaning with food. I knew that Alan and I would be in our family's thoughts and prayers.

No sooner had Thanksgiving passed than Christmas loomed. But two weeks into December a fever of unknown origin confined me to my quarters at The Hotel de la Marine where all the nurses from Base Hospital Number 5 were billeted. It was directly across from the Casino. The French had condemned the hotel before the war. When we moved in it was very dirty. The hotel backed in to a hill at the rear so we had a very up and down effect with narrow dirty stairs in most unexpected places.

Nonetheless the hotel did have some rather endearing charms. Nearly every room had two or three large mirrors, old French gilt minus the gilt. Some rooms also had a fireplace that took the chill off wintry nights when a cold wind swept off the Channel searching to invade nooks and crannies and sap our warmth. When it wasn't too cold it was relaxing to sit in front of the fireplace and smoke a cigarette. We were also usually able to get the London papers on the day that they were published. This source of news was much better than at Number 11. News there consisted primarily of rumors and they changed so fast that we never believed anything until it happened.

Two days later I returned to duty as a head nurse. But after three days the fever once again flattened me in my quarters, this time for nine days. I wasn't the only member of Base Hospital Number 5 who had succumbed to the ailment that was probably a precursor to the flu.

I was secure in my room on the evening of December 22nd when Boulogne was bombed without warning. Many of the 170 casualties, including men, women and children were taken to the already overcrowded Number 13 General Hospital. Personnel worked throughout the night removing the dead from the streets and demolished buildings. The raid was both brief and devastating, occurring in a densely populated area when many people were out for an early evening stroll with no hope of taking cover.

Despite the bombing, the nurses and men decorated the Christmas trees placed in all the wards. On Christmas Eve a chorus of nurses, officers, and men sang carols in the wards. Perhaps it was a good thing I couldn't participate. Members of Base Hospital Number 5 described me as an accomplished singer, provided no one was near enough to hear me. Each patient received a present and the cooks provided a Christmas dinner complete with English plum pudding for dessert. We nurses had a festive buffet supper in our mess.

In addition to the holiday cards that I received from home (our presents didn't arrived until the following spring), I had a Christmas card from Sir Thomas Lipton. He had sent a card to each member of the unit. How well I remember that afternoon at his country house in May. We had arrived from New York after ten days at sea and were to have about a week in London. Sir Thomas had invited us to lunch and tea the following Sunday, a fine day, sunny and hot. As soon as we arrived he presented each nurse with a red, white, and blue bouquet.

Entertainment followed a very nice luncheon, with claret served side by side with lemonade. Then we posed for still and moving pictures. Finally the call for tea came. We had the real Lipton brand, an abundance of bread and butter, sugar and cream, with "Shortbread" and candy to top it off. While speeches were made, the ladies at our table smoked and pitied us because we couldn't smoke in uniform. Sir Thomas gave each nurse a box of candy before we boarded the buses for our London accommodation.

That day in May seemed far from this winter's short days with their penetrating cold and dampness. The first few months of 1918 we cared for patients with fevers of unknown origin, bronchitis, trench foot, and old wounds that were horribly infected. My medical officer was Doctor Tom Goethals. He told me that Doctor Cushing, who came in to see some wounded soldiers, said that he couldn't get the dressings in his wards that I had on hand. Tom was very pleased and passed his pleasure on to me. Neither of them knew how long it took me to wangle what I wanted out of the British Sergeant in charge of supplies. He enjoyed being kidded and I kidded him out of his Red Cross supplies. I took pleasure in having on hand what was called for.

The summer of 1914 I had taken a four-month post-graduate course in administration at Massachusetts General Hospital. The course prepared graduates for positions as hospital superintendents. Among the topics we studied were methods of contracting for hospital supplies. Kidding was not mentioned.

Because of our comparatively light work load, some nurses went on their first leave since arriving, but all this changed in mid-March when the Germans launched the Second Battle of the Somme. In only ten days they ripped apart the Allied defensive system and hurled the British and French armies back for 35 miles along a 50 mile front.

Although casualties were heavy, at first most of the wounded Tommies went to hospitals to our south. But beginning on March 23rd we received convoys of gassed and wounded soldiers. In early April the Germans launched a new phase of their offensive and we received untreated stretcher cases directly from Armentières. For the next ten days wounded and gassed soldiers, as well as those with severe head wounds, inundated our landing platform and reception hall. The hospital was already full, but the wounded kept coming.

Just as the wounded filled our days, so air raids filled our nights. The Germans were trying to smash Boulogne because all British reinforcements had to come through here. The dread of the raids was cumulative. When the siren sounded at night we nurses scampered from our rooms to a dugout in the cliff behind the hotel. Many of us would have preferred to take our chances in a warm dry bed, rather than a wet hole in the ground. The nurses on night duty of course stayed with the patients. Sandbags surrounded all the medical huts, the Casino itself, and some had even been placed between the rows of beds in some of the wards.

Finally things quieted down enough so that on May 20th, I was able to take my first leave. It was almost a year to the day since I'd arrived in France. I was more than ready for a change.

FOR THE DURATION

I LEFT BOULOGNE ON TUESDAY THE 28TH OF May at 8:30 p.m. in a wagon-lit or sleeping car. They will reserve them for sisters, but always with the proviso that no brass hats are coming through to Paris. Another of the Number 13 nurses was with me so we had a very pleasant night with no foreigners. We arrived in Paris at 11:30 Wednesday morning.

I hadn't visited Paris in 1910 when I went to Europe with the Forbes children so this was my first time in the city. I decided to devote a day to Paris and rocketed around the entire day. I thoroughly enjoyed burning up the boulevards. The stores were mostly going full blast except on the *Champs-Élysées* where most of them were closed or else devoted entirely to Red Cross committees and workrooms.

That evening I left on the 8:20 train for *Evian-les-Bains* on the shores of Lake Geneva for six days. The journey to Evian was in 1st Class carriages sitting up all night by way of Culoz. Three Frenchmen, an American Ambulance driver, a Scotch padre, and I shared the carriage. The English-speaking contingent hogged the outside windows and had a very pleasant time until 11:30 when it became necessary to carefully arrange our feet, pillows, and overcoats with what comfort and grace we could manage.

Each Frenchman had at least five cushions and two blankets and looked daggers at the open window. The *courant d'aire* nearly finished them.

I was much diverted by the experience of this night of traveling alone. Really it is quite simple and the English officers are so very kind and thoughtful that it is very pleasant. I changed trains at Culoz easily, but the padre and the American nearly missed their train while putting me on mine. We parted hastily.

After Bellegarde we began to go through the lower mountains up and up. It was good to see actual rocks and trees again and the change from coastal air to the thinner lake air was most refreshing.

Evian is a little place and is entirely given over to the repatriates. The convoys that came made for interesting sights. Seven hundred French people who are being relocated arrived at 6:30 a.m. and another 700 twelve hours later. Six trumpets and six drums greeted them. Anything more pathetic than the dancing joy of the old and the young I have never imagined. They keep time to the music and hop up and down. Then often two or three groups start a song when the first trumpeting stops. They march through the station to the street and then the quarter-mile to the casino. Red Cross ambulances transport the very old or sick. Evian has both an adult hospital and a children's hospital. The entire countryside is given over to housing.

At the casino the repatriates are fed a solid meal of soup, bread, meat, potatoes, a glass of wine, and chocolate. Then they go through the clerical department. An information card is filed for each person and there's a secretary for each letter of the alphabet. This department also delivers mail and telegrams. The repatriates meet their friends. The adults go through the secret service bureau. A doctor examines all the children and if they're sick, a French woman tells the family what will happen. Then the repatriates have a shower bath and receive fumigated clothing. After that they are very rapidly dispersed. They are sent to their homes, which may be temporary or permanent. They are cared for entirely by the French.

The whole operation is French organization except the children's clinic, dispensary, and hospital.

My seven-day leave passed all too quickly and I was soon back in Boulogne. One of the first things I'd promised myself that I'd do was write to Barbara, Donald's wife. My second eldest brother, a graduate of Harvard Medical School, had specialized in psychiatry and mental hygiene. Later he'd married Barbara, whose father, Dr. Walter Channing, had established the Channing Sanitarium, Wellesley, Massachusetts in 1879. It was advertised as a "small country community caring for no more than 35 patients." Men and women, old and young suffering from mental and nervous disorders, or in need of rest and convalescence went there for care.

Although I felt refreshed when I got back to work and fully intended to write to Barbara right away, it took me longer than I expected. By now I should have realized the devil of chopping off more than I could consume. When I did write Barbara, I told her I was making every attempt to straighten the line and come in strong on a correspondence offensive. Go while the going is good, I thought.

I saw Alan in July. He told me that I looked very well, that I was cheery, and apparently contented. He was right. Since returning from my leave I continued on as associate editor for *The Vanguard*, a position I had agreed to in May. This was Base Hospital Number 5's monthly publication and the American Expeditionary Forces' first publication. We featured poems, sports and news items, information about concerts, and information about personnel transfers and promotions, commonly referred to as "Camp Notes." Members of the unit had founded the monthly paper in July, 1917, for their families and friends. Unit members continued to edit and distribute it.

As if a prelude to our Fourth of July party, we had a severe air raid the night of July 1st. The enemy dropped 80 to 90 bombs on Boulogne. Four hit near Base Hospital Number 5, breaking windows on one side of the Casino. No personnel were hit, nor were any of our 584 patients. But over the next few days several nurses and men developed minor neuroses. We called it shell shock.

Members of Base Hospital Number 5 celebrated our second Fourth of July in France with a Gala Day of Sports. Events included a 50-yard dash (free for all), a potato race for ladies, a 50-yard dash for officers, a sack race, and a three-legged race for ladies. Last but by no means least, we had a thread and needle race. Chaplain Peabody and I placed second in the finals.

Shortly after the Fourth of July party was over the "Whizz- Bangs" began to appear. The daily "Whizz-Bang" first appeared in the middle of September, 1917. It was the unit's first attempt at producing a daily paper. It ceased publication for a while but resurfaced in July. Shortly after its resurgence, Miss Walsh and I engaged in another literary effort. We wrote a new production entitled "The District School" and staged it in the enlisted men's hut.

In mid-July the tide changed for the Allies. The German High Command had been planning to take Paris. But together the French, American, and British thwarted their attempt. We received several convoys of American patients, but work in our district was low-key because most of the fighting was to our south. Fewer patients didn't mean any less excitement. We had air raids almost every night later in the month and throughout the month of August as the Germans tried to interrupt the British lines of communication. Finally, in late August we painted a red cross on a white background and put it on the roof of the Casino. We also erected more sandbags. August was marked by a great water shortage in Boulogne. The hospital water supply was frequently shut off which made it difficult to keep the wards clean.

Our workload increased greatly in August. Since mid-June we'd received no walking wounded, only stretcher cases and "special" cases, patients who needed more intensive medical and nursing care. This put extra pressure on us, although as soon as patients could walk we evacuated them to convalescent camps. These camps were actually hospitals for ambulatory patients. By the end of August we had treated 2,890 sick and wounded soldiers. More than two-thirds were British, the remainder Americans.

We'd had major changes in personnel. Miss Hall, our chief nurse, had been called to London in May for duty as Chief Nurse, American Red Cross, for Great Britain. Miss Rose Butler succeeded her as out chief. Moreover, one nurse had to be sent to England because she was so upset by an air raid. We didn't think she'd ever be able to rejoin us. And several nurses had to be hospitalized because of the strain of the work. Night work during the air raids was the worst.

In August I had in my surgical ward rather the less severe type of case. Amputations, and now and then, compound fractures. The through and through bullet wounds were, of course, septic, some more than others. Wound infections were particularly troublesome because they often led to amputations and sometimes death.

We used the Carrel-Dakin method to treat the infected wounds. This was a method of irrigating wounds with an antiseptic solution called Dakin's solution. Dead tissue was first cut away from the wound. Then a series of rubber tubes were placed at all depths of the wound to deliver the hypochlorite solution of fixed strength to the tissue. The smallest tubes were placed in the deepest part of the wounds and joined with glass connectors to ever-larger tubing. Then every three hours or so the nurse opened a stopcock, allowing the Dakin's solution to flow from a liter glass bottle to the infected areas. The wounds seemed to clear fairly well.

For the 47 beds in my ward I had five personnel, two orderlies and three nurses, including myself as the head nurse. That made about 24 patients to each working nurse and orderly. I filled in all the holes that I could, but I had considerable bookkeeping the first thing in the morning which made helping with patients difficult.

The orderlies swept and washed the rubber sheets and basins, waited on patients, gave some baths, changed some dressings, and did some treatments. The sisters made the beds, gave treatments and medicines, took temperatures, pulses, and respirations, and did dressing changes with the medical officer.

Because our dining room was small, two seatings served each meal. The head nurse went to second breakfast at 8 a.m., a half-hour later than the other nurses. It was a nuisance because I just didn't get things done as

I wanted before the medical officer came on at nine. By 9:30 we were ready to dress wounds and from then on it was a constant hustle of dressing changes until 12 noon. I did just about break my neck to get through at noon, so that I could do my routine work in the afternoon.

Dinner came up at 12:00 p.m. We stopped changing dressings for about 20 minutes, got the supplies made up for the sterilizer and then went for our own dinners at 12:15 and 1 p.m. The hours off were from two p.m. to five p.m. or five p.m. to eight. This made the working hours fairly short, but when a rush came we lost the time off. Moreover, in slack times there wasn't a great deal to do so I didn't enjoy my spare time as much here as I would have at home.

In the afternoon we did dressings or made supplies and gave treatments. We started to take temperatures at 3:15 p.m. and rubbed backs and did treatments again at six. That, with the countless drinks of water, "fix my pillow, sister," and all the rest of the stuff that came up such as linen count, commanding officer's visit and adjutants' inspection, the day was gone before I knew it.

I got very fond of a great many of the patients and missed them when we sent them on to Blighty. I have had lots of amusing letters and cards from them. I'll keep them to look at when I'm 80 odd years.

One of my pet patients was a private 1st Coldstream Guards. He was a dandy, a dental mechanic from Liverpool in private life. He had lovely blue eyes and a very cheery smile. He was fond of puzzles and books and I spent several spare minutes with him.

Another of my pets was a Scotch lad, a barber from Fife, Keith Bauffshire. I hadn't heard from him for a long time after he went up the line. He was such a dear. I knew he'd be in for a stiff time. He certainly was a live wire. He was a Lance Corporal and was the company runner for the 9th Gordons. The 9th Gordons were sappers, trench diggers who put up the barbed wire entanglements. Dirty work in no man's land most of it because the runners carry all the messages back and forth from the working parties to the command. You had to be a good scout to stand that racket and get away with the goods.

My "routine" and that of many other members of Base Hospital Number 5 changed drastically in September when we were assigned to Mobile Unit Number 6. Nineteen other nurses, three medical officers, 30 enlisted men and I entrained for Deuxnouds in the Argonne, southwest of Nubécourt. This really depleted the personnel of Number 13 General Hospital at a time when all staff was needed. But we'd been asked to go and off we went.

Mobile units operated approximately 30 miles from the firing line caring for "non-transportable" patients. The average mortality rate was 90%. Traveling exclusively by motor truck, these units could erect a 250-bed tent hospital in 18 hours and evacuate it in a third of the time. Mobile Unit Hospital Number 6 saw some of the heaviest fighting in the Argonne. Shell fire and hospital raids were nearly continuous.

On September 25th, the day before the opening of our offensive in the Argonne, we were still short of supplies and personnel. We nurses had been the first to arrive, followed several days later by batches of officers, enlisted men and wagons. It was a somewhat surprised outfit that found itself a Mobile Unit temporarily placed in what was destined to be a stationary hospital for head cases only, in an old château in a small isolated French town. Captain Harvey, who had left Boulogne the month before, was "sitting on the lid" and in possession of such articles as he had been able to retain, by fraud, funds or persuasions, from the French staff which had just evacuated the place. Those articles ranged from pig 1, potato patch 1, market garden 1, to such rare products as coal and petrol and some cans of sterile dressings from the New England Surgical Dressings Committee which were cached in an old barn. And what is more, wounded began to arrive about the time Mobile Number 6 did, together with many surgical teams from diverse sources, all of whom had to be cared for.

I was a head nurse in this unit. We worked 12 hours a day caring for severely wounded soldiers. Each shift a surgical team was on duty, together with a triage officer, ward nurses and orderlies, and stretcher-bearers.

For eighteen days we were operational at Duexnouds and during that time we cared for 819 patients. It was said that the average time between wound and admission to our unit was 7 hours due to our proximity to the front. By October 14th, we were ordered to move again, this time to Varennes. Due to shelling the nurses were unable to move until October 24th. This new location was about 15 kilometers from the front line. As the enemy fell back, the line was farther away, nearly 45 kilometers. And with that distance, the time between a soldiers' receiving a wound and his arrival for care increased to nearly 24 hours. There was talk we would be moved again, to be nearer the front. But by November 8th, it was evident there was no need. The enemy was collapsing.

The Armistice was signed on November 11th. Our work continued but we soon stopped admitting and the unit began to prepare for a possible move to Germany. That, too, became unnecessary.

Effective November 30, 1918, 19 other nurses and I were temporarily assigned to Evacuation Hospital Number 18. We were to go to Briey, the coal and iron mining area of France that the Germans had occupied before the first battle of the Marne. When we arrived on December 1st, we joined the hospital personnel in their attempt to clean the unit and organize the chaos they'd found. They'd been at it for a week and it took another week to finish the job.

Before being transferred to Briey, Evacuation Hospital Number 18 had been in St. Mihiel. It took 85 motor trucks and 15 ambulances to transfer the personnel and equipment. The hospital they took over had been a French civilian hospital.

The Germans had vacated the building only four days before the Evacuation Hospital Number 18 took it over. In fact, a German medical lieutenant and eight enlisted men were still at the hospital, awaiting a pass through the allied lines. In addition to the German personnel there were a number of French civilians and soldiers and a few American and German soldiers who had been kept by the German hospital.

By the time we arrived, the personnel of Evacuation Hospital Number 18 had done a great deal of cleaning and repairing. But much more was needed. Obviously the Germans had done no cleaning for a long time. Owing to the plumbing being in very bad repair, the building reeked with the odor of unflushed sewerage.

The complement of the Field Hospital, from whom Evacuation Hospital Number 18 had taken over this occupied French civilian hospital, was too small to do anything but take care of the patients.

Two things had badly handicapped Evacuation Hospital Number 18's cleaning and organizing efforts of the first few days. Within 48 hours after arriving, more than 1,200 patients were admitted to the hospital. The divisional sanitary units just ahead sent all their patients back so they could move on with their divisions. So more than 1,300 patients occupied the hospital, as well as surrounding tents and barracks which had been thrown up to take care of the overflow. The personnel of Evacuation Hospital Number 18 told us that cots were placed two deep in the corridors, and the recreation parlor and every other available floor space was utilized. The men were all fed and had a sleeping place, either bed, cot or stretcher, but they had very little room to move around.

Finally, on the third day, the overcrowding was relieved. A hospital train was brought up to within 15 minutes ambulance run of the hospital to speed evacuation.

The second great handicap was the lack of water. An electric pumping station with a high tank supplied the hospital. But the water came from a reservoir quite some distance from the hospital. An electric pumping station of very limited capacity filled the reservoir. The electricity to power this pumping station came from Strassbourg in German Lorraine. On any given day at least one of these links in the chain of supply was broken. The result, of course, was that water could be obtained but rarely.

As if the overcrowding, filthy conditions and defective plumbing were not enough, the chimney from the main cooking range was out of commission. The Germans (Boch) had plugged it with bricks. So feeding the total of 1,500 odd mouths was a problem. Moreover, the Germans had taken every piece of equipment that wasn't nailed down. They had cut the electric wiring in the X-ray laboratories off sheer with the wall, so as to leave not even a single inch of useful wire. Their spoils also included most of the lights so that much of the hospital was in darkness either partial or absolute, from four p.m. till morning.

By sheer hard work and determination, by the end of my first week at Evacuation Hospital Number 18 the personnel had put the hospital in shape to meet any demands. We had erected a number of portable German buildings which increased the hospital's capacity. So we were able to dispense with most of the tentage which had hastily been put up during the rush.

Effective December 18th, 1918, I was transferred back to Base Hospital 5 in Boulougne. But I couldn't leave Briey until the 29th of December. So I spent Christmas there. Considering the state of affairs when the 19 nurses and I arrived, it's hard to believe that a month later, we had a dance. The officers and nurses of the unit gave it in conjunction with the 166th Aero Squadron and the 110th Infantry. Then on Christmas day we gave a party for the French children of Briey and nearby areas. We had more than 500 guests.

The Christmas tree for the children of the neighborhood was a really delightful experience. It was their first real Christmas since 1913.

The crowd of youngsters, quite a few with their parents, exceeded our expectations. All shapes and sizes, but all dressed in their best, they filled the great corridor and then overflowed into the courtyard. With rosy cheeks and sparkling eyes, they struggled to catch a glimpse of Santa Claus, who was holding forth in Chapel. We all thought these children much more orderly than a crowd of American children would have been. At last, we got them to form a line and we gave each of them a ticket. The ticket entitled each of them to a present, as well as a chance on a splendid toy automobile or a doll. As they walked excitedly past Santa Claus, his assistants distributed the presents. To add to the festivities, the band of the 110th Infantry played in an adjoining room. Eventually the tree was bare. Everyone had gotten something and in cases, more than one something. Some didn't want to leave. They were quite happy to hang around for a long time. We were pleased to have had the party for them. Long after the guests had gone—some had required considerable persuasion—we talked about who had had more fun, they or we.

A while later we had a visit from the *Medecin—Inspecteur Sabatier, Directeur du Service de Sante' du 14th Corps*, Army of France. The Inspector was favorably impressed with all that he saw. But when he when into the Dental Office and found a Poilu in the chair being treated while a half dozen Americans, including an officer were waiting, he became even more impressed.

I got back to Base Hospital 5, January 1, 1919. Then came a welcome leave of absence from the 3rd or 4th through the 12th, with permission to visit Paris. Reserve nurses Ruth E. Hawkins and Cora L. Thompson had the same leave. We had been together at Mobile Hospital Number 6.

From the 17th to the 26th, I had another type of leave. Sick leave. For the first two days I was sick in my quarters, but then spent the 18th to the 26th in the hospital. Perhaps exhaustion was the source of my illness.

We received orders to demobilize Base Hospital 5, but it wasn't until March 6th that I was transferred to Brest for embarkation to the United States, aboard the S.S. George Washington. I reported to the nurses' demobilization station, which was the Hotel Albert in New York City, on the 25th of March. I was happy to be back in the U.S. after 22 months as an Army Nurse. After a few days in New York City, I left on March 31st for Chestnut Hill in Boston. My experience in the Great War had left me weary, but proud of the work we had done.

Thoughts of the war end abruptly when I realize I am nearing Rosebud. The drive from Winner has been uneventful, a good thing since my thoughts were overseas. But, as I consider the next part of my plan of work, I doubt that uneventful will be a correct adjective. I am about to encounter the field matrons in their own districts.

JUNE 21, 1966—FROM ALBUQUERQUE TO SANTA FE

"THANKS FOR DRIVING TODAY. I'M A LITTLE TIRED so I appreciate the chance to be a passenger," Melody said, leaning back in the seat with her eyes closed.

"Are you feeling bad or are you just worn out?" Alice asked as she maneuvered her Karmann Ghia into the stream of northbound traffic. Shifting smoothly into high gear, she considered whether to mention what was on her mind or to let Melody sleep.

"No, I'm just fine, just glad to be able to rest a little. I'm not comfortable letting down much when I'm at home." Melody spoke with her eyes closed. "I listened to Miss Gregg's third tape last night. World War I must have been an awful experience for everyone who was in the combat. But, she said it was a great opportunity for the nurses."

"In a way, I can understand that because for the individual nurses, it was a chance to do important work and at the same time have experiences they wouldn't be likely to have in the jobs most nurses had at the time," Alice said. "Back then most registered nurses did private duty in people's homes or were the head nurses or superintendents in hospitals. Students did the rest of the hospital staff nursing. District nursing or visiting nursing had been a part of the beginnings of public health nursing in the U.S. before the turn of the century. But it was only after the war that there was a greater recognition of the value of public health nursing as a means to emphasize disease prevention. So, before the war, most of the opportunity for nurses was in hospitals or doing private duty." Alice paused for a moment, then continued. "Many nurses had their training at a hospital and worked in that same hospital for their entire careers. Going off to the war was a big change from that pattern. I think that nursing, well actually women in general, made changes in the early nineteen hundreds that created opportunity for all the years since. There was women's suffrage; Margaret Sanger beginning to make birth control information available so that poor women didn't have to just endlessly bear children; there was Jeanette Rankin, who was the first woman elected to the House of Representatives. That was the time of the first feminists, around the turn of the century and the early nineteen hundreds." Alice looked over at Melody. "Don't take what I'm about to say the wrong way," she said. "I've been wondering why, with the opportunities we have now—I have now—I'm not taking any of those opportunities. Here I am, engaged, about to get married and go to work in some hospital, period. Oh sure, I'll make choices—the colors for the bridesmaids' dresses, which hospital to work in, maybe even whether to take the pill so I won't be a mother immediately. But that seems like so little when I think I could do more. That's why I'm still thinking about the Peace Corps. But I still haven't mentioned it to anyone but you." Silence from the passenger side drew her attention. Melody's gaze was fixed on the Sandias.

It seemed like minutes before Melody asked quietly, "You don't think that getting married and going on as you planned is enough?"

Hesitantly, Alice responded with the question she had been holding back, "Is it enough for you?"

"Truthfully, I don't let myself take the time to think about that. I made a commitment when I married Brice. Everything since then is a matter of living up to that promise. So, I guess that makes a lot of possible choices—about work and purpose in life—seem not to be possible choices at all. I can't just think about me, I have to always consider all of us." As she spoke, her hands closed protectively over her slightly protruding belly.

"Sometimes I get so frustrated with myself. Why can't I just settle down and be happy?" Alice asked. "I mean, I have all the things a woman's supposed to want and lots more than most people and it sounds like I'm complaining." Crossing her heart in a mock oath, she said, "I promise to shut up now and focus on this project."

When Melody laughed at her scout's honor sign, Alice said, "Thanks for listening. You're a good friend."

They continued in silence until they reached the outskirts of Santa Fe. Melody stretched and turned toward Alice.

"Now, about reminiscing, I read the Butler article from the bib and in it he mentions that life review is often a highly visual process. Maybe that's why she's able to close her eyes and tell her memories so vividly. It also suggests that the process of life review is something that can be aided by reminiscence and that life review may be a normal part of human development, part of developing identity, but one which typically happens in later life. From that, I think that while we may help Miss Gregg by asking her to reminisce, the benefit to her may be something we never know about. That she may find ideas or connections she hadn't looked at until now as she recalls events and people in her life. She may or may not want to or be able to talk about the meaning of those ideas and connections," Melody said.

"That's the way I understand it, too. And she could reminisce and do life review alone but encouragement may help. Makes me wonder about what I'll be reviewing when I'm her age. She's had such a full life. And if her current manner and the content of these stories are any indication, a part of her identity that's been in place for a long time is a good sense of humor and an interest in other people," Alice said.

"Goodbye Miss Gregg. Thank you for this next tape and for your time." Melody held the older nurse's hand as she spoke. Standing together she and Elinor embodied contrast, Alice realized as she looked at them. Tall with dark curly hair and olive complexion, her body and face blooming with pregnancy, Melody was "young womanhood." Elinor, with slightly stooped stocky body; gray once-red hair refusing to be contained; and slow gait was "old womanhood." Yet Alice saw something of the same in them. They both had what she called "nurse's eyes"; eyes that appear kind, concerned, intelligent and deeply intent on the other person. These were both people for whom conveying empathy and providing comfort came easily because it was genuine.

"Please call me Aunt El. Everyone else does. I'm so glad you both were here today and that we had time to chat. Next time you come I want to hear more about your curriculum in nursing school. Meanwhile, I'll get to work on another installment. Be careful on your way home."

As they left the driveway, Alice said, "I just love these pictures. The one taken when she graduated from Waltham Nursing School shows her as the ideal picture of a nurse, to me. And, isn't this one of her from the war just great? It's almost artistic and so clearly shows her strength and fatigue at the same time. I'm so glad she let us borrow them to copy."

"Yes, I'm going to make copies for each of us to keep besides the ones we'll use in our report. We'll want to remember her. I think the batteries in your recorder will hold out if you want to listen to this new tape while we go back to Albuquerque. No sense wasting a good hour," Melody said as she slipped the tape into the player.

INCURSION INTO BLACK PIPE

"He died Thursday at midnight. The service is tomorrow and I think that we should go." In the 30 below zero temperature every word of Lottie Rasch's greeting hangs like a cloud in front of her face.

"Who died?" I ask, getting my clothes and pocketbook out of my car.

"Mr. Perry. He was at the conference last month at the Agency. I'm sure you met him."

In fact, I do remember him. Tactful and kind, he impressed me as being a man of principle.

"He worked with the Indians here for sixteen years," Lottie says as we walk up the snowy path to her cottage. "At first he was a day school teacher, but for the last few months, he's been the farmer in charge of the Little White River district."

Lottie really wants to go to the funeral and I see no reason not to. After all, I'll learn more about the community and prairie geography.

Monday at first light we leave for White River, 60 miles away. With the temperature still 30 below zero, I tie several gunnysacks around the radiator. As I grapple with the bags, I wonder if the Bemis Bag Company made them. Lottie and I securely fasten the celluloid curtains in my Model T Ford runabout, wrap ourselves in blankets, and wish for heat.

Despite the gunnysacks, the radiator freezes and we steam into White River. "The Masonic Order is conducting the funeral," Lottie says, "and I'm just sure the whole town will be there." Confirming her prediction, she gestures with her gloved hand at all the buildings on the main street. "See, all the businesses are closed."

J.H. Perry wanted to be laid to rest in Indian country, among the people with whom he had worked and associated. The funeral is simple but full of the ritual of his Masonic lodge. When spring comes he'll be buried in the White River cemetery. But until the ground thaws, he'll rest peacefully in the woodshed.

All the way back to Black Pipe the engine overheats and the radiator steams. "Wasn't it nice that the whole town turned out for the funeral?" Lottie asks. "It just shows you how much the people thought of Mr. Perry. Did you notice that even a few Indians were there?"

"Yes, I did. Is it unusual for them to attend the funeral of a white person?"

"Not if they like him."

"How do the Sioux care for their dead?" I ask.

"Most bury them underground just like white people do. But they began doing this only about ten years ago. Traditionally they placed a body with its wrapping in a tree or on a burial scaffold. They didn't bury the body underground because they were afraid the soul couldn't escape."

"Why did they change their custom?"

"The whites began tearing down the scaffolds looking for artifacts. You see, before the Indians wrapped a body, they tucked personal belongings and offerings of food next to it to comfort the soul."

"That's interesting," I say and mean it.

"Yes, the Indians did have some very strange customs. In fact they still do. Have you been to any of their ceremonies yet? Probably not," she says answering for me. "After all, you've barely arrived."

Somehow I don't think that my attendance at the wedding of Francis Flood to Joseph Running Bear last week on November 27th counts as one of "their ceremonies." After all, the couple was married in the Catholic Church at St. Francis. In the evening, a dance was given in their honor at the Council Hall in Rosebud. Everyone enjoyed "Billy's Melody Boys," which, according to the *Todd County Tribune*, is an orchestra we all should be proud of.

"What about the strange customs?"

"Well," Lottie says, clearly warming to the topic, "adultery and illicit relationships are shameful problems."

I never considered either a custom, but I'm sure that Lottie will enlighten me.

"I'm surprised that Superintendent McGregor or Dr. Eddleman didn't mention it to you."

Even if they had, which they didn't, I wouldn't tell Lottie. As children growing up, my brothers and sisters and I were never allowed to gossip or to say things about people. Carrying tales was strictly forbidden.

"Some Indian couples like to think they're married just because they've agreed to live together. Of course, this marrying by Indian custom isn't a legal ceremony. It's just another of their immoral tribal customs. And if this isn't bad enough," Lottie says, gathering steam, "some legally married Indian couples divorce by 'Indian custom.' Then one or both of them move in with a new husband or wife. All the while they're still married to their original spouse."

"What's the Indian custom of divorce? I've never heard of it."

"The couple simply separates. A man who wants a divorce announces that he's 'thrown his wife away.' A woman who wants a divorce puts her husband's belongings outside the house. Can you imagine such behavior?"

"Does this sort of thing happen in the Black Pipe district?"

"Indeed it does. But believe you me, I make sure that both Superintendent McGregor and Dr. Eddleman know about every incident!"

I'm sure you do, I think to myself. I wonder what else I'll learn in the next three weeks with Lottie.

As soon as we get home I begin trying to thaw out the radiator. I wrap it snugly in an old army blanket and pour boiling water into it. Three kettles later I finally can drain it. Had I left it frozen all night, I would have needed a new engine block for sure.

The next morning Lottie has an office day. Indians come to get treatment for a variety of ailments, including colds and eye infections. One elderly woman has rheumatism and a very bad toothache. The tooth really needs to be pulled, but all we can do is give her aspirin.

Late in the afternoon the day school teacher brings a seven-year old boy to us. Small blister-like areas cover his trunk and the skin between his fingers and toes. I can tell that he's been scratching the areas and he says that they itch, especially at night. While I continue to examine him, Lottie makes the day school teacher comfortable in the living room.

"Do you have a wash tub, Lottie?" I ask.

Never dreaming that I'm about to transform her kitchen into a clinic room Lottie hands me the tub. Aghast, she watches as I give the boy, who's badly infected with scabies, a sulphur bath. This tidy six-room cottage is Lottie's home. She doesn't like sharing it with sick Indians, and I'm sure she doesn't relish sharing it with me, especially now. She's probably wondering what I'll do next.

Lottie's been in the Indian Service more than 30 years and for at least ten of these she's been the field matron at Black Pipe. Thirty miles in any direction from a doctor, it's the most isolated of the field matron districts. The district's only school is a small day school. Like a rural public school, it offers the first three grades. Unlike a rural public school, the day is divided between academic instruction and work. In the morning the children learn to read, write, spell, do math, and master English. The rest of the day they work. The boys may learn to mend fences, to farm, and to make small repairs around the school. The girls help the cook prepare and serve the dinner at noon. They help clean the school and they may also learn how to care for babies and chickens.

The Indians like Lottie very much and are accustomed to coming to her for help. She has a telephone that occasionally works, so she can call the doctor in case of an accident or sickness. But Lottie's not a nurse, and according to her monthly reports for the past year, health care is last on her list of field matron activities. Her priority, at least on paper, is quilting. She has several quilting frames and encourages the Indian women to make lovely patchwork quilts. She also teaches them how to can fruits and vegetables using water-bath processing. They come to her for jars, lids, and rubber seals.

According to the official guide and manual, quilting, food preservation, and the sexual conduct and morals of the Indians are all responsibilities of a field matron. Quilting and food preservation are included in the aim of Domestic Instruction. Providing moral guidance, and urging the Indians to abandon their "immoral" tribal customs for those of a civilized people are subsumed under Practices and Customs. To Lottie, Practices and Customs are far more interesting than Domestic Instruction.

While I'm finishing the sulphur bath, Lottie says, "I told his mother weeks ago how to apply the sulphur ointment. I also told her to wash his bedclothes. And still the boy is infected."

In a way I feel sorry for Lottie. Being dependent on others for transportation hinders her ability do her job. She can advise the mother, but she can neither show her what to do nor observe her carrying out the instructions. I ask the boy how to get to his home. He smiles and mentions several landmarks to make sure that I can find it. Like most of the 15 students at the day school, he lives within a few miles of it.

Lottie assures me that she knows exactly where the boy lives. "Well then, tomorrow we'll call on his family," I announce. "We can show his mother how to apply the ointment and at the same time we can examine other members of the family."

"I'm not sure what good going out there will do," Lottie replies. "You've already treated the boy. But if you think it'll help, we'll go."

I don't think that going will help, I'm certain that it will. Having a clear idea of the family's home environment will help us understand them and the problems they face. And I know that I can teach more by taking care of people than by just talking to them. I learned the importance of home conditions and of teaching by doing in my nurse's training.

I had entered nursing school in 1906. Dr. Alfred Worcester had established the Waltham Training School for Nurses, in Waltham, Massachusetts, in 1885. Twenty-one years later it remained the only four-year training school for nurses in the United States. All other programs were three years. But it wasn't just the length of the program that separated Waltham from the other schools. Waltham provided more theoretical training, a probationary first year, and district or visiting nursing.

The three-year programs were hospital-based. They believed only in hospital training for their student nurses. The Waltham Training School believed more in home nursing than in hospital nursing. I spent the first month of my probationary year out in the district. Then came lessons in chemistry, anatomy, medicines and hygiene, massage, and domestic science. Scientific knowledge was considered as important as the art of housekeeping. During the probationary year we all learned how to bring our best self into action. Over the next three years of the program, I was trained in private nursing in patients' homes, in district or visiting nursing, and in hospital nursing. The Waltham Training School trained nurses to serve a community, not an institution.

Next morning Lottie and I easily find where the boy lives. The 30 below zero temperature has held, making all the roads, creeks, and gullies traversable by Ford. Even before we knock, the boy's mother opens the door of the one room cottonwood log cabin. Her younger son is sitting quietly in his father's lap. We all smile. The family has just finished their breakfast of fried bread and coffee.

Minimal light comes through the two small windows, but I see two mattresses on the dirt floor, a table, two chairs, and a stove. Bundles of herbs, probably for medicinal use, hang from the rafters. Flour sacks filled with corn and beans, which they had raised last summer and dried, also hang from the rafters. Containers of lard, flour, and sugar, supplies that they can afford to buy at the store, are piled in a corner.

As soon as I finish examining the older boy, his father smiles, says "Please," and hands me his younger son. He's also infected with scabies. So I show the mother how to apply the sulphur ointment to all skin from the neck down, especially the finger and toe webs. I leave enough ointment for the parents as well.

Lottie and I call on four other families who live in different parts of the Black Pipe district. At least one member of each family has come to Lottie in the past two weeks because of colds, eye infections, and in one case, a burn. These home nursing visits give me an opportunity to follow-up on their treatment, to talk about cleanliness and sanitation, and to get a first-hand look at living conditions. All these families live well below the subsistence level of white people.

We get back to Lottie's about five p.m. The house is stone cold because we're short of fuel. By the time we get a fire going, carry water, and take care of the cow and hens, it's nearly 6:30. The cold weather makes work move a little more slowly. As we're getting supper, Lottie asks, "What did you do for Thanksgiving?"

"Miss Post kindly invited me to dinner."

"Was it just the two of you?"

"No, there were several of us."

"Yes, of course there would be. She's a very nice young woman. I'm sure she wanted you to meet some of the other people at the agency. Who else was there?"

"Miss Gravez, Hans Larsen, H.P. Davis, Miss Woodbury, and Emery Rusho. You probably know all of them."

"All of them except Emery Rusho. Let me see," she says, cataloging the diners. "Miss Gravez is the public school teacher, Hans Larsen is the chief mechanic, H.P. Davis is the agency farmer, and Miss Woodbury works in The Office. Who's this Emery Rusho you mentioned?"

"I believe that he's a merchant."

"At Rosebud?" asks Lottie pressing for details.

"He said he lived in Carter."

"Well, I don't know anyone in Carter," she says as we sit down to eat.

During supper Lottie is quiet. I'm sure that visiting the Indian families in the district with me increases her feelings of inadequacy. These visits and the sulphur-bath-in-her-kitchen incident have surely destroyed any good will that I may have established by taking her to Mr. Perry's funeral.

For the remainder of the week and all of the next, Lottie and I continue. We treat the ambulatory patients who come to her cottage and we visit Indians in their homes, providing bedside care and home nursing. We see patients with trachoma, tuberculosis, tonsillitis, pleurisy, rashes, and a variety of skin diseases such as pustular dermatitis. One day we have a clinic of twelve people at Lottie's. Once again I talk about cleanliness and sanitation.

All agency personnel work six days a week, so Saturday I return to Rosebud. Just as I did last weekend, I meet with Superintendent McGregor and Dr. Eddleman to keep them informed. Superintendent McGregor is the first to admit that he knows little about health care. Despite this lack of knowledge, however, his concern about the health of the Indians on the reservation is genuine. Dr. Eddleman views medical practice as being limited either to the hospital or the home. My public health activities don't seem feasible to him. Yet, both men are supportive of me and interested in my work. In other positions that I've held, I had only one boss. Here I have three, the Superintendent, the doctor, and the Red Cross.

"What's the general situation at Black Pipe?" Superintendent McGregor asks me.

"It's difficult," I respond. "The Indians desperately need nursing care. And, because the district is so far from the agency, cooperation between the field matron and the various employees is essential."

"Miss Rasch can be somewhat uncooperative," volunteers Superintendent McGregor.

"Living alone in that isolated district for the past ten years with only her cow and chickens for company has changed her disposition," says Dr. Eddleman. "She's become withdrawn. She's physically able of doing the work, but her mental attainments are very limited. Now, tell me about the medical work of treatment at Black Pipe."

Mentally I compare the field matrons whom I met briefly last month, and I think about their monthly reports that I've read. "The medical work is the same everywhere," I explain, "if we disregard a field matron's personality and the availability of transportation. The field matron dispenses drugs and home remedies and attends to ambulatory patients. She makes home visits and provides bedside care. But these duties require a great deal of time because of the expansiveness of the territory that she covers and the poor roads."

"In view of these realities, do you think these duties are worthwhile?" Dr. Eddleman asks.

"Absolutely. They provide many opportunities for teaching. A field matron who has the requisite knowledge can easily teach cleanliness, sanitation, food values, and cooking. Moreover, she can easily talk about good housing and good care of animals." And yes, I add silently, home life and morals.

"All of this said," Dr. Eddleman replies, "field matrons are not graduate nurses. Their judgment of cases is simply not reliable."

He's absolutely correct. They're the first to tell you that they're not trained nurses and because they aren't, they can't be expected to know about health care.

After a few more minutes Dr. Eddleman leaves for the hospital. I'm going to check my mail and then go to my room at the Employees Quarters. My trunk arrived from Faith's earlier this week, and I want to unpack it. As I stand to leave, Superintendent McGregor says, "Nella and I would like you to join us for Christmas dinner. We want to ask you before you make other plans. We sincerely hope that you'll accept our invitation." I do with pleasure and appreciate being included. Christmas is only eight days away.

Monday morning I'm back at Black Pipe. After bitterly cold and snowy weather for nearly the first half of December, the temperature increases 90 degrees. The result is mud and a lot of it. Other than visiting the day school this week, I expect that my last week with Lottie will be much the same as the first two. We'll be "at home" for the Indians who come for help and then we'll slip and slide to home visits.

We've just finished breakfast when someone knocks. Lottie opens the door to an Indian woman holding her four-year old son wrapped in a blanket. He has tetanus. We're able to contact Dr. Eddleman by telephone, but unfortunately Rosebud Hospital has no tetanus antitoxin serum. It's expensive and given only after tetanus develops. But Dr. Eddleman arranges for a hospital in Sioux Falls to send serum to Black Pipe. An hour after speaking with him I watch helplessly as the child dies in rigid convulsions.

"Tetanus is prevalent around Black Pipe," Lottie explains. "It's just one of those things."

"Just one of those things," I repeat, stifling a grim laugh that neither Lottie nor the child's mother would understand. Four days later the serum arrives.

Much to Lottie's relief I leave Saturday morning, off to what she would probably call my next incursion. Like Miss Stoll, who's demonstrating public health nursing in New Mexico, my parting cry is "MUD."

A NEW LINE OF WORK

I've got a lot to learn about a lot of things, but Indian ways top the list. I don't understand Indian thinking. It seems to me to be ruled far more by feelings than reason. The Sioux live in the present, utterly lacking foresight, either for success or disaster. My most recent example involves a four-year old Indian child who lives with her parents between Parmelee and Rosebud. Her entire arm has been covered with pustular sores for three months. I thought that her father would take her to the doctor and consider leaving her at the hospital for a few days, especially as her mother has a tapeworm and could get treatment at the same time. But no, the father didn't want the child to cry. And all they wanted was to go to the Christmas Tree party at the boarding school. So they passed within 50 feet of the hospital and never turned in, either going or coming home. And yet, for the Sioux, children are their most precious gift.

Perhaps my new line of work will enlighten me about Indian ways as well as those of the Indian Service. The new year has just begun and I'm looking forward to spending time at the Rosebud Boarding School. I set off alone in my Ford with only a few clothes and my pocketbook. I'll keep my room at The Agency while I'm at the Boarding school, but I'll live temporarily at the Employees' Club in Mission.

Long before I cover the flat one and three quarter miles from Mission to the Boarding School I see its many buildings. From a distance it looks like a small town; tall and short buildings resemble pieces of a mosaic. Edward J. Peacore is principal of the school. I know him slightly because I met him in November in Superintendent McGregor's office. Today I find Principal Peacore in his office in the basement of the three-story brick school building.

"Welcome," he says. "It's good to see you again. How was your drive from Rosebud?"

"Fine. The road was frozen. So not once did I have to get out and push."

"Good. Driving around here can be challenging. But from what I've heard, you're dauntless. Road conditions aside, I'm pleased that you'll be with us awhile. I think you'll be impressed with the school. We try very hard to give the children a good education so they can take their place in society. We offer all grades from first through sixth. Although some children arrive having already completed the first three grades in one of the nine reservation day schools."

"Where do the children go after the sixth grade for more education?" I ask.

"Unfortunately for the majority of them their formal education stops here."

Reservation and non-reservation boarding schools are the government's attempt to create a new kind of Indian: an Indian who is detribalized, fluent and literate in English, economically self-sufficient, hard working, and self-disciplined. To accomplish this goal the government takes children as young as five or six away from their parents and, insofar as possible, away from Indian life. The government boards, lodges, clothes, and educates the children. It provides medical service and amusement and pays transportation costs from and to their homes. Per Congress' decree a boarding school can spend only between $225 and $250 per student each year.

The half and half system of government boarding schools keeps the cost per child lower than would be otherwise possible. Vocational or manual training supplements academic instruction. The children attend classes half a day and then work, study, and play the other half. They do all of the work that is done by paid help in white boarding schools. The children literally work their way through school under the direction of the few white members of the school staff.

"What's your opinion of the half and half system?" I ask.

"I think it works," Principal Peacore says. "The children learn the three Rs. And equally important they learn skills so that they can be self-supporting. We've made a change this year that should help children advance more quickly. All children in grades one through three will be in school all day. Previously they worked half a day just like all the other children here at the school."

"It will be interesting to see how it works out."

"Now, getting back to your visit," Principal Peacore says. "I understand that you and Dr. Eddleman will be examining the children. I've spoken with Miss Helmhout, the school nurse, and you can use the dispensary for your work. Miss Helmhout is expecting you today so why don't I introduce you?"

"Thank you. I appreciate your courtesy, but you must be very busy. If you tell me where her office is, I can introduce myself."

"Well, if you don't mind, that would be helpful. You'll find her in the girls' dormitory. Her office and the dispensary are on the first floor at the opposite end of the building from the two large ward sleeping rooms."

I wonder how Miss Helmhout feels about sharing her work area, but before going to see her I accept Principal Peacore's offer to explore the school building. Passing the reception room in the basement I see benches snug against the walls. Next come a storage room, a playroom, and two water closets. All sanitary facilities are in the basement.

Academic lessons start at nine a.m. The curriculum is standardized. The Indian Office prescribes the course of study and each child, regardless of his proficiency in English, does the same work. It seems to me that a uniform curriculum stifles independent thinking but perhaps that's the government's intent. Independent thinking and assimilation may be diametrically opposed.

By the time I find the four classrooms, two each on the first and second floors, the children are sitting attentively at their desks. At the front of one room the teacher points to today's lesson on the blackboard. The students are neatly dressed. The girls wear their long hair in braids, but the boys all have short hair. Their beautiful long black hair is cut when they enter school.

I wonder what it must be like for the children to be at the Boarding School. They're here for at least nine months of the year with little or no family contact. Families can visit once a month, but sometimes they're turned away and sometimes they can't make the trip because it's too far.

Life at the boarding school is regimented and institutionalized. The day begins at six a.m. and every hour is accounted for. Even personal care of teeth is a scheduled event, five minutes after breakfast, ten after supper. Evening activities vary according to the day of the week. Study hour is usually Monday and Wednesday, Tuesday is religious instruction and choir practice, Thursday is a movie, Friday is general assembly, Saturday is games or a social, and Sunday is talks by different ministers. Activities for the children stop promptly at nine p.m. The staff has lights until ten-thirty p.m. when the electricity goes off. After that, kerosene lamps are the only source of light.

The regimentation of the boarding school is in sharp contrast to the freedom that Sioux children have at home. Beginning early in life, they're treated as adults and encouraged to make decisions. Their parents don't yell at them and never spank them. Punishment, which is rare, takes the form of a loud scolding by each family member. The child doesn't like to be scolded in front of others so quickly learns to behave.

By the time I finish looking around the school building it's mid-morning. Dr. Eddleman is coming this afternoon so I'd better find Miss Helmhout. I head for the girls' dormitory, an imposing three-story brick building with an arched main entrance. I find Miss Helmhout restocking the medicine cabinet in the dispensary. "You've come at a very opportune time," she says. "The two sick beds are empty and no one is waiting to see me. It's a good thing you didn't come any earlier. I had so many children here that I wasn't sure where to start."

"How many children do you usually treat in one day?" I ask, glancing at the health posters on the wall.

"About sixty, mostly for eye or skin problems. Perhaps you'd like to do some of the treatments while you're here."

I'm not sure if Miss Helmhout is joking or not. But she's more than pleased when I accept her offer.

"Although I treat sixty children each day," says Miss Helmhout, "I see more than that. They come at daily sick roll and then, with permission of a teacher or matron, at other times, usually for first aid. Nearly all the children do some kind of manual labor. So sometimes they get hurt while working. And of course, brush burns are common especially when the children are playing. When a child falls, the surface of the skin usually gets scraped off."

"Are tuberculosis and eye diseases like trachoma major problems among the children?" I ask.

"Most definitely. This year about one hundred sixty children or sixty percent of our enrollment was excused from school because of tuberculosis. As you know, we don't have any facility for treating them here and they won't go to the sanatorium schools because they're so far away. So, they go home."

Home, I think, to unsanitary living conditions that contribute to the spread of the disease. Improving their nutrition with milk and cod liver oil would accomplish something. That means a lot of work for me on diets and even more work for me with parents on budgets. (This is a new word on the Rosebud. I haven't yet learned the Indian name for it.) It will also mean a special request to the Commissioner for an adequate supply of cod liver oil. It must be in the form of emulsion because the Indians who receive the plain oil use it for tanning hides.

"We also have a fairly large group of students who have arrested tuberculosis," Miss Helmhout continues. "These students rarely gain weight and are to have some special nourishment between meals. We're striving to keep trachoma under control and seem to be making progress."

Just before the noon dinner bell rings, Miss Helmhout invites me to dine with her at the employees' new mess hall. There she graciously introduces me to many of the staff. They include teachers, matrons for the boys' and girls' dormitories, engineers who manage and operate the heating and lighting plants, the farmer who looks after the school's garden, the farrier who runs the blacksmith shop, and a seamstress who manages the sewing room. The mechanical and domestic employees are also teachers. They instruct the boys in industrial arts and the girls in domestic arts and science.

Soon after one p.m. Dr. Eddleman and I are busy examining children. They come to us in groups of eight. I greet them in Sioux and call them by name in hopes of putting them at ease. But they're very shy and quiet. They speak only when spoken to and then somewhat hesitantly.

I find the Indian names, which are translations of the Sioux, most delightful. But I have a dreadfully hard time connecting names with faces. Only a couple of weeks ago, a fat old squaw sitting on the ground, smoking a cigarette on the sunny side of The Office building was introduced as Mrs. White Woman. But to me she is the same squaw who five minutes earlier had stepped quietly up behind me in my office at the Agency Day School to watch me type. I learned that this woman was not Mrs. White Woman, but Mrs. White Wash or Mrs. White Cow or any other white thing that I may or may not be able to remember. The Elks are either Jumping, Foolish, Two, Crazy, or Yellow. It's far more difficult than the Cabots of Boston! And of course, nothing pleases people so much as recognition by name. I shall keep trying.

While Dr. Eddleman examines one group of children for chronic and contagious diseases I perform a conventional school health examination with another group. I weigh and measure them and check their vision and hearing. I examine them for gross muscular disabilities, enlarged neck glands, enlarged tonsils, and mouth breathing and ask if they have chronic or frequent colds. A nurse in a public school does the same type of examination. It's a standard part of public health nursing in any state public health program. The idea is to identify problems early so that they can be corrected.

In November I developed a record keeping system that was a combination of the Red Cross, National Organization of Public Health Nursing, Indian Service, and the Child Health Demonstration of Mansfield, Ohio. It's working well here and helps me document my findings efficiently. Accurate and up-to-date records are invaluable, but unfortunately often were missing before I introduced my system.

Dr. Eddleman and I manage, but just barely, to examine 16 children by five p.m. He can't come to the Boarding School every day and the school has a capacity of 265 children, ranging from six to 18 years of age. At this rate we'll need three weeks and then some to examine all of them.

Within a couple of days we identify several children who need to have their tonsils and adenoids removed. As soon as the parents give their consent, Dr. Eddleman will perform the surgeries at Rosebud Hospital. The children will go in squads of four. Nellie and Martha Andrews, Lenora White Hawk and Gilbert Dillon are in the first squad.

Having examined the mouths of more than a few children, I've noticed differences between Indian and white children. The Indian children have superior dental health and fewer cases of bad oral hygiene. Their throats, however, are smaller and they seem to have more cases of enlarged tonsils. Most of them show pus pockets quite plainly.

I've just returned from yet another visit to the pupils' dining hall. I want to learn about the diets of the children and visiting at mealtime is the best way to see what they have to eat. By the time I got to the dining hall at seven a.m., the children were already standing by their places waiting for the signal to sit. Breakfast was rice with raisins and cream, bread, syrup, and coffee. Dinner one day last week was roast beef, macaroni, potatoes, pickles, hot rolls, and coffee. And supper on another day was fried hominy, cold meat, applesauce, corn bread, and milk.

The cook prepares the meals with help from the older children. A baker, also assisted by children, does all the baking for the boarding school. It's not uncommon for them to bake 900 cookies, 40 cakes, and 400 loaves of bread in one day. The children not only help prepare the meals, but also help serve them and clean up. Students Agnes Nightpipe, Kate Quickbear, Dorotha Leadercharge and Rebecca Goodelk proved themselves excellent helpers in the dining room.

As much food as possible is raised at the boarding school. Six hundred acres were under cultivation last summer. Unfortunately, supplies of fruits and vegetables are limited and available only in season. Menus tend to be heavy on starches, meat, stew, and gravy. Servings of milk and milk fats such as cream and butter are limited. The school has a dairy herd of 150, but that's too few cows to produce the daily recommended quart of milk per child.

Much work needs to be done about nutrition. The teachers present dietary facts in the classroom. They teach the children the importance of a proper diet and its principles, but the latter are noticeably absent in the dining room. I'll try to get the boarding school to plan for more milk and to stop serving the children coffee. It really puts a crimp in my health talks on diet.

One of the people I've gotten to know is Miss Della Fisher. She's between 40 and 50 years of age and has been in the Indian Service many years. As matron of the girls' dormitory she has charge of about 100 girls as well as the building in which they live. She probably influences the lives of the girls more than any other employee. Living in the dormitory with them she tries to create a family atmosphere. Basically she's a teacher. She helps the girls learn healthy habits, self-discipline, housekeeping, and the proper care and repair of clothing.

Like most boarding school employees, Miss Fisher doesn't understand why I'm here. She associates nurses with the personal service found in hospitals. The role of public health nurses in health education and disease prevention is unfamiliar.

While I'm waiting for Dr. Eddleman to come to the dispensary, Miss Fisher stops to talk.

"What is it like for the children when they first come to the Boarding School?" I ask, watching a little girl walk silently down the hallway her head bowed.

"Nearly all of them are homesick for a while. They usually get over it, but until they do they're more quiet and shy than their classmates. Some children cry and mope. Homesickness truly affects their mind and spirit. If children are going to run away, chances are they'll do it during the first few weeks of school."

"You say they usually get over homesickness. Does that mean that some of them don't?"

"I remember one child, poor thing. She was inconsolable and she stopped eating. We thought we'd either have to send for her parents or have someone take her home. But at the last minute she began to eat and settled in."

Listening to Miss Fisher I can only imagine the fear, isolation, and separation that the children must feel, regardless of how hard the staff tries and how well they treat the children. It must be worse if the child understands only a little English. Yet some people believe that boarding school is positive. The children have food, clothing, and shelter, which is more than they might have at home. But surely there's a better way for Indian children to have the necessities of a healthy childhood than ripping them from their roots. I suppose, however, that this thinking would be in complete opposition to the government's plan for their assimilation and "civilization."

"And of course," Miss Fisher continues, "just nearly everything about the boarding school environment is new to the children unless they have brothers or sisters who've been here before them. If they do, then they have some idea of what to expect. One thing that fascinates all the children at first is the toilet room, wash room, and bathroom. The amount of toilet paper that the children use is sometimes astounding," she says smiling.

Indeed, I think, children accustomed to using a privy or the out-of-doors, must find indoor toilet facilities quite novel, even if they are in the basement. I have to confess, however, that I wouldn't have liked to walk down one or two flights of stairs to the toilet in the middle of the night. As a child I was afraid of the dark. One time Richard jumped out at me from a dark corner. Father caught him in the act and promptly turned him over his knee. I burst into tears. I always cried when someone else was hurt, but when I was hurt, I laughed. Richard later told me that the spanking didn't hurt much because he was wearing corduroy pants.

"Boarding school must make it difficult, if not impossible, for the children to develop a normal family life," I say.

"Yes, it does. And the isolation and separation that they feel here at first often recur when they go home. They take with them the habits and ways of the white culture. But that culture doesn't fit when they return to the conditions of their birth and early childhood. A young Indian man who'd been to a boarding school once said that he felt like an apple—red on the outside, white on the inside. I think many children who go to boarding schools feel this way."

A tragic position for anyone, I think to myself. But somehow it seems even worse when those involved are children.

Since I arrived I've been helping Miss Helmhout give treatments in the dispensary every day. I've seen so many diseased eyes that I'm not sure I could tell a normal Indian eye if I saw one. Perhaps Indians have redder conjunctivae than whites. I've identified two classes of eye problems, a chronic conjunctivitis and an acute exacerbation of the chronic. The chronic seems to inconvenience the children very little. They usually tell me that they recently had "sore eyes." When the chronic form suddenly becomes worse, the children complain of more or less tearing and the inner surface of their eyelids looks like velvet. Miss Helmhout treats the children at the Boarding School with good results; unfortunately the same conditions exist even among the pre-school children. I'm convinced that any constructive health work must start with the children.

The days of the rough and rugged cattle country are just disappearing over the horizon. But for the boys here, the "manly" way to be has not. They all imitate the conventional moving picture "tough guy" and Wild West hero. The younger boys believe that if you're a "cowboy" you don't need to have wounds and sores treated. So twice as many boys need treatment for sores as girls, and the boys' sores are twice as dirty as the girls' are. The older boys slouch horribly so of course the small ones do too.

Poor posture among the girls is due to a certain attitude of shame that is part of modesty and the proper behavior of Indian women among strangers. The women hang their heads and answer in whispers or not at all. The result is a characteristic pose that is hard to describe. The only hope is that they admire the erect posture of the white girl. Only the bold ones dare assume it, however. This may be the first step in Indian Feminism! Posture, after all, reflects attitude.

Last evening I attended a party for the December honor roll students and the night before I watched the boarding school basketball team defeat the Pine Ridge Boarding School team. The previous week the Rosebud Boarding School team beat the fast Lakeview team, but in the process one player had a tooth knocked out and his lip was badly bruised. So the audience got to see this Red Cross nurse in action. Tonight I'm sitting in my room at the Employees' Club in Mission trying valiantly to write my monthly report. At the beginning of every month I vow and declare that I'll send my report off on time, but somehow the end of the month arrives and I'm not finished. Sometimes I've not even started.

Another four or five days and my three weeks at the Boarding School will be over. Dr. Eddleman and I have examined 230 of the 265 children. We'll finish on odd days spread out over the next few weeks. I came to the Boarding School to get acquainted with the children and I have. Moreover, I've discovered the general attitudes of the teachers and matrons toward the children. I've also learned about the organization of school activities. I've learned much and found much that can be done. But I have so much yet to see and learn that I can't stop to do all that is staring at me. And now a speech and another new experience await.

JUNE 23, 1966—ALBUQUERQUE

"Sorry I'm so late. Brice wasn't feeling good this morning so it took me a little longer than usual to get things organized," Melody said as she closed the door to the study room.

"Baby Brice or Big Brice?" Alice asked. Simon and Garfunkel were singing "Sounds of Silence" from her portable radio. Waiting for Melody's answer, she turned her head and wiped away a tear.

"Big Brice. He's the bigger baby when he feels bad. He's okay, just hay fever. But what's wrong with you? I can tell you've been crying."

Turning off the radio, Alice faced her friend. "Yes, I have been. But I'm through."

"You'll feel better if you talk about what's upsetting you," Melody said.

"I'm afraid I'll start crying again. I'm so mad at Carlos and I'm upset at myself for being so…oh, I don't know, so uncertain," Alice said.

"Uncertain?" Melody echoed, just as she had learned in their nursing class on Therapeutic Communication.

"Yes, I'm uncertain." Then she laughed realizing she was the object of a therapeutic communication technique. "It does work, doesn't it?" Beginning again, she said, "I'm uncertain about getting married in December, for one thing. I made the mistake of being less than enthusiastic about Carlos' mother wanting me to start working with her on plans for the rehearsal dinner. That's months away! I mean she's a very nice person and she's just trying to please Carlos, but I'm just not ready to think about the wedding. And the way he acted—accusing me of not loving him. If I did, he said, I'd try to make his family happy, meaning his mother. And my mother's just as bad, already asking about the invitations and reserving the church." Alice sounded near tears again. "What's wrong with me? Do you think I'm afraid? Of course, I argued with Carlos and told him I thought that it would be nice if people realized I have a lot to think about with my schoolwork and don't have time for all this planning right now. Then he really set me off by making some remark about 'how difficult could nursing school be?', as if what I'm doing is all just common sense, not real education for a profession." Spots of color rose in her cheeks as she continued. "Anyway, lots of things were said that probably shouldn't have been. He could see I was really hurt, and he apologized. I thought I was over it, but thinking about it this morning, I got upset all over again."

After a long pause and a deep breath she said, "You're right. I do feel better now that I told you. Please promise you won't tell anyone what I said. I'm probably just going through a phase," she sighed as she opened her notebook and smiled at Melody.

"You can say anything you need to and trust me to keep it to myself," her friend replied solemnly.

"I'm ready to work now. Do you want to talk about that last tape of Miss Gregg's?" Alice asked.

"Okay, if you're sure you're ready." Melody turned to her notes. "One thing that struck me was that principal at the boarding school saying that she was dauntless. And he said it as a compliment. How do you suppose a person becomes dauntless? I looked up the word in the dictionary—cannot be intimidated or discouraged, fearless, bold. I think it would be wonderful to have people think of me that way."

"I think a person becomes dauntless by having the courage to choose to do things that aren't ordinary. And the more a person succeeds at those things, the surer they are about their ability to handle challenges. So they are bolder. Miss Gregg went off to World War I and had all of those hard experiences but saw it as opportunity and as something exciting. After a person has done something like that, it might not seem so difficult to go off to the Wild West to demonstrate how public health nursing could help the Indians. It probably helps if you are encouraged as a child to have lots of different experiences," Alice said.

"I'd like to try to raise my children that way—to experiment, to learn they are able to do things that are out of the ordinary," Melody said.

"What if this next one is a girl? Will you do the same with her? You know, let her climb trees, trap snakes, go camping by herself, repair a car?"

"Good question. When I was a child no one told me I couldn't do those things, but I was encouraged to stay clean, be careful, do things indoors. Miss Gregg actually seems to have enjoyed being outdoors in adverse circumstances, testing herself," Melody said. "If I have a daughter, I hope I'll have the courage to let her do more. Did you notice that in the Indian school they seemed to emphasize that same type of female and male difference? Girls were taught to sew while boys did farm work outdoors. That might have been influenced by both the Indian and white cultures of the time."

After a moment's silence, Alice said, "I can just see Miss Gregg as a nurse. When she was out with Miss Rasch, the field matron, she just saw what needed to be done for the families and then set out to do it, including taking over the kitchen to give a sulphur bath. But she was also sensitive to Miss Rasch's feelings. In fact, treating people kindly and taking care to accept them and their culture seems to be a big part of how she approached her work. Hearing her story makes me eager for our public health nursing course next year. I'd worried before about how it would be to work alone out in the community without all the support of hospital equipment and other personnel. But I'm beginning to see that the best place to accomplish any disease prevention or health promotion is in homes, schools and community organizations. No one's real life is like what happens when they are hospitalized. But, their real life is where illness develops or health is preserved." Alice looked back to her notes, then said, "Did you notice she got involved in the community right away? She attended a funeral, a wedding, a ballgame, and an honors day assembly. She could've just gone to her room and gotten her reports done, but she chose to participate in the community. I think that must have helped her be effective."

"I know we're supposed to be thinking about how this reminiscing is affecting the person doing it, but I'm just so interested in the stories she tells. She does seem to be enjoying telling them and visiting with us." Melody hesitated, "Are we doing anything for her?"

"Just being with a person can be helpful to them. We don't have to be giving meds to be doing nursing," Alice said. "Sometimes I have to remind myself of that. Another thing I was interested in was the difference in how people are affected by isolation. There was Miss Rasch who had been without transportation for all those years. She apparently accepted that and just drew a line around herself, saying 'I quilt and can food and watch these scandalous Indians marrying and divorcing.' She mostly lived vicariously. Miss Gregg seems to have carried her sense of purpose and her background with her. She stayed connected to the outside world by bringing it in her mind to bear on this new situation. When she didn't have her car, she took the stage. When she didn't have the patient records she needed, she developed them. She knew that keeping statistics has been important to nurses since Florence Nightingale's day as a way of demonstrating effect and of guiding action. And all of this was in the nineteen twenties!"

Smiling at Alice's enthusiasm, Melody asked, "Are you feeling better now?"

"Oh sure. I'll be fine. I just need to figure out what I want to be when I grow up, I guess. Here's the new tape that came this morning. We can listen to it now and we'll be going to Santa Fe again next week. Meanwhile, I'll work on being nice to Carlos. He probably isn't really to blame for my bad humor."

She looked up from setting up the tape player, "I wish I knew Miss Gregg a little better. I might ask her advice."

PACKED TO THE FLAPS

I'VE GIVEN SEVERAL TALKS AT CHURCH MEETINGS since I've been at Rosebud, but this is a first. I'm to be interpreted. The Sioux language seems to have many more words per square inch than English, so I'll have plenty of time to think about what to say next. The challenge will be to remember it. Because I'm giving much the same talk that I used on the Chautauqua circuit, the memories of the summer of 1919 crowd my mind.

When I got home from the war in March 1919, I was restless and had itchy feet. So early in April I wrote to Miss Clara D. Noyes, Acting Director of the American National Red Cross in Washington, D.C. asking about available positions on Chautauqua. I knew that the Red Cross was going to use circuit Chautauqua to bring the war and peace story of its nursing service to the American public. I told Miss Noyes that I was interested in the work because it was a chance for me to improve my public speaking skills. Moreover, it was a good opportunity to bring important subjects before active minded people.

Americans had a desire for personal self-enrichment and self-improvement. But some lived in cities and towns that were either too remote or too small to attract nationally known entertainers and lecturers. So these communities contracted with a commercial Chautauqua company for five to seven days of amusement and education presented under canvas at the local fairgrounds. Chautauqua offered something for people of all ages and nearly everyone in a community attended.

Circuit Chautauqua was a combination of two favorite 19th century forms of adult education: lyceum and permanent Chautauqua. Lyceums were non-commercial associations where local members or visitors from other town lyceums lectured. Permanent Chautauqua, located on the shores of Lake Chautauqua in Fair Point, New York, was a full-fledged summer school.

Mid-May I was at American National Red Cross headquarters getting instructions about the message I was to deliver over the summer. The message was to contain something for everyone in the audience. I'd begin by talking about my overseas experience. Then I'd suggest ways that

a community could advance the Red Cross peace program of public health. Finally I'd try to interest young women in nursing as a profession and to stimulate enrollment and interest in the American Red Cross.

With me at Headquarters were 14 of the 23 other nurses assigned to the summer Chautauqua circuits. We were scheduled to visit all states except Massachusetts, Rhode Island, Connecticut, New Jersey, North Dakota, and Nevada. Nine of the 23 nurses were veterans of the Chateau-Thierry-Argonne offensive. Some, myself included, had served in surgical teams and mobile units that operated close to the front. One nurse had been a member of a "shock team." Several others had served with the American Ambulance Hospital that had been established in 1914, thanks to the generosity of wealthy Americans.

Many of the nurses assigned to Chautauqua had citations for courage and devoted service during the war. Chautauqua would be a new experience for us in more ways than one. Throughout nurses' training we'd been taught to go quietly about our business and to avoid publicity. Circuit Chautauqua, however, thrived on publicity. Posters and local newspapers announced the pending arrival of Chautauqua Week. Articles introduced the musicians, civic leaders, literary talents, theatrical performers, and Red Cross nurses who would expose audiences to new ideas and customs, to national and international issues, and to popular forms of entertainment. We'd been chosen for Chautauqua because we knew about public health nursing and had served overseas. But we'd be sharing the bill with some of the best professional entertainers in the United States.

In less than a month I was again in Washington, D.C. This time I was on my way to join a five-day Chautauqua circuit team in Lincoln, Nebraska. From early June until early September I would travel through the Midwest with the Standard Chautauqua group. We'd present programs throughout Nebraska, Iowa, Colorado, Kansas, and Missouri, as well as in Farmington, New Mexico, and Pine Bluffs, Wyoming. I had never done any public speaking but that didn't daunt me. I was to give the same speech 92 times in 93 days and thought it would come easier as I went along. I had heard that practice makes perfect.

Our Chautauqua opened with "Ye Old New England Choir." Dressed in the costumes of each period, the Choir sang songs of four decades of United States history. In the evening Paul "Sunshine" Dietrick left them smiling with his lecture "The Sacrifice Hit." Princess Te Ata's Indians and her assistants were part of the second day's program. They sang Indian songs, performed Indian dances, and told Indian legends. Clarence L. Burgderfer, "The Funny Man," completed the day. He kept them laughing for an hour. On the third day "The Lockhart Trio" performed and Ex-Congressman Finley H. Grey of Indiana spoke about The League of Nations. Audiences on the fourth day were treated to the music and comedy of "The Bohannans." And Dr. Martin D. Hardin, one of the leading pastors of Chicago, spoke about "The Spirit of America." He heartily applauded the Red Cross and ended his speech with an appeal for The League of Nations.

The Cremona Orchestra and I were the fifth day performers. The Orchestra included six college girls and a young man. Five of the girls played the violin, one the cello. The pianist doubled as their manager. Sometimes I felt like a chaperone. The Orchestra provided a prelude to my lecture in the afternoon and then in the evening they gave a full program of instrumental and vocal numbers.

Many of the communities that sponsored Chautauqua were 20 miles from the nearest railroad station. Most had populations of less than 1,500. City folks may have had their fill of war stuff such as Liberty loan and war drive campaigns. But rural citizens were eager for tales of heroism and courage especially when linked to patriotism. People wanted to meet the nurses and soldiers who were coming back from "over there."

Sometimes when we arrived in a town the community band and local soldiers marched in front of me. Later when I stepped onto the stage in my white silk uniform, regulation white oxfords, white silk stockings, and Red Cross nurse's cap, the band played "The Rose of No Man's Land." As soon as the applause died I described my two years in France. As a member of the Peter Bent Brigham Hospital unit (Base Hospital Number 5), I had gone over before our boys did. And I stayed four months after the armistice was signed in November 1918.

I told them that only a year ago I had been at Chateau-Thierry, where we evacuated 3,000 wounded in one night. Then I described in vivid detail how we got out ourselves on six hours' notice as the Hun got our range. Suddenly those long lines of khaki in the front rows went wild. I had to wait several minutes for those soldiers to settle down. Then I continued with a view of the humanitarian work that the Red Cross carried on worldwide. I praised the efficiency of the Red Cross workers. The help of the women of the Red Cross organizations in America contributed greatly to our success overseas.

Proceeding with my speech I explained how the Red Cross work would now continue in the United States. A nation's health could be measured only by the health and strength of its people. So the Red Cross had organized to furnish trained nurses in every city, town and community in America. These public health nurses would care for the sick. Moreover, they would teach people how to prevent sickness and how to live healthy lives. Health, not disease, should be catching, I added.

The Spanish flu dramatically demonstrated the need for trained nurses. Between September and November of 1918 a highly lethal strain of influenza swept the world. Between 20 million and 40 million people died worldwide. In America the death toll was an estimated 675,000. The flu devastated many communities in America because of the shortage of trained nurses. There were not enough to care for the sick and the disease continued unchecked.

Our nation drastically needed trained public health nurses, I continued, and various opportunities were open to women. Single women interested in the nursing profession could enter a training school. Many offered scholarships and some specialized in public health. Graduate nurses who wanted to pursue courses in public health nursing could apply for Red Cross scholarships and loans. But women didn't have to be nurses to contribute to public health. Wives and mothers could take the Red Cross Course of Instruction in Home Hygiene and Care of the Sick. They would learn how to keep their families healthy and how to nurse ill members.

As a troubadour of health I had to be flexible and unflappable. In mid-June I was speaking in Grafton, Kansas, when seven white hens joined the audience in the canvas tent. They took their time finding satisfactory seating, clucking as they passed down the middle aisle. Selecting empty chairs near the front, they perched on the backs and then promptly proceeded to demonstrate their concern with my wartime trials. They put their heads under their wings and slept. The audience loved it.

In the same month I spoke in Durango, Colorado. The tent was packed to the flaps. Even though the sides were rolled up for cross ventilation in the intense heat, two women fainted. I had put a little too much gore and vivid detail into my speech. My first instinct was to stop and render first aid, but the show had to go on.

In Genoa, Nebraska, in mid-August a bush pilot was giving airplane rides for one dollar. I lost my entire audience when he revved the engine. I waited patiently on stage until they drifted back in. Then I continued where I had left off.

Because the Cremona Orchestra and I were the fifth day performers, we always helped our crew take down the tent after the evening's performance. That night or the following morning we'd move to the next town. Occasionally we traveled by train, but usually we went by car or bus.

As nomads we stayed in small hotels, private homes, or boarding houses. Once in a while we met the other four teams on our circuit.

By September my feet had well and truly stopped itching. I was glad to return to Boston. I'm not sure how much public health nursing I sold to anyone except myself. But I had been reintroduced to the West and knew that I preferred it to stodgy conventional New England.

Now, little more than three years later, I'm looking at an audience that is Indians of all ages. Each baby is wrapped securely in a little patchwork quilt and carried in the mother's shawl. Once tightly wrapped, the baby is unwrapped only when the mother gets home. Rosebud is not conventional and is anything but dull.

MY STAR DAY

"I've never seen anything like it—a horse committing suicide."

"I've certainly never seen anything like it either," says Mrs. McDonald from the passenger seat of my Ford. "All tangled up in that barbed-wire fence and lying there beating its head on the frozen ground."

"Why didn't someone shoot it? Put the poor thing out of its misery. Especially when everyone said nothing could be done for it, that it had lost any ability to respond to human touch."

"I thought about shooting it. But can you imagine the news item in next week's *Todd County Tribune*?" asks Mrs. McDonald laughing. "'Miss Elinor Gregg, Red Cross Nurse, and Ida H. McDonald, field matron and wife of district farmer, P.C. McDonald, shoot mad horse'."

We're headed back to Wood after another day of visiting Indians in Mrs. McDonald's district of Butte Creek. Since I arrived in Wood the first of February I've met many of them. Depending on the nature of their illness, they either travel to see Mrs. McDonald during her Office Day or send someone for her. Over the years the Indians have learned that they can count on her and they do.

Today we've treated Indians who have sore eyes, tonsillitis, and rashes. "That new mother and baby we saw earlier today both look quite healthy," I say.

"Yes, they do," says Mrs. McDonald. "I helped her deliver two weeks ago. Sometime around the twenty-seventh of January, if I recall correctly."

"Do most of the Indian women in this district have their babies at home?"

"Yes, and the white women as well. It's more practical because Wood is so far from the hospital at Rosebud. I've delivered a lot of babies in the district, but I'll never forget the first time I delivered twins. I hadn't been here very long. The temperature was zero and the Indian mother was in a tent that was banked with snow. We had a wood burning stove inside the tent, and the stovepipe stuck out through the top. I boiled lots of water and everyone survived."

"I'm sure it's an experience you won't forget." As soon as I utter these words, the memory of a delivery that I did alone some twelve years ago floods my mind. The baby was alive at birth and appeared healthy. He was alert, peppy, and pink. Twenty-four hours later he was dead. He just quietly died. I've never known whether it was my fault or not. I've always thought that I might have held him back too long for fear that the mother would tear. No one ever said it was my fault, but I've never known for sure.

Mrs. McDonald's voice interrupts my thoughts. "It was memorable," she says, "and not just because the mother had twins. That was when I learned about the Indian custom of having a woman who'd just delivered walk around a pole until it was encircled with blood. Some women would literally die of exhaustion. Or at the very least, an old tuberculosis infection would flare up because of the extreme blood loss and they'd never really recover. Thank goodness that custom has gone by the wayside."

"As I recall you came to Rosebud as a field matron in nineteen-nine. How did you make your home visits then?"

"I had a top buggy with the finest team of white horses you could ask for. Many's the day I'd leave after an early breakfast, make my visits, and get home late that night. That team always got me where I needed to go. Then in nineteen-eighteen I married Pat. He owned an automobile, and since then he's been driving me."

Walking into the warm six-room cottage we find Mr. McDonald sitting at the kitchen table drinking a cup of coffee and looking at the mail. The cat's dozing in front of the hard coal heater, and Midgy, the McDonald's white dog, practically turns herself inside out with excitement when she sees her mistress.

After supper we move to the sitting room and the cat jumps onto my lap. "I wonder what it is about stroking a cat that's so relaxing?"

"I don't know," Mrs. McDonald says, looking up from her knitting, "but it has that effect on me too."

After a few moments of comfortable silence, Mrs. McDonald asks, "Have you always been a public health nurse, Miss Gregg?"

"No. I started out doing factory nursing in a cotton manufacturing company. Then I did training school supervision and hospital management."

"I always thought it would be exciting to be a nurse in surgery," Mrs. McDonald says.

"Well, it certainly can be. My only experience with that was in nursing school. The worst operation that I scrubbed for, the patient died on the table. That finished me for operating room nursing."

"I can see where it might," she says, smiling.

I'm enjoying my visit with Mrs. McDonald or as the Indians call her Winyan Omani, which means woman who travels. She's a good housekeeper and cook, and more knowledgeable about sickness than Miss Rasch. Come hell or high water, Mrs. McDonald carries out her field matron program. Maybe that pot of coffee that's always on the back of the stove keeps her going. It's as strong as lye.

Two days later, on one of the coldest days we've had this winter, I wave goodbye to Mr. and Mrs. McDonald. I'm leaving a bit later than I had planned, but I may still be able to reach Rosebud in time.

Back at The Agency I find Ellen C. McArdle in the hotel lobby. She's the field supervisor for the Central Division of the American Red Cross.

"I hope you haven't been waiting long," I say.

"About an hour, but that's fine," Miss McArdle says. "I knew you were in the field. I've enjoyed watching the people come and go here at the hotel."

I visited the Central Division Office in Chicago on my way to Rosebud. I spent half a day with Miss Minnie Ahrens, the Director of Nursing for the Division. But because Miss McArdle was away, this is our first meeting.

"Just before you walked in I was thinking about all that's happened in the past five months," she says. "In September I was here surveying the Rosebud and Pine Ridge Reservations. They were being considered as an assignment for one of the Red Cross Nurses that we'd loan to the Office of Indian Affairs. Now it's February, and you've been here three months."

We walk to my office at the Day School. Miss McArdle asks me to tell her about my activities at Rosebud. She's read my monthly reports, so I decide to talk about some of the larger issues rather than individual Indian situations.

"Tuberculosis is a major problem," I begin. "Every patient has such a long and involved history that I often think that only the most diligent and intense social work will accomplish the desired results of improving health care."

"I understand," Miss McArdle says.

"Let me give you just one of many examples," I say, wanting to make sure that she does understand. "Last month the doctor, a field matron, and I spent an entire day visiting two women with tuberculosis. The first woman, who lives about fifteen miles from the agency, had practically no money, and her husband was gone. He's a rascal too slippery to catch. The woman's fifteen-year old daughter was home from boarding school, but rather than caring for her tubercular mother, she was racing around.

"The second woman, according to the person who summoned the field matron, was dying at home. We drove ten miles to see the woman, but no one was there. We finally found the entire family forty miles away. They were traveling in a squaw wagon during the day and pitching their tent at night. They told us they were on their way to a church meeting. We suspected that this was a pretext for bringing the man within range of easy moonshine. Our suspicion may be quite unfounded. We'll never know. But we did know that after traveling one hundred thirty miles at a top speed of twenty miles an hour, we'd spent all day driving around, and accomplished nothing."

"I can see that it's difficult to keep track of the tubercular cases," Miss McArdle says.

"And plans for social work and relief policies are far more important than I anticipated." Having Miss McArdle's company is such a pleasure that I want to tell her everything at once. "The Sioux are by nature kind and unselfish," I continue. "They believe that people are far more important than things. Years ago a hunter would give part of his game to the needy of the tribe. This social custom of giving continues today and not infrequently at the person's own expense. So it's important for me to be able to help them when necessary. But this requires that I know the family, which takes considerable time and study."

During the next two days, we talk more about conditions at Rosebud and my plans, and we visit several of the 1200 Sioux living in The Agency district. Finally, on the third day of her four-day stay, Miss McArdle interviews Superintendent McGregor and Dr. Eddleman about my work. Returning from the meeting, she says, "Well, there's no doubt about it. They're both glad that you're here. They tell me that you're taking considerable initiative and they're impressed with your work, to say nothing of your being out in all kinds of weather. I want you to know that Commissioner Burke agrees with their evaluation."

Despite the positive comments, I hear a "but" coming. I know that Miss McArdle doesn't entirely approve of my giving out medicines on standing orders from the doctor. Yet this is the only way of treating some of the Indians. Dr. Eddleman could not begin to see everyone who needs treatment.

"As we discussed the other day," Miss McArdle says, "you've done well in these first few months. I believe, however, that you should be organizing your future activities along different lines. I told Superintendent McGregor and Dr. Eddleman that I thought you should have regular children's clinics at the nine day schools. Dr. Eddleman didn't seem to think that it's feasible because even now the doctors can't see everyone who needs medical care. Of course, I told them the final decision was up to the three of you."

The plan doesn't seem workable to me either. Too many emergencies keep the doctor away, and the Indian women will make a two-mile trip only if they need immediate medical care or if food is going to be served. Moreover, I'm going to the Pine Ridge Reservation in about five weeks. It seems more sensible to continue as we have been. I'll deal with individual situations and people as they come or as Superintendent McGregor and Dr. Eddleman send them to me.

During Miss McArdle's visit I've refitted as to laundry, sleep, and ideas. As soon as she departs on the 16th, I leave on a short day trip. The terrific windstorm that we had three days ago has long since passed, but not the 20 to 30 degrees below zero temperatures. As I head south in my car with my sheepskin coat wrapped snugly around me, I'm reminded of one of the first times I came out this way. It was late November and I was riding horseback to reach a family living in an area inaccessible by my Ford. I had put a tin box of pills in my pocket. Not until I was mounted did it occur to me that my bronco might mistake the rattle of the pills for a rattlesnake. But he didn't. Riding across the prairie, down the gullies, and fording the stream was all that it should have been—plenty of bright sunshine, blue sky, fresh air, and a wise little cow pony with lots of pep.

I've always liked the outdoor elements, probably because I played outside so much as a child. Mother always said that the four elements of earth, air, water, and fire were necessities of childhood. But I like these elements even more in the wide-open spaces of the West. Mother still doesn't understand why I prefer the West to New England.

"Why do you want to bury yourself in the wilds?" she asked when I told her that I'd decided to take the Red Cross position in South Dakota.

Yet, in 1882 she herself had moved from the effete East. Despite its malarial air, Hartford, Connecticut with its population of 40,000 was stimulating, delightful, and liberal, but my father had accepted a call in the West. He was to be the minister at the First Congregational Church in Colorado Springs, Colorado.

William Jackson Palmer had built Colorado Springs on the protected side of Pikes Peak in 1871. This resort, 75 miles south of Denver at an altitude of 6,000 feet, offered well-to-do people from back east the beginnings of culture and refinement. Built on the order of cosmopolitan Newport, Rhode Island, The Springs provided an amenable climate, invigorating mountain air, tranquility, better health, romance, and adventure.

My parents arrived in April 1882 with James, Faith, and Donald, three of my eldest siblings. Colorado Springs had few businesses, but the population of 5,000 was intelligent, refined, and had high moral standards. The city had no saloons, no electric lights, no telephone, no bicycles, and no means of public transportation. It did have a railroad, a gentleman's club, and a newspaper, *The Colorado Springs Gazette*.

Mother may have forgotten what The Springs was like in the early days. But she surely would have termed today's eight-mile drive from the agency to St. Francis in my Ford as being in the wilds.

I've been to the Catholic Boarding School at St. Francis several times, but the contrast between it and other schools still impresses me. The enrollment of 400 is about equally divided between boys and girls. The boys are under the care of Jesuit priests and Brothers and the girls are under the care of the Sisters of St. Francis. The children are well fed and clothed. Their lives are well regulated. The continuity of service on the part of the Fathers and Sisters makes for a certain dignity and charm missing from the other schools. The spirit is cheerful. But I do wish that the children were not herded together in such large groups. There are many disadvantages to them, though many economic advantages to the school.

Parents of children at a church school like St. Francis are allowed to visit more than those whose children attend the government boarding school. Never a day passes that some family isn't camped just outside the fence. They sit patiently all day in the warm hall, waiting till the children get spare time. The parents bring all sorts of treats—food and candy—that aren't good for the children. But what is one to do? The prohibitive method never works in dealing with them. Substitution is the only way.

The school at St. Francis, which offers grades one through eight and two years of high school, has been in existence since 1886. But a fire in 1916 destroyed it, the church, and the living quarters. The Fathers (Black Robes as the Indians call them) believe that the children set the fire in response to a rule that forbade them to speak Dakota either on the playground or in the school. This rule is usual in government boarding schools. Since the fire, the Jesuit Brothers and boys have planned and rebuilt the entire plant with very little outside help. It's not completely finished, but it's fireproof and everything about the place looks clean.

As soon as I approach the attractive Spanish Mission style buildings, Father Beuchel and the Sisters greet me. Father Beuchel, who's been among the Sioux for 30 years, knows more about them than anyone. He speaks to them in Dakota. The Indians say that he knows their language better than they do.

The Sisters very kindly give me a small office where I can examine the children. Even so, it's no light task to examine Indian children all day from 8:30 until 4:00. They must be handled with great gentleness. Even then, they whisper answers most of the time. They're easily discouraged. Even one mistake in English usage, if I comment on it, often sends them into a silence nearly impossible to overcome.

Health examinations are just the half of my efforts at St. Francis. A variety of other public health nursing activities demands my attention. For example, one day I examined 55 boys, made two pre-natal visits, gave a gargle to a man with a bad sore throat, saw a baby with "spasms" (tubercular, I'm afraid), and did paper work from seven o'clock until my watch stopped. It must have been after midnight.

Now it's barely eight a.m. Saturday morning, the 24th of February and I'm back at the agency for the weekend. "Superintendent McGregor wants you to go the office right away," the Indian Chief of Police says, summoning me.

I have the usual green-carpet qualms. I never outgrow them. In a matter of minutes I'm on my way, public health nursing bag in hand.

"A sixteen year old girl is about to have an illegitimate baby," Superintendent McGregor says, "and I want you to bring her to the hospital. Dr. Eddleman is on another confinement case, and Dr. Porras is sick." Dr. Lorenzo Porras is the physician for the reservation who arrived in December from Pennsylvania to help Dr. Eddleman.

"The prohibition detective will drive you to the girl's home."

When we arrive the girl is lying on the kitchen floor, atop the filthiest bedding that I've ever seen. Although she speaks English, she won't tell me how long she's been in labor. Nor will she let me examine her. A woman of 70 accompanied by her blind husband of 80 is the girl's only helper.

Although the girl had agreed to come to the hospital, she's trying to avoid it by having the baby at home. I decide to risk taking her the six miles to the hospital. The combination of a Red Cross nurse and a prohibition detective is too much for her obstinacy, so she packs and grunts her way into the back seat of the Ford-Touring. I know that it's a crazy risk on my part, but the back seat is surely cleaner than her bed. And I know that the moral effect of going to the hospital and not giving us the slip is worth a good deal—though I feel pretty sorry for her, too.

The baby arrives three minutes away from the hospital in spite of the prohibition detective at the wheel. I'm chiefly concerned about how to get the girl out of the Ford and onto the ground. Fortunately it's a mild day, and we're able to hail the driver of a passing truck who helps us get her out of the backseat. Shortly, everything is all right. I haven't run one of these shows on my own for some twelve years, and then not in a Ford-Touring. I want a Ford ambulance from the War Department quick!

Almost as soon as I get back to the agency, I leave for Okreek, 30 miles away. Curiously enough, the original name was Oak Creek. But when Oak Creek applied for a post office and mail service, the United

States Post Office Department told them that only one-word town names were acceptable. (Talk about centralized authority in action!) So the people of Oak Creek suggested Okreek, which was approved.

I'm in Okreek to give a talk on motherhood at a meeting of the Motherhood League. Somehow I feel particularly well fitted for the occasion. The Motherhood League is a nondenominational and educational group for Indian women. Its purpose is to do everything possible to increase the interest, knowledge, and ability of Sioux women in motherhood. The aim is to give them information that will help them take better care of their homes and children.

I have put in much office work at Rosebud on the Motherhood League, interspersed with the health examinations at St. Francis. Like the phoenix rising from the ashes, the Motherhood League promises to be a very valuable adjunct to my development work, a very feasible method of working with mothers. I'll make the Motherhood League the center of my Fair demonstrations later this summer. Only because Mrs. McClosky, who is one-fourth Indian, asked Superintendent McGregor for permission to organize the Motherhood League, do the Sioux women have an organization for themselves. A constitution and by-laws are being printed in Dakota.

This is the third monthly Motherhood Meeting I've attended. But well I remember one of the first. I was eager for a success, but an awkward division of opinion about where to hold it led to rather sparse attendance. Finally, we ate a picnic lunch in a large room on the top floor of the jail. The room had a few benches, but most everyone sat around a blanket on the floor.

We waited for more people to arrive. Then I spoke for an hour about health, sanitation, healthy babies, and public health. I drew again on an old Chautauqua speech. Only about half of the audience understood English so Mrs. McClosky interpreted for me. Several new babies and toddlers were in the audience, but children never distract Indians. The children are not scolded, nor do they require much watching; they are never noisy or querulous.

The polite way for Indian women to listen is with heads bowed. With the women sitting motionless on the floor with their foreheads almost resting on it, all I could see was the parts of fifty black scalps. The only way I could tell if they approved of my speech was if they laughed. If the subject was serious, they gave the equivalent of the English "Hear, Hear," only it is "Do, Do" or "Oh, Hun." The N has the French value as in "*nonne.*"

Quite a few Sioux had fought in the World War. So I ended the speech with a comparison of fighting germs instead of Germans. We could conquer both I assured them. At that point, I was startled when a very old woman clapped her hand on her mouth and gave the victory cry. The younger women smiled and told me this was the proper thing for the older women to do whenever a vanquished enemy was mentioned.

Refreshments of cold cornstarch soup—almost pudding, with pounded chokecherry, seeds and all—and coffee followed the meeting. We used the jail plates, but all the women had brought their own tin cups and spoons. Not having been forewarned and therefore having no spoon, I licked my soup from the plate. Perhaps that was unseemly, but no one appeared to mind.

Today's meeting in Okreek lasts until four o'clock. Then five women talk with me about their ailments. Two miles up the road I visit a baby dying of tuberculosis, and then half a mile down another road a man with tuberculosis. After all of this and a 30 mile drive, I arrive back at Rosebud about nine p.m. Barring the childbirth-in-the-Ford incident I could put in a day like this almost every day. My Star Day—the best so far.

In the midst of this month's health examinations at St. Francis, general paperwork, work on the Motherhood League, getting ready to go to Pine Ridge, and the "usual" activities, I had taken two 18-year old girls, Alice Bear Shields and Rosa Hunts Horses, to the eye specialist in Omaha. Their extreme near-sighted vision is about 20/100 (normal 20/20). Dr. Charles Gifford had operated on one of the Indians used in the design of the bas-relief that adorns our nickel. Dr. Gifford truly likes the Indians and never charges them for his services.

The girls had never seen a train so the trip was quite an adventure. We had a delightful time in the stores in Omaha riding in the elevators.

The girls squealed with excitement like two little pigs. And the Five and Ten Cent Store was pure rapture!

Unfortunately their eyes were too far-gone to do much, but at least we know that we've done everything we can. I, myself, have learned much about the eye, and I have much more to learn. Mr. McGregor has asked that the Government send us an eye specialist in May. I could get an enormous amount of help from him and could round up several good-sized eye clinics for adults as well as school children. I hope that this will pan out.

March arrives and I have to push hard to finish up at the Catholic Mission Boarding School by mid-month. Yet, much remains to be done. In February I kept track only of the tubercular cases and one little heart case. The task of following up on all the other work is impossible. To leave all this nursing work incomplete, not followed, and scarcely cared for by any stretch of the imagination, aggravates my sense of justice to these people more and more. Well I realize the administrative difficulties, but these people need care. They are responding to these beginnings so very well that I regret that my job is so analytical. I wish that it were more intensive and detailed and that it involved providing more direct care. Even then, one nurse would not be enough. I could use ten public health nurses tomorrow.

I may flatter myself, but I have begun to feel that the Indians see me as a help. They have such a talent for organization that they are more lenient with my inability to be everywhere at once. Also, they are accustomed to isolation. I would find it much more advantageous to put eight months in on Rosebud and give an extra month or two beyond my contracted year, so that I can play fair to Pine Ridge as well. The six months is simply not fair to Rosebud. I was so green when I came here, that I spent fully two months learning the major ropes of the Indian Service organization—not to mention the Indian. I know I could do much more, if I had more time.

JUNE 30, 1966—
SANTA FE TO ALBUQUERQUE

"MAYBE IT WAS THE WRONG THING TO DO, TELLING her about Dwight. What do you think?" Melody asked as Alice turned from the driveway onto Old Santa Fe Trail.

"No, she could tell you were sad today as soon as she saw you. Why shouldn't you tell her? She's a nurse, and it's natural for her to want to help. It's a big part of who she is."

"It did help to talk to her. I understand a little better now that I'm not just sad, but also really angry. I think this whole war is wrong and then it's so personal when my favorite cousin is killed in it. He was just twenty-one, my age. We were always together when we were little. I'm glad Uncle Junior and Aunt Lou live near their daughter at Silver City. Shirley's older than Dwight and I and a good person. She'll be a help to them."

"Miss Gregg, Aunt El, as she reminded us to call her, is so wise. Besides giving me a chance to talk and to cry, there's something about her that made me feel stronger. It was as if she absorbed my sadness and gave me back. . .comfort, I guess."

Glancing at Melody, Alice saw that although her usual smile was absent, the earlier sadness had been replaced by calm. "When is the funeral?" Alice asked.

"It's on Sunday. I told my mother I'd let her know tonight about whether I can go. She and Dad said they'd come through Albuquerque to pick us up on Saturday. Brice said he didn't want to go. Says he hates funerals. I'd almost decided not to go, just to keep the peace in the house, but I've decided now I will go. Mother will help me with the baby. It really would cause an uproar if I left him here for Brice to take care of. I'm not surprised he won't go. He's always pouted anytime Dwight called me and made ugly remarks about him writing to me from the places the Army sent him—like 'You'd think he was a boyfriend, not your relative'."

"Is he always so possessive of you?" Alice asked.

"It seems a little less since we've been married. When we were dating, it was so romantic—he wanted to be with me every minute. He says it's because he loves me so completely and needs to know I feel the same. I do love him, but sometimes it's hard to breathe. He is devoted to our little family and works hard for us. It sounds like I'm complaining, and I don't mean to." After a minute's silence, she said, "Let's change subjects now, okay?"

Alice marveled at her friend's ability to focus on their work regardless of any turmoil she was feeling. "Sure," she said. "Here's something I was thinking about. I'm going to see what I can find in the library about the Red Cross. Apparently it was a very influential organization in those days. And Aunt El's work with the Red Cross certainly affected her career. I'd like to ask her about that, but I hate to interrupt the way her story is unfolding."

Melody nodded. "I was thinking about that part where she mentioned how she still wondered if she was responsible for that baby dying. It showed me she's not only a strong, remarkable person, but a very human one too. Recalling after so many years that she might have made an error. That's strength and humility. I took a lesson from that."

"Maybe this next tape will have some more about her family. I believe we were right about some of her early experiences helping encourage her to be dauntless. She talked about her mother believing outdoor activity was essential for children, not just for the boys. I'd like to know more about her family because I believe that so much of what a person does with their life is affected either positively or negatively by family," Alice said. Noticing Melody checking her watch, she said, "Are we going to be all right with the baby sitter's schedule?"

"Yes, I'll be there in plenty of time to get the baby. I'm hoping to get home and have a meal ready and the evening routines over with before I tell Brice I'm going to the funeral. Everyone is calmer after a good meal," Melody said.

"You put a lot of effort into keeping things calm at your house, don't you?" Alice said.

"Seems like it," Melody replied.

"I think you're a better woman than I am, and a better wife than I'll ever be," Alice said, turning into the campus parking lot.

MORE THAN I CAN CHEW

If I hadn't had to wait for them I would have arrived earlier. But they've been no trouble and helped me push through the mud in one bad place. "They've been picked up down the line in Nebraska," Mr. McGregor said. "They've run away from Holy Rosary Mission School and have to be taken back. Will you take them with you?"

How could I refuse? Somehow I've missed the Chief of Police and have to bungle around looking for the jail. I finally find it, turn over the two Indian boys and come on to the Boarding School to find a jolly game of basketball going on. So, I stay to watch for a bit.

Superintendent Tidwell knew that I'd be coming to Pine Ridge. It was only a matter of time. Just as Commissioner Burke had written Superintendent McGregor, so he had written to Mr. Tidwell.

Unfortunately, when I arrive, he is sick. So I spend a day or so before getting my assignment made. Mr. Tidwell is cordial in a reserved sort of way, "Welcome, Miss Gregg. I am sorry I could not see you until today."

"Thank you, sir. It was not a problem, because I had time to get settled and to write some reports I've been neglecting," I reply. I don't mention that after driving the 100 miles from the Rosebud Agency I was happy to stretch my legs. Nor do I mention the two young charges who'd been my traveling companions. Health, not law enforcement, is my business.

He launches into a quick rundown on the Reservation. "There are approximately seven thousand five hundred Indians living here in four counties within the Pine Ridge Reservation, about four thousand five hundred fifty-eight square miles. As you know, the Agency is near the Nebraska state line and about three hundred people, both white and Indian employees and families live here. I think the settlement, with the homes, churches, the Indian day school and the county school is quite attractive and well kept."

"Indeed, this is a very pleasant appearing Agency settlement," I say.

He smiles with a proprietary air. "You may also know already that we have no field matrons on this reservation, and our doctor is temporary, until a regular Civil Service appointee can be found. He's very busy with the large territory to cover. So, I'm not certain just what your work can entail here. But rest assured, we will cooperate in every way as Commissioner Burke has directed."

As he speaks I notice his eyes stray often to a large stack of correspondence on his desk. He obviously has work to do. "Mr. Tidwell, thank you for your time. As I know you have informed the employees of my arrival, I'll be happy to introduce myself to everyone. I will make certain to keep you informed of my plans. I appreciate your cooperation and I know that Commissioner Burke and the Red Cross do as well."

That was a little more than a week ago. Today and March will be gone. The tops of the bushes in the creek bottom look red. A robin and meadowlark have come. I know, because I saw them, and they sang for me. I have brought a blanket, the O.D. blanket which last month I pinned around me squaw fashion with a horse-blanket safety pin for an extra skirt on those fearfully cold drives. Five years ago, I was wrapping up stretcher cases in them in France. I am lying out in the warm spring sun just under the lee of the bluff that skirts the crest at the Boarding School at Pine Ridge.

I have examined children with the doctor all morning at the Holy Rosary Mission School. There were 148 boys. The doctor looked at their eyes, noses, throats, teeth and neck glands. There are lots of bad tonsils and no way to take them out without money. Hot Springs and surgeons are 65 miles away. The Indians here are not so willing to have operations as the Rosebuds.

Overall, it seems the Indians here are more docile than at Rosebud. They have no field matron to complain about and seem to have fewer cliques. Perhaps their manner has something to do with their history. I'm learning bits of their past from here and there. Inaccurate as some of the details I hear may be, I do know that the Wounded Knee Massacre occurred here at Pine Ridge in 1890. When it was over, some 300 Sioux were dead at the hands of the U.S. Army. I'm told that men, women and children were shot and over 150 were buried in a mass grave. It's hard to believe it's been less than 35 years since that. That tragedy had to have an effect on the survivors and on the next generation.

My public health education at Simmons College certainly has made me see things differently than I might as a hospital nurse. The Red Cross paid my tuition for the course, which was one academic year in length. It was definitely a good investment for me and for the Red Cross. Although I could not take a permanent assignment immediately after I completed the program in June 1920 due to my father's poor health, I was well prepared. I had a temporary assignment in New Hampshire, near the family from that time until his death in May 1922. After he died, as soon as my mother was situated, I was eager to put my knowledge to a real test. The courses built on my Waltham Training School background and firmly convinced me of the interplay of the community and the health of the individual. We studied municipal and industrial sanitation, bacteriology, biology and infectious disease, home nursing, education, sociology and social services. All that was followed by four months of intensive field work in and around Boston. Not a day goes by here on the Reservation that I don't apply something I learned.

I'm back at the Agency. "Mr. Tidwell, to keep you up to date with my activities, I begin tomorrow examining pupils at the Government Boarding School. I will also spend some time on the day schools." I am reporting, following channels, something I believe Mr. Tidwell is keen on. "I expect to stay until sometime the first week of May. I'll go back to Rosebud. Then I hope to return and stay here from September through January."

"Yes, well, that will be fine. Are you getting cooperation?" he asks.

"Oh, yes. Perhaps I have been too slow in saying that I am getting every help from the Indian Service employees. Nothing that I have asked to have changed has been refused and every courtesy and consideration is given me both personally and officially. The missionaries are willing to cooperate heartily, as well." I don't think it's necessary to mention my assessment of the obstacles here. The impediments all revolve around meager resources, limited personnel, and impossible transportation difficulties. He's most certainly aware of those problems.

As I have his attention, I continue. "There are two aspects to the health work in the boarding schools which are equally important. Of course the actual care of the sick does not come in my province at all. My two considerations are the factors that go to keep each individual child well and the education which that child is receiving both as to its own health and the health of the community of children in which it lives. The same is true of the day schools, only on a smaller scale. By examining individual children, I gain information not only about that child, but also about the group. Based on that information, for example about what illnesses are prevalent or where development is lagging, I can then make plans for further action. That might include changes in diet, alterations in school activities, or teaching of health information to pupils. The possibilities are almost endless."

I draw a breath to continue but stop short. I see I have lost his attention. No matter—I've accomplished my main purpose, to make an official report of my activities.

The contrast between Mr. Tidwell and Mr. McGregor is sharp. Both seem to be principled and just men. But where Superintendent McGregor is warmth and personal attention, Mr. Tidwell is procedure and calculation. McGregor is very interested in my work and sees it as important to the lives of the people of the Rosebud. Mr. Tidwell is courteous but seems to see little reason for my being here. He just wants another doctor. And he's probably right. Why turn up health problems when nothing can be done about them?

I noted another interesting difference. Mr. McGregor is Chairman of the very active Red Cross Chapter at Rosebud. Clearly he is instrumental in its success. There is no active chapter at Pine Ridge at all. Mr. Tidwell has explained that the Indians here are too poor to support others in need. Ah well, no one said this would be easy! I come to a halt as I leave the Agency, hoping I haven't been uttering my thoughts aloud as I walked.

Talking to myself is useful though, because I now realize what's been bothering me. I am somewhat staggered by the job of starting work here. I think I am biting off more than I can chew, in six months. I know so well that the greatest force in health work is content and follow-up and putting through plans. That is even more true with the Indian than with the white. To the Indian, the white man's word is not as good as his bond. The Indian waits to see just how you will make good before he will traffic with you. I do not want to start what is not going to be carried out. I know that I could sail in here for six months, flap my wings, talk and sail out with little done and nothing left to build on. And thinking about what needs to be done after what I've begun at Rosebud, I know that there I must spread myself thinner and see the whole reservation. The whole thing depends on cooperation among the people and there is a lot of bickering and dissatisfaction that must be dealt with by talking with them individually and in groups. The Motherhood League is one way to get group work started, but that takes time also. Also I don't want to undermine the field matrons' work until I know if there is to be someone to follow up my lead. Yes, that's it. I must have more time. One year is certainly not enough.

"Miss Ahrens, it's so good to be able to talk with you. Our being here together at the conference in Minneapolis is such a good opportunity for me to have your counsel," I begin.

"Please, do tell me all that's on your mind. Things often become clearer just with the telling, I find," she says warmly. "I've read your reports as they come in, but I know there is much you think but don't write."

I launch in without further encouragement. "Now that I've been at Pine Ridge several weeks, in regard to the school children, I am beginning to feel that I know my ground. I can begin to make some judgments of value as to their health and as to ways of improving their health. Most of the sickness is of the respiratory tract. The mucous membranes and the skin are the most susceptible to infection. There are two great obstacles to carrying out plans for improvement of individual health or in the schools' education for health. There are only barely enough teachers to carry on the extremely heavy routine as now organized. The groups are so large as to be very unwieldy. I soon found that out when trying to teach some breathing exercises to seventy-five girls from twelve to eighteen years one evening in the gymnasium. The teacher that has this enormous group every Monday night during the year simply cannot make much headway. In the school classes, the ages are very much mixed and no attempt is made to separate the mentally deficient. Throughout the whole system, it is impossible to give enough individual supervision. With that, I am amazed at the results that are at present being obtained. I am certain that other teaching staffs would never put out the effort.

"The other great drawback is insufficient funds to get the right equipment. It is a tight fight for the Superintendent and the Agent all the time to get the bare necessities, let alone make any change that involves expenditure."

Miss Ahrens nods but says nothing.

"Let me give an example," I say. "In making sanitary inspection with the Superintendent of one school, I criticized the sanitation in the dairy. Not that they were neglecting to do what could be done with what they had, but that what they had was quite inadequate to produce clean milk. My objections were agreed with, but funds are not available at present for change. In this case I consider the fact that the children are not at present getting the best milk to be of minor importance compared with the fact that the dairy boys are getting trained in producing dirty milk. Their answer will be 'That's the way we did it at school.' Future babies and children will suffer"

Having Miss Ahrens' ear and her full attention make me realize how much I need this sort of discussion. Isolation has its disadvantages. "I realize that above all, I need more time for the two reservations. I can't begin to make too strong a plea for carrying on this work with Red Cross funds if the Government cannot swing it right away. In fact, I believe that two or three years of Red Cross work would hand the Government a much stronger organization than they could develop in the same time themselves."

"What would you propose, specifically?" Miss Ahrens asks.

"I haven't thought through a full proposal yet, but I do have an idea. There is a territory twenty-five miles from the Pine Ridge Agency where I can do a piece of intensive work. The population is about one thousand two hundred fifty, an average population for a county nurse, I believe. There would be six day schools in the area. In many ways the conditions would be typical of the Indian Service and yet comparable to white service. I want to settle there in September and carry them through January. This runs over my year, but I hope that some funds will be left from the original appropriations that could be applied to my salary.

"I cannot begin to do justice to these two reservations, not to speak of myself in a constructive demonstration in less than fourteen months. Getting the confidence of the Indians and the employees of the Service has eaten up two months of Rosebud time. Of course I can do it in less time on Pine Ridge with that behind me. The advantage of taking a single district on Pine Ridge is, first, that they get very little medical service. It would be the key position to develop. Second, it gives excellent material for a sound report on the cost and the possibilities of the cooperation of the Indian. More work could be done as the distances would be so much smaller."

"After you've considered this more, write me with your thoughts. In the meanwhile, I will be thinking about it also," says Miss Ahrens.

May already! I go back to Rosebud this week, and I have promised myself I will complete my April report before May fills my thoughts. It is so difficult to feel I am doing justice to either reservation, but I know the summer at Rosebud will be very busy with work on the Five Year Plan and I am eager to participate.

I find on Pine Ridge the same conditions that lead me to think that all the efforts should be put on the tuberculosis and eye problems. The teachings on cleanliness and proper food are the foundation work but the fact remains that the sick are getting no care, and until this is remedied by some type of clinic or sanitarium that the Indian can and will patronize, the task of good home supervision is hopeless without nurses and doctors. At a minimum, there's need of an X-ray to make some sort of near guess as to the progress of the involvement. Another need is a Sun Lamp to treat the gland cases; another, a much larger quantity of cod liver-oil to give out to the undernourished babies and young children. The year's supply is gone now! When you stop to consider that they do not have any butter in their diet and very little whole fresh milk, the necessity for supplemental oils is very apparent. There is no seafood and a great deal of goitre enlargement. Another scheme I have been studying out is a sanitarium school for these tubercular children in the early stages. An abandoned day school property would be quite possible, with tents with wooden floors. But that is far in the future I suppose. One thing that I am convinced of is that we will never succeed in getting sick Indians to go 1,000 miles away from home to a hospital. It is hard enough to get them to come to our own hospital on Rosebud. Pine Ridge is a little nearer the Hot Springs facilities, but they are woefully deficient in all surgical matters. The removal of the diseased tonsils would be a great help in preventing the further infection of TB glands.

Ah well, will I ever learn? The report I submitted, for April, before leaving Pine Ridge, struck a nerve with Mr. Tidwell. He retorted that I was applying "white" standards. That was in reference to needing an X-ray and Sun Lamp. And he said the homes are the problem with Indian health because the children do fine as long as they are in the Boarding School. And to clinch it, he said emphatically that there was no sense to supply cod liver oil because Indians just won't take it. He is such a nice man and treats me well, but he is convinced that there is nothing to be done about health except to add more doctors. I definitely have a challenge at Pine Ridge. Even if I did not also have Rosebud, Pine Ridge alone could consume all my energy. But, since I am back here at Rosebud, I am even more hopeful that something good can be demonstrated here.

"Well, Miss Elinor Runs Reckless, you certainly made the Memorial Day celebration impressive. Marching along with all the children up to the cemetery—you in your full uniform. It was a picture worth saving," Mrs. McGregor says. "You are such a good organizer, and the Indians just love the pageantry. I know the reason they cooperate with you is because you participate; you don't just tell them what to do."

"Yes, it was a great deal of fun. I enjoyed it as much as the children did," I smile. The children were very cunning; all dressed up in their best, walking up the long dusty road to the cemetery on the top of the bluff. I spoke a little about patriotism and the unselfish service of those soldiers and sailors. We decorated the graves. Old High Horse made a speech at the grave of Spotted Tail, the Big Chief of Rosebud, who made the final treaties with the government. He gave his own interpretation of the flag. The stars show that we are a great nation united, the blue is the uniform of the soldiers and sailors, the red is for the blood that has been shed to give us liberty and justice, and the white is for the honesty and honor of the people.

After the decoration of the graves, there was a community picnic, a speaker, and baseball. The Boarding School band came over to supply the music. It has all been very nice and I am sorry I will have to leave early to get back to Pine Ridge for tonsil surgeries tomorrow.

"I'm concerned about you, that you may be working too hard. All your traveling . . ." Mrs. McGregor says.

"I'm trying to keep a finger in the pie by going back and forth from Pine Ridge as much as possible, but a hundred ten miles in a two-year old Ford runabout takes a good deal of energy. I'll try not to overdo, but there is so much to be done. Me and my Ford are pretty good pals. She only fails in gumbo and that only because I can't ride and push at the same moment," I laughingly reply. Mrs. Mac is a good friend to be concerned, I think.

Now it's June. As of this week, the Rosebud Reservation officially has a Red Cross Health Station. It is also my new living quarters. The Arrows had lived here and now that they're gone Superintendent McGregor assigned it for my work. It will be homey and I will do all I can to make it a demonstration of cleanliness and neatness of the sort we advocate for disease prevention. The front room will be used as an office and I'll try to keep one day a week as an office day. Those who know ahead that they need to see the Red Cross nurse can come on that day, but I'll be available at other times when I am here. They can catch me coming and going from my other duties.

I have a visitor coming this month, Miss Florence Patterson. I am eager to have her advice and her company. She's had much public health experience and has been doing a survey of some of the Southwest Reservations as the other part of the Red Cross effort to help the Indian Service. Perhaps she'll see a way for me to accomplish something meaningful for both reservations.

"Yes, my dear, you were exactly right when you wrote in your report that you've bitten off more than you can chew. There's no way that one person, regardless of how tirelessly you work, can do a good demonstration of field nursing in such a large territory. Add to that the factor of two different reservation administrations and it's impossible to do anything more than dabble. With your permission, I want to talk to Miss Fox as well as to Superintendent McGregor about confining your work to Rosebud and extending your term of assignment at least until next July," Miss Patterson says. She's now been with me for three days as I went about my routines. She's supposed to be on vacation but doesn't seem to mind that this is work. As part of her own work she supervises Miss Stoll who is doing a demonstration similar to mine on the Jicarilla Reservation in New Mexico.

We've made a trip to Pine Ridge and several home visits here on Rosebud, along with an office day here at the Health Station. Regardless of whether it's office day or not, there are an average of five visitors a day—for advice, medicine, or sociability.

"I know that you have mentioned this concern in at least two reports, but my independent observation in addition to that may be what is needed to convince the Red Cross and Commissioner Burke. Will you consider it interfering if I do this?" she asks.

"Interfering? Hardly!" I say. I am so heartened by her desire to help. Once again I realize how easy it is for isolation to reduce one's sense of choice. I must always stay in contact with my colleagues, I am convinced.

July arrives rapidly. Mr. McGregor and I went out today to Cut Meat working on the house-to-house survey as part of the Five Year Plan. "Runs Reckless, I've sent a letter to the Red Cross headquarters with a copy to the Commissioner asking that you be stationed for the next year exclusively in Rosebud. I hope that letter, along with Miss Patterson's effort, will get an affirmative response. We do have so much here that you can accomplish, particularly with the tuberculosis problem," he tells me.

He's given me the Indian family name, Runs Reckless, as a compliment, I think. "I hope you're right. I do appreciate your interceding.

Although I feel badly about Pine Ridge needing so much as well," I responded.

"That's true, but if your work pays off, perhaps all the reservations will get field nurses," he said. I nod as I line up the family for the picture. I take photos of each family we visit and get to check on the home environment and family health while he and the farmer check on the farm-related situation of the family. All of this information will be the basis for the Five Year Plan for Rosebud. In the process, I get to check particularly on the babies and the pre-school children.

"Mrs. White Elk, I will put your baby's picture in the gallery I'm making for the fair next month," I explain as she poses the youngster.

The Annual Fair in August is where I'll have the picture gallery, an exhibit of a good layette, an outfit for a premature baby, weighing day, and as many health posters as I can muster. The picture gallery is going to be very attractive, I think. I do so much want to show some things to be proud of. There is so much to be discouraged over. Up to ten months the babies do pretty well but the mothers look very badly in need of other nourishment. After about 18 months the babies begin to fail.

At the last meeting of the Motherhood League, I complimented them on how many good housekeepers I had seen in my visits with Mr. McGregor. One of them spoke up and said she thought that I had too many weeds around my house. It is quite true the place is full of ragweed as my poor nose testifies daily and hourly. So I told the story to the stableman and he has been out with the mower.

I had good news today! I am to be assigned exclusively to Rosebud for another year. That made me eager to start planning. However, the survey work and planning for the Fair took precedence. Today was a typical survey day. We saw about 30 families, made about 75 miles, worked from 8 a.m. to 8:30 p.m. and had our picnic lunch in the shadiest spot we could find.

I have found many frank cases of TB among the adults and many suspects. The babies with sore and dirty heads are legion. Itch and impetigo run riot. Of course I don't know what these skin cases really are but I suspect most of them are low-grade staphylococcus or streptococcus infections. Oh, to have a skin man for a couple of weeks! But I see no way to arrange it yet. My two big problems, related to these visits and the cases I find, are to dispense the essential remedies with instructions as to their use and to follow up the first visit by a second within a reasonable space of time. Home supervision in the adequate sense of the term is not possible. I keep one day in the office at Rosebud as strictly as possible but usually have a few calls to make after five in the evening. There's always the temptation to work as long as it is light but I am going to try to take life a bit more easily in September as six weeks of hay fever has eaten up most of my gimp.

Blessed relief! I'm sitting in my cozy house with my feet up. I need a rest after three days of Fair. Everyone did seem pleased with the things we did. Next Fourth of July or next Fair I hanker to try a pageant by the Junior Red Cross. This time I wrote a song for them to sing. It was in honor of the mothers and went to the tune of "Maryland, My Maryland." They did a grand job. Anything symbolic and spectacular goes like a streak. The children know how to do it instinctively and the elders appreciate it enormously. If I had the time to prepare it I could run a good afternoon of counter-attraction to the all-consuming Indian dance.

The dogs and coyotes are giving their usual midnight concert. The roads are in prime condition and I hate to think of winter. My Ford must have a new top but otherwise I think that it will weather another winter. The human frame is supposed to renew itself every seven years and in the Indian Service a Ford is almost human!

WHAT'S TIME WHEN YOU CONSIDER ETERNITY?

"I DON'T SUPPOSE YOU HAVE MUCH OCCASION to repair flat tires in Pittsburgh, do you Helen?" I laugh as I hand her the little jack. This is our second blowout since leaving Rosebud. But our trip to the Black Hills is actually going along quite well. Since Helen Bigelow arrived in late September, 1924 she's been everywhere with me as I work. And now we're taking a quick vacation trip for her to see the Badlands and the Black Hills before she returns on October 12 to her own work with the Child Welfare Bureau. She and I had both worked at Cleveland City Hospital and were both in the War. Although we were with different units over there, we have lots in common. She's a good friend.

"Elinor, I don't see how you and 'Lizette' have managed this whole year of travel on this reservation. The paths that are called roads out here are little better than wagon ruts," she says.

"True enough. Some of the supplies for the Agency are still delivered by freight wagon from the railroad in Crookston, Nebraska," I say while taking off the wheel. I rejoice that it isn't raining.

I explained some of the history of the Black Hills and the Badlands as we began the 150 mile initial step of our trip, so Helen was prepared. She'd particularly liked the story of the gold rush of 1876 that had turned Deadwood briefly into a thriving city. I estimate that at our present rate of 25 miles an hour, allowing for blowouts and a roadside lunch, we should reach the southeastern edge of the Badlands by 3 p.m. As it's only 11 now, we have plenty of time to talk out here on the prairie before the buttes and crags of the Badlands demand attention. We'll stop in Rapid City and then go west into the Black Hills. We've made no more definite plans than that. We'll just see how the spirit moves us.

"Helen, you've been such a good sport about the rather primitive conditions out here. I guess that you haven't forgotten roughing it like we did in the War. You haven't said a bad word yet about 'Chick' either. I'm quite impressed," kidding her a bit.

"I don't believe I ever heard an outdoor toilet called a 'Chick Sales' before. But no, it would be very bad manners for a guest to complain of the facilities. A well-brought-up woman would never show bad manners," she says. She's a kidder too. "I intend to write your mother when I get back and tell her just how impressive your work at Rosebud is. She has no idea. I imagine that's because you don't tell her. Mothers enjoy boasting a bit about their children's exploits. So you really should give her more to go on."

"I do well to just fit in writing her a letter every week or so," I answer.

"Perhaps if you weren't quite as involved in the activities on the reservation that aren't health related, you'd have more time to yourself," Helen says.

"That's true. But I wouldn't be able to do really good public health nursing without being involved," I say.

"I suppose that painting the place cards for the banquet the other night, as well as being one of the speakers, comes under the heading of 'involved in the community'." Helen is joking about my recent artistic endeavor for the banquet honoring some of the attorneys in the suit between the Sioux and the government in regard to the claim to the Black Hills land.

"I thought of it more as an act of creativity, good for my artistic soul," I say. "Mr. William Spotted Tail, one of the other speakers, was most complimentary of my design. But regarding time to myself, we are taking a vacation, you've noticed," I point out.

"That we are, and I'm having a grand time." After a thoughtful pause, Helen says, "I'm interested in knowing something else, Elinor. I wonder if you've considered what it is that drives you to do this work. After all, with your background, you could have lots of other positions, far less difficult ones."

"Yes, I have thought occasionally about that," I nod. "Several things go together, I suppose. First, there's the adventure of being in this more primitive place. And of course, there's the need. So much need." I pause a moment. "There's the work itself. Whatever I invent, if I'm able enough, I can do. That's so different from jobs where everything is all predetermined."

"Pioneering in more ways than one, then," Helen assesses correctly.

"Yes. As far as why those things are important to me, I can't say exactly, but I wonder if my father's influence has something to do with it. I was reading not long ago, a letter to Alan he wrote in January of nineteen twenty-two, before he died that May. He wrote it as his principles for living, I think, saying, 'this is the life which is life indeed'. This is what he wrote,

1. As regards the body, to seek for ourselves and for all others, insofar as we can secure it, health.

2. As regards the conscience, to seek for ourselves and insofar as we can to bestow upon all others, truth.

3. As regards the conscience, to do ourselves and to help others to do the right.

4. As regards the heart, to love God supremely and our fellow man as ourselves.

5. As regards the aesthetic sensibilities, to cultivate and to foster in others the quick and wide recognition and promotion of beauty.

"He also mentioned, not as an essential of life but as contributing to its joy, a sense of humor.

"None of that accounts for my preferring the Wild West, but perhaps it does relate to choosing this work. There could be many ways to live a life that met those essentials, but on most days, this place, these people, this work seem a very good way and a good spot for me to try to do that." I stop speaking, a little embarrassed at myself.

Helen urges me along. "Now that you know you're to be at Rosebud until next July, what have you planned?"

"I'm thinking about what to put in my report of the first year's work and how to tie that to the plan for next year. The next year's plan is rather simple—three main things—first, to establish a routine that could be carried out in each district if nurses were put in; second, to make records of families that would be of value to succeeding nurses; and third, to try a simple experiment in health education on a small group of school children where the entire routine of the child is under my control," I reply. "Those are my main plans, the ones I might have some actual ability to complete. But at the same time, I hope to influence the superintendent, the physician, and other employees to be concerned enough about health to see how everyone's work actually can have a positive effect on the Indians' health. Everything is related. In the long term, doing something about preventing tuberculosis and trachoma rather than burying the dead or assisting the blind must be everyone's concern. Then eventually something might get done. Oh, Helen, you've let me get started preaching again!"

"But you do it so well," she laughs. "Your father would be proud."

Today's October 27, 1923 and I may actually get a few minutes to straighten up here at the Red Cross Station. I've been away for several days doing the TB clinics.

The Red Cross chapter paid for Dr. Katz, the chest specialist, to come and conduct clinics one day each in St. Francis, Wood, Mission, and Parmelee. At St. Francis, we were at the Catholic Mission school. Dr. Katz brought his secretary and I took Mrs. Jordan, an Indian woman who works in the office and knows the people very thoroughly. We couldn't examine the whole school but called out those whom we knew to have come in contact with the disease. Also I sent out a letter on Red Cross stationery to all the families of that district whom I knew were ailing. We examined 79 people of whom 37 were negative, 23 active, and 17 suspect, less than 50% definitely negatives. Pretty bad. Fifteen active cases in school. The government doctor isn't altogether to blame. It's a physical impossibility for him to cover the work here even after a fashion.

Each of the four days went much the same, slow going. It is a terrible job to get the people out of their clothing. They are very shy and slow to get ready. The lowest number of active cases was in the Boarding School at Mission. The total figures for the four clinics were 396 examined, 200 negative, 56 suspects, 144 positive. It would be difficult to say whether this percentage would increase or decrease if the whole population were examined. At any rate there is no doubt that the Indian wants help, medical help. The good old myth that has comforted so many Indian Bureau physicians no longer holds good. The Indian wants help and can spot medical bunk almost as well as I can. How in the world can I supply help for them? No sanitarium, no money, not even a doctor just now, no home nursing, no registered nurse at the hospital. I can't bear doing such poor work much longer unless some pretty strong backing in development comes along.

The frustration I'm feeling does have one beneficial effect. I took it out on the house. Now all three rooms are clean and neat and I am worn out!

"Nella McGregor, do come in. I'm here alone, feeling sorry for myself. Let's have some coffee," I say to the superintendent's wife. I'm happy she's come to visit.

"Sorry for yourself because you're alone?" she asks.

"Goodness no, just frustrated by the lacks—of money, of equipment, of good medical personnel in the Indian Service. Probably a big part of my upset comes from the TB clinics we just finished. The only benefit that can come from all the work is to be able to give accurate reports on specific numbers of cases. That's because, in reality, we won't have much possibility of getting good treatment, and even less of improving diet, home situations, and knowledge on the ways to prevent more cases. And to top it off, I've been out of luck for transportation much of the month.

"The government agreed to supply my transportation but the request for permission to buy a new car has got beached in some quiet little Washington office or else blue-penciled before it reached the eye of Mr. Merritt or Mr. Burke," I say.

"Has Mr. McGregor tried to help?" she asks.

"Of course, he's done all he can at his level. Perhaps I expect too much. One would think the matter might move faster. I started the wheels September sixth. But then the extra special order for a hundred bottles of cod liver oil I sent out June twenty-seventh has only just now come!" I say.

"I can see why you would be frustrated," Nella says.

The coffee smells good. I smile as I pour and say, "Governmental speed is miraculous. It does make me think of my father, the minister. I know what he would say to me right now. He'd say, 'Ah, Elinor, what's time when you consider eternity?'"

My first full year ends as November closes. "Lizette" is officially retired. Perhaps she'll provide some spare parts as needed. My new Ford coupe, 1924 model, with a Red Cross on the side, has arrived. Bless Mr. McGregor, he figured a way to have it purchased with local Red Cross funds. I would still be afoot or on horseback if we'd waited for Washington's approval. It's been a hectic month with several trips taking patients to the hospital in Pierre and to the eye specialist in Omaha. On one trip (in Lizette), I didn't get started back here until noon. In White River my generator went fluey and I had no lights when I tried them as I was climbing Horse Creek hill. I was too mad to go back and too tired to go on, but as there was a moon, I did go on and got to Rosebud at 7:45 p.m. Tiring to say the least, but my services are definitely in demand. I am convinced that the Rosebud Sioux Indians are ready for this work. The thing is sold as far as they are concerned. The next thing is to sell it to Mr. Burke and Congress.

Perhaps it was fatigue that made me pessimistic back in November. The trip to Boston for the holidays and the time to rest were both welcome. I laughed aloud today when I read in the *Todd County Tribune* that I had "returned with renewed energy"! How could they tell, I wonder? One thing that did set me up a bit was my meeting with Commissioner Burke. Though it was a bit bold, I scheduled an appointment and showed myself right there in his office in Washington, D. C. I told him directly about some of my experiences here; that his idea of using nurses rather than field matrons is a good one, based on what I've been able to do; and about my idea for an experiment with a six week camp for some school children as an effort to improve their health knowledge and health habits.

He asked questions and listened attentively. I believe he was truly interested. Now, whether any of that will have an effect depends on the members of Congress. After our meeting, I understand even more clearly than before, how much the opinion of individual members of Congress can affect both policy and budget. Not only does he have Congress as a concern, he also must tread carefully among other influential groups and individuals interested in the Indians, or their land, or the minerals or forests on their land. I do not envy him his job.

But today it's February and Commissioner Burke is thousands of miles from here and I return to my work. Now that I've put the Red Cross Station back to rights by dusting, straightening, and seeing to the woodpile for heat, I'm ready for business. The cold weather is keeping visitors away this morning, so I'll use the time to visit Mr. McGregor and report on my meeting in Washington.

"As I talked with the Commissioner, the plan for the camp became even clearer to me. I'm so glad that you agree we should try this experiment. To have that small group of children and supervise their living situation, nutrition, hygiene, schedule, education, even for six weeks all with an eye toward how their health can be improved can be very instructive, I believe. Of course, I am tempted to aim too high and expect that they'll all be washing their hands before meals and demanding green leafy vegetables at the end of it. But realistically, we could put ten pounds on them each and have them smiling, at least. And perhaps we'd have less coughing and fewer sick days, to boot." I'm talking fast, excited.

"You're really eager to do this aren't you? Did Mr. Burke promise any money for a teacher and tents for the camp quarters?" Mr. McGregor asks.

"Of course not. I didn't make a formal request. It wouldn't be my place to do that as a Red Cross employee." I'm quickly back to earth. "I also know that bad weather or any of a hundred other obstacles can prevent our doing this. But I do hope to try. As I mentioned before, I want to do it at the end of April, the 23rd through June 4th," I say.

"Go ahead with developing the plan and I'll do what I can. But without extra funds for a teacher, I can make no promises," he says.

"Oh, Mr. McGregor. I do understand your financial dilemma. I hope you don't think I'm complaining. I just want to make you aware of my visit with the Commissioner. By the way, I did mention to him that you are most supportive of my work," I'm quick to add.

"I'll do what I can," he promises.

That was early in February. Looking back, now that it's April, it's easy to see all the things that prevented our doing the camp. Paramount was the lack of funds for a teacher. Mr. McGregor appealed to Washington, but no extra funds were to be had. All of March was muddy roads. Travel was impossible and no one expected me to go. Still I got so sick of putting people off with talk of getting stuck half way, blizzards and broken springs that I took to horseback one afternoon starting at two o'clock and getting in at 8:30 having made 26 miles round trip. The real reason they sent for me was to see if I would work a sick baby to get an aunt out of jail for bootlegging and gambling. So the sore muscles of the following few days did not seem commensurate with the good done! It snowed every day of the month except three but the frost was coming out of the ground all the time.

The hospital boiler burst and I took a patient into my house. He was a post operative from the Murdo hospital where they had loaded him up on opiates and turned him loose with some kind of abdominal fluid giving him terrific pain. He came in a Ford truck from 30 miles north and couldn't be turned away. So I spent the rest of the month doing special day and night duty along with the usual callers at the house plus some home work. I learned later that he had cirrhosis of the liver.

Even though I'll have to give up the idea of the camp, the planning has been done and could be used another year. There's no doubt the demand for my services is strong, so I'll continue working as if there will be other nurses here to join in or follow up. Maybe Commissioner Burke will make that happen.

"Miss McArdle, you have no idea how happy I am to see you. There's so much to talk about. But first you should meet my housemates here at the Red Cross Station. This kitten is Dumbbell. She's true to her name. Out back there is my horse Folly. Perhaps you'd like to ride while you're here. I have been trying to ride some every day. Besides being good for the horse, I think it might help with my reducing campaign. I weighed recently and found I was up to a hundred seventy-three! By avoiding most food for a while, I've gotten down to a hundred sixty-five, but I aim for one hundred forty-seven." I stop, realizing she's smiling and shaking her head.

"You do have lots to tell, don't you?" she says.

Laughing, I say, "Yes and most of it is more important than my weight and the menagerie. I really do need your advice about next steps."

Taking Dumbbell into her lap, she says, "No better time to begin than now."

On the trip back to Rosebud from Winner where I had picked her up, Miss McArdle and I had kept to general topics of conversation, saving the work until we arrived here. One major point of discussion had been fresh fruits and vegetables. Now that it's June there's bounteous variety available in Winner, though none in Rosebud. We loaded up strawberries, asparagus, lettuce, pineapple, cucumbers and tomatoes. We agreed we'd not look at a potato for days.

The cat jumps from her lap to chase an imaginary mouse. Miss McArdle turns her full attention to me. "Tell me what you've been thinking about."

"I know you read my reports, so you are aware that the tuberculosis problem is one of my greatest concerns. In May, the doctor and one of the hospital staff, the district farmer and I spent fifteen days working eight a.m. to six p.m. on the house-to-house survey. We traveled four hundred seventy-seven miles. The result was that of four hundred twenty-three examined, forty-eight percent were either positive or suspect for tuberculosis. While this house-to-house method was hard work, we got a record of the home conditions which could not have been possible in the clinic method. However, follow up work can be done by home visits and the class-clinic method." I pause, organizing the jumble of my thoughts.

"The question that troubles me is where to begin. I do so wish that the Indian Service would consult the National Tuberculosis Association for administrative advice. I can't see why such important things should be left to the almost inevitable blunder of people unaccustomed to handling so complex a medical problem. I feel sure that there are two almost separate problems. The first is the care of the existing cases. Second is the preventive work. They are interwoven but neither is being adequately managed at present. The first necessity for any program is trained personnel. The second necessity is assurance of a continued policy, something more than demonstration, and third is proper institutional facilities for care.

"I don't know what Miss Patterson will report from her survey in the Southwest, but I cannot imagine that it will be much different than here. I believe this demonstration has shown the benefit of a public health nurse. And I will have, by the time my present term is up here, good routines and records for another nurse to follow. But without a more definite program on the part of the Indian Office in Washington I begin to doubt the practical value of my services. The Superintendent has not the medical knowledge to organize the medical work and push it along. The doctor has not the administrative sense to cooperate with the Superintendent, nor has he the initiative to push the work through regardless of who gets the glory. The organization, with the reservation medical personnel answering to the Superintendent rather than to a medical supervisor actually impedes the work, I think." I shake my head and think of the incredibly slow pace at which any work seems to proceed in the Indian Service.

Miss McArdle says, "I am not certain of all the content of Miss Patterson's report, but I have heard that she feels the organization is, as you identify, a great problem. In fact, I believe she's gone so far as to say that under the present organization, there would be no sense to place field nurses on the reservation even though they could potentially do much good."

"I wouldn't go so far as to say that, probably because I am eternally an optimist. If Commissioner Burke sees field nurses as something desirable, then adding them, even to the current organization could be a first step toward change," I say.

"Yes," she agrees, "that's a perspective that has merit. But there are many who haven't the patience to wait for change, particularly when the circumstances are primitive and the work is difficult. Frankly, I don't know how you've done what you have here."

"If it weren't for the adventure, the beauty of the place and the interesting people, perhaps the work would be too much," I say. "I don't know what next year will hold, whether the Red Cross will want me to stay on, the Indian Service will add positions for field nurses and want me to stay, or what. There's too much to do to spend much time thinking of that. And I suppose I will hear soon as I am only promised here through July. I do know that at least I have gotten under their shirts about tuberculosis. Dr. Eddleman has written a letter to Washington saying he is alarmed and suggesting some rather drastic changes. Mr. McGregor has been in communication with the Commissioner on the subject each month. Surely some good will come of all that. In the meantime I'll just make the most of each day. Enjoy the enjoyable parts and dismiss the rest. And speaking of enjoyable parts, we should get ready. We're attending the Graduation Exercises at the Boarding School this evening," I say, tucking away any thought of the future beyond tonight.

JULY 7, 1966—ALBUQUERQUE AND SANTA FE

CLOUDS GATHERING LOW IN THE WEST SUGGESTED the possibility of showers later in the day. The usually dry desert air carried moisture that made the inside of the Karmann Ghia cloying. "Sorry there's no air conditioning. I usually like to drive with the windows open," Alice said as they got into the car. "The vents will probably be enough to keep you from melting. Does being pregnant make the heat seem worse?"

"Maybe it makes me less willing to tolerate it gracefully," Melody said, smiling. "In fact, I just may be less tolerant in general and I could blame it on being pregnant. My mother told me never to make any big decisions during a pregnancy because a woman's emotionally unstable then. I don't know if I agree with 'unstable,' but I do know I'm less likely to keep my thoughts to myself. And I probably cry more easily even though I hate to cry. It seems so. . .weak, I guess."

"You've been crying? Oh yes, last weekend was the funeral in Silver City wasn't it? Was it hard for you?" Alice asked.

"It was so sad. And I was so confused about how I was feeling. One second I was angry at the minister for saying how glorious

Dwight's death was in the cause of peace and freedom. Who knows if it had anything to do with peace and freedom? He died because he was following orders. And the next I was angry with Dwight for thinking that joining the Army was a smart thing to do because he couldn't find a job and didn't want to spend four years in college.

"Then I was so sad and sorry for my aunt and uncle because they just seemed unable to believe it was real. The last time they saw him was in January, and they'd just gotten a letter from him the day before the notification of his death came. I hardly recognized them. They both looked like they'd aged twenty years since I saw them at Christmas. I know my uncle must have been feeling guilty because he'd encouraged Dwight to enlist, telling him it would be a good way to decide about his future. A lot of Dwight's high school classmates were there. One of them told me that Dwight was the only one from their high school to die in Viet Nam. I managed not to say what I thought, which was but he won't be the last if this war continues."

Alice didn't speak, but nodded. She drove, silent. Melody was quiet, staring at the road and recalling the weekend as the miles between Albuquerque and Santa Fe passed.

"I feel wrong telling you what I'm about to say, but I need to," Melody said. "Brice acted worse than I've ever seen him when I told him I was going to the funeral. He just blew up, made no sense; started accusing me of all kinds of awful things. At first, I tried being reasonable, telling him I'd just be gone two days and I'd be with my parents the whole time. I thought maybe he was worried that something might happen to the baby and me—you know, a wreck on the road. But, that wasn't it. He was just awful," she shook her head as she paused. "The more I tried to be reasonable, the less sense he made. He went on and on until I was crying and just about ready to say I'd stay home."

"Has he ever hit you or threatened you?" Alice kept her eyes on the road as she asked.

"No, it's all just words, accusations and telling me that if I ever left him he'd take the baby away from me, things like that. And not listening. It's like a two-year-old's tantrum. Once it starts, it just goes on until he wears out. It's better if I just don't say anything when he starts," Melody said. "I'm ashamed to be telling this, because he's not always that way. He can be a really nice person. We've had lots of good times."

"That doesn't make it wrong to need to talk about how you feel and it also doesn't make it right for him to act that way," Alice replied. "Oh, Melody, I'm sorry. I shouldn't criticize Brice. I don't even know him. But it upsets me. I know you would never speak that way to him."

"Here's what's even worse to me. Mother and Daddy got there just as this tantrum was going on. And it was like he was another person when they came to the door. He was all smiles to them. He never said another word about my not going. He helped load the car and told us to be careful." Melody began crying as she spoke, "I called when we got to Silver City, you know, to let him know we made it all right. There wasn't any answer. After I tried three more times before bedtime, I decided I wouldn't try again. So I don't know when or if he was home while I was gone. Since I got back, he hasn't spoken to me.

"Most things I can put out of my mind and focus on work that needs to be done, but this is really hard. I know what he expects is that I'll apologize and promise to stay home and never go anywhere without him. But it's so unfair. He could have gone. I asked him to."

Alice interrupted, "Does he drink or do drugs?"

"No drugs. He drinks beer sometimes, but he wasn't drinking that morning when he started all this. Well actually, he'd started the evening before. You remember, I said I was going to have dinner ready when he got home before I told him? Well, it didn't work, I guess. As soon as I told him, he started in with the hateful remarks about Dwight. Then he just got up from the table and went to bed, slammed the bedroom door." Melody dried her eyes. "If I'll just give in, the way I usually do, everything will be fine in a couple of days. But besides hurting my feelings, this has made me mad. I shouldn't have to apologize."

"Did you talk to your mother about this, at all?" Alice asked.

"Oh no, I wouldn't," Melody answered quickly.

"Why not?"

"I'm not sure. I think she'd tell me I need to work it out—that it's my responsibility to do my best to make our marriage work. And like I told you, I feel so guilty telling it because it makes Brice sound like an awful person. I wouldn't want my parents to know, to think that."

"Does he do this often?" Alice asked.

"It seems like it's been quite a while since a really big blowup. I keep thinking that there's some way for me to be, to make things smooth all the time. I ask myself if it's something I'm doing that makes him worse. I'd try to change if I knew what it was. Maybe I'm unrealistic. Maybe all married couples argue," Melody said.

"I think most couples argue, married or not. But it sounds like Brice is unreasonable, like it's more than disagreeing," Alice said. "My parents argue but it sounds more like a heated discussion than anyone having a tantrum. I don't know. I guess I don't know what's typical either. But it's something else to think about. I don't think I could live with Carlos if he had that kind of temper. But now that we're talking, I really don't know that he doesn't. He was pretty close to being like a child when we had that argument about the wedding."

"We're nearly there and I'm a mess. Do I look awful?" Melody asked.

"You look fine. It's impossible for crying to ruin your makeup since you don't wear any. There, when you smile, you look fine," Alice said, encouraging her friend.

The three of them talked about the weather, current events, and the nursing program at U.N.M. Noticing that their usual hour-long visit was nearly over, Alice decided to ask a question she'd been thinking over.

"Miss Gregg," she began.

"Aunt El," she prompted. "I'd like for you to call me what all the young people in my family call me. Being Aunt El to them has been one of the pleasures of my life."

Nodding, Alice began anew, "Aunt El, as we were listening to that last tape, I was wondering how you came to be so committed to your job with the Red Cross. Did the organization have some special meaning for you, to make you feel so strongly about your work?"

"I suppose I did, and do, think the Red Cross is very worthwhile. In the days before there were local, state and federal agencies to provide health education, health care and social services in remote areas, it served many unmet needs.

"Of course, you know that before there were regular military nursing services, the Red Cross was also the reserve for providing nurses for war service. Only after the First World War were the military services created in their present form, and then with the aid of nurse leaders who were veterans of the Red Cross wartime service.

"The county nursing services supported by local Red Cross chapters demonstrated what later became the state and local public health nursing services. The themes of cooperation and collaboration were well entrenched in Red Cross programs, always directed to encouraging local people to help their own. I'm telling this as if it happened in an orderly fashion, but actually the developments differed in each state and locality. Today, Red Cross work continues to include disaster relief as it always has but also health teaching, first aid, and water safety education. All of that remains important. But to answer your question, while I felt the Red Cross was worthwhile, it was not a commitment to the organization, as such, that kept me going in those days. If anything, it was a commitment to myself. I truly believe that the only way to be of value to others is to first be of value to yourself. One of my standards is to do your very best at any work you choose to do. So I wouldn't have been satisfied with myself had I not done the work the best I could. Nor would I have been satisfied if I hadn't tried to enjoy myself every day. That's a part of taking care of something you value—yourself. Without that, you have nothing to give. The well runs dry.

"Back to your question again. I'm not certain I have ever felt a commitment to an organization. To people, to a person, to an ideal or a value, yes. But suppose an organization once represented an ideal and then strayed from it. I would remain committed to the ideal but not to the organization. Yes, that's it, an organization is a means to accomplish an ideal or demonstrate a value. That's where commitment should lie, with the value."

Both Alice and Melody were silent as they considered her response.

"You look thoughtful," Aunt El said. "This is the kind of discussions I often had with my brothers, Richard and Alan, in particular. Thank you for causing me to think about that. In fact, I should thank you for choosing me for this project. It has caused me to recall many things that I enjoy thinking about. Not just the events, but the people, the turns my life has taken. Oh, I did have one thing that I wanted to show you. Melody, reach over to that basket beside the table and put it up here, please."

Elinor reached into the basket and handed each of them a rock. "You asked me how I could remember some of the stories so clearly. These stones help me to recall. I began with my first trip to Europe choosing just one from some place I visited on each trip. So I have a stone for every journey that I've taken. It becomes a quest within each trip to find just the right stone. Each one has to be different because each trip is unique. The one you're holding, Alice, is from the South Dakota Badlands."

"The contents of this basket represent a lot of trips. Have you always loved to travel?" Melody asked.

"Always. One of the only things I regret about my age is that traveling is not as easy for me now. I especially enjoyed driving. Road trips, even with the occasional flat tire, were one of my favorite recreations. Seeing something new, meeting new people, being free to roam—yes, I love traveling."

They'd reached the outskirts of Santa Fe on the return trip to Albuquerque before either of them spoke. When they did it was simultaneous.

"Did you—oh sorry."

"It never came—oh, me too! You first."

"Commitment, I never before thought of commitment as being other than a promise to another person or some strong attachment to an idea or value or goal—strong enough that it could guide your actions, help define choices. But I never thought of having a commitment to yourself," Alice said.

Melody nodded, "Exactly what I was thinking about. That disagrees with all the things I've been taught about 'being selfless is good—being selfish is bad.' Of course, those were rules I learned as a child when things were much simpler to me. What do you think would be different about you if you had a commitment to yourself? Or maybe you already do have and hadn't thought of it in those terms."

Frowning slightly as she concentrated on finding the correct words, Alice said, "If I use the word selfish as a positive not a negative term, then I think I am somewhat selfish; somewhat committed to me. You're right about things being simpler when you're a child. Everything then seemed, or was presented by parents, church, and teachers as being black or white, as if the choice of action were always clear—one right, the other wrong. I see more and more that there are shades of gray that make some choices very difficult. Doesn't everyone have multiple commitments? And if that's so, is it ever possible for it to be clear what is right to do? For example, I think that I have two commitments conflicting. One I made to Carlos, by becoming engaged—or I guess by being in love with him. The other one is to myself. In fact, I recall thinking, not long ago, that I was being selfish to want to delay the wedding. It would be a lot simpler if I just quit thinking and marched right along, wouldn't it?"

She looked across at Melody who responded without turning her gaze from the building clouds.

"Easier? Probably. Best for you? Probably not. Oh, I don't know. I'm certainly not one to give any advice. But if you accept the idea that it is important to have as one of your commitments, a commitment to yourself, then conflict seems almost guaranteed. There will always be the possibility that acting on one, such as yours to Carlos, will make it necessary to ignore some of your other values, such as having a life beyond home and family, or having adventure. It's hard, isn't it, being analytical about an emotional subject—and commitment is emotional, not just intellectual."

"Your turn. How would you be different?" Alice asked.

"I can't really answer that yet. I've made a habit of not permitting myself to analyze my own life too deeply. But I am going to think about it and I want us to talk about this again. I can tell you this—it makes me uncomfortable," Melody said.

"Maybe your skirt's too tight," Alice spoke softly.

"Shut up and drive," Melody said, laughing. She turned on the radio. The Beatles sang "We Can Work It Out" as they approached Albuquerque.

"See you tomorrow. We have lots more to work on for this project," Melody said as she got out at her car.

"Two o'clock at the library?" Alice said.

"Have you been waiting long?" Melody asked as she joined Alice at the library entrance.

"No, it's just a couple of minutes after two. I was early. I walked from my apartment and I guess I was moving faster than I realized," Alice said.

"What had you moving so fast?"

"Just thinking," Alice answered.

"About delaying the wedding?"

"Yes, that and a lot of other things. I'm so tempted to just cancel the engagement, to get this whole thing over and give myself a clean slate. But I really do love Carlos. I hate to hurt him and I hate to lose him. I've changed so much in the year we've been engaged that if he proposed today, I doubt I would say yes," Alice said.

"Is it only you who's changed? Is something different about him?" Melody asked.

"I doubt he's changed in any big ways. It's just that now I know him far better than I did. And I'm not sure we want the same things from life. You know, if no one was allowed to get married until they're at least thirty and then only after they've lived together for at least six months, it would help a lot," she laughed. "My parents would just die if they heard me say that."

Melody smiled. "Yeah, but your idea is probably a good one." They settled in a study room and she continued, "You said something just now about 'just get the whole thing over.' Let me tell you what I was thinking about—it's related, a little, at least. By the way, I had plenty of time to think last night because Brice stayed in the garage working and not speaking to me.

"Aunt El was recalling how she worked and it sounded to me like a big part of what she did was to take small steps each day with an overall goal in mind. She was flexible about the small steps and about her plan for the year. But her overall goal of demonstrating a role for the public health nurse on the reservation was what she kept in mind. She didn't try to solve problems in one big leap. And I think because of her optimism, she could accept that she couldn't control how everything would turn out. Then there was what she said about making a commitment to yourself. How if you don't, you run dry—nothing more to give.

"I was trying to analyze myself—my own situation with Brice. Well, analyzing came after being emotional. First, I was thinking in big leaps. I would just give in, apologize, and do everything he wants, the way he wants. I was even considering dropping out of school and staying home with the kids. That was a big leap—kind of 'I'll show him. Let him see how he likes that.' That would settle things, at least for now. But then I realized that I would be unhappy, even if it did make him happy. I really want my degree and I want to work, not just work, but be good at my work as a nurse.

"If instead, I take small steps and have the overall goal of having a reasonably happy marriage, for both of us, then I'll start considering what makes me happy too. That's making a commitment to myself. And each day, I'll keep that in mind. Today's small step was being pleasant, but not apologizing.

"Maybe you could consider what taking small steps would mean for you," Melody hesitated when she noticed the look on Alice's face, a sort of puzzled frown. "It's just a thought."

"How can you be so analytical about things—you amaze me. And you're probably exactly right. Let's see, a small step would be to say definitely that I need to delay the wedding until after I graduate. If I'm willing to live with all the probable results of that—which may be—Oh, yeah, see, I'm trying to control the outcome of everything, how I feel, how Carlos feels, what he'll say or do. And that doesn't make sense. I can only be sure of how I feel and what I do. Looks like I need some practice with the small steps approach," Alice said.

Melody said, "You could apply the same approach to considering the Peace Corps. One small step would be to request more information. Another would be to meet with the recruiters when they come back. Anyway, 'small steps instead of big leaps' is the theme of this little sermon and I intend to try it."

Alice patted Melody's arm. "It didn't sound like a sermon. Thanks for telling me what you're thinking. It helps me to have another, more objective opinion. And speaking of opinions—here's one. My opinion is that we'd better get to work."

Melody nodded, "Okay, let's talk about the last tape a little more before we listen to the new one. You first."

"Listening to Aunt El, I'm convinced that public health nursing is what I want to do, even though we haven't had the clinical course for it yet. It's so different from hospital nursing. You'd really have a chance to make a difference in how people live and how that affects their health, not just help them through an illness or surgery. Those acute problems are important, but I think my personality is better suited for public health," Alice said.

"I'm leaning that way too. One of the things that frustrates me about hospital work is that you really don't get to know the patient and family well enough to help with preventing future illnesses. Even though we're educated to consider the whole person, family and environment, we can't have much overall effect in the short span of a hospital stay. Not that care and comfort in an illness aren't important, but since we learn a lot more, I'd like to be able to use it," Melody said.

"Listen to us, talking about ourselves. This reminiscing project is supposed to be about Miss Gregg. Is she getting anything from it?" Alice asked.

Melody quickly replied, "Yes, I think she is. Recall her mentioning how our discussions reminded her of her brothers?"

Alice nodded, "Yes, and those principles for living that her father wrote—that surely seemed to please her."

"Those principles were impressive to me, profound. I think I'll type them up to save," Melody said, making a note to herself.

Without looking up from her own notebook, Alice said, "Maybe you could do it up in needlepoint."

After a couple of beats, the comment registered with Melody who said, "Yeah, or maybe have it printed on a T-shirt! Turn on that tape, joker."

THIS IS THE BERRIES

I'M TEMPTED TO DANCE, BUT THERE'S NOT MUCH room here in the Red Cross Health Station in Rosebud. So, I'll be content with just rereading Commissioner Burke's letter, once again. It's dated July 9, 1924. I skip the first paragraph where he explains about his intention to get the Red Cross involved on the reservations and his wish to eventually replace field matrons with nurses—old news. Here are the good parts. "The first step towards reorganizing the field matron force is to secure a proper person as a supervisor, and that is what prompts me in writing this letter. In addition to the splendid record which you have to your credit in the Red Cross organization, we have been favorably impressed by what you have demonstrated and accomplished since you have been on the Rosebud reservation. We believe that you would be the right person. . . salary of $2,400 a year. . .headquarters would be here, but your duties would require you to be in the field much of the time…your reports would be direct to the Commissioner…wire me, collect and proceed to Washington for conference at your earliest convenience."

How much room is there for negotiation, I wonder. More salary would be nice, but I doubt that will change. But the title must. Nurses, nursing surely must be part of my responsibility. That has to be clear from the beginning and the title of the position is where that starts. My thoughts spinning, I fold the letter and stride purposefully (though I'd prefer to dance) toward Mr. McGregor's office. He'll have good advice, I'm sure.

"I guess this goes to show that it's possible for good work to be noticed even if you're in the most remote outpost. You will take the position, won't you?" he asks.

Before I can answer, he continues, "Having someone in Washington who understands and cares deeply about the health of the Indians may be the only way we'll ever get the TB problem under control. It's not that Newberne and the others don't care, it's just that you've seen it from the point of view of the people who are affected—people who die before their time, needlessly."

I think, "What can one person really do?" But my optimism prevents my saying that. Although I was just recently near despair myself, I see this letter and the position it offers as a peg to hang hope on. "I know that I alone can do little to improve things, but I know there are many in the service who do care. And maybe, through this position, we can add some nurses who will make a positive difference on some of the reservations. Most importantly, I think the Commissioner is genuinely in favor of making health care a priority or he wouldn't have created this job," I say.

"As much as I hope you'll take the job, I am sorry you'll not be here at Rosebud. And as much as I want you to succeed in Washington, I want you to remember that Congress ultimately determines the budget, the real engine that drives our service. I guess what I'm trying to say is go but don't forget us—and do what you can but realize the limits," McGregor says solemnly.

I nod because I don't trust my voice. Tears are threatening to fall as I think of leaving the McGregors and the other friends I have here at Rosebud.

One thing I've already decided. I'll never spend August in Washington, D.C. again if I can avoid it. The heat and humidity are almost unbearable. I've not yet settled on a place to live, so I'm at the Hotel Grafton. Pen poised above a sheet of hotel stationery, I realize I'm woolgathering. I should write Mother. Instead I'm reviewing the first days of the beginning—ah, I do love firsts—new sights, new people, new work.

This is the berries—the berries may be gooseberries, but the salary is better, the job entails travel and the title is Supervisor of Field Matrons and Field Nurses for the Indian Bureau, Department of the Interior. Some berries, boys! My superior officer is the Commissioner himself. That is a fair start at least. I've got most of what I wanted embodied in my powers and authority and duties.

It's late and I should be tired, but I'm invigorated, have been since I arrived here, even with the heat. Learning the ropes is proving most interesting. There are some cumbersome regulations which I will have to devise means of circumventing but I believe that will come on as I find the right way to get hold of the individuals on my staff on the inspection tours.

There is so much red tape to swallow and inwardly digest. The number of funds from which different things are paid is 1,100! The restrictions trip you up at the most unexpected points. I have not begun to get all the threads in place. It's going to be jolly good fun when I do.

Since I can't be still, I might as well begin packing. I'm leaving this week for my first official tour. The itinerary takes me back to Rosebud S.D., arriving on August 16 and brings me back to Washington on November 15, in time for Congressional budget hearings. During the three months "out," I'll be in South Dakota, Montana, Wyoming, Kansas, and Minnesota. Of course, that itinerary is subject to additions or changes depending on circumstance (and perhaps on whim).

The Sioux Health and Education Conference at Rosebud is officially over today, August 23, 1924. The best result of the conference is the report I'm polishing up for signature by Mr. Peairs, Education Supervisor; Dr.

Stevens, Medical Supervisor; Mr. McGregor; and me. Boldly, we think, we are submitting this to Commissioner Burke on the topic of tuberculosis among the school children of the Rosebud and Pine Ridge reservations. We mention that approximately 44% of those children have tuberculosis in some stage. We urge a temporary plan to be followed by a thorough survey of both reservations to result in a more comprehensive plan. This temporary plan includes: 1) using the agency hotel for a general hospital and converting the hospital to TB care; 2) having Special Physician Culp sent to do a complete survey of all the school children; 3) appointing two field nurses to Rosebud. I hope that some good will come of this. Mr. McGregor has taken up the torch on the tuberculosis problem and I would so like to see all the work that was done before I left result in some improvements. Of course, the disease in the children is only a part of a larger picture. It is almost impossible to prevent tuberculosis when the nutritional status is poor, when living conditions are not sanitary, when ventilation is poor and when there's no understanding of contagion.

A long-term plan must attack all of that. If only there were something curative that could be done, aside from rest, outdoor air, and good diet, then perhaps an all-out assault could have dramatic effect. But in the meantime, we must soldier on doing as much as we can.

Writing—I can see that's going to be a big part of my work in the job. Before I left Washington, I received a memo—"your earnest cooperation in meeting the requirements set forth will be appreciated"—telling me exactly how to write reports (circulars on the subject were attached) and to whom they must go. With the number of stops I'm to make on this trip, each requiring a report, my pen hand will soon be a claw. As there's no traveling secretary sent with me, I believe I must learn to type!

"Richard, Donald, it's so good to see you both. Isn't it fine we could all be here at Glacier National Park? My visit to the Blackfeet Reservation made this the perfect spot to meet. Let's rent horses right away, shall we?" I'm chattering eagerly to my brothers.

"Elinor you don't look any the worse for wear, so far. But I can't help thinking all the travel in backwater regions is going to be trying," Donald, my psychiatrist brother says.

"It might be if it weren't for the excitement and the challenge out here. I know from my time at Rosebud that very little is routine. Each day is different. Even when I'm in Washington, it's all still new. It's a big job with lots of detail and the first year will all be learning," I reply.

"You and Richard both seem bound to do exotic things. You know he's thinking of moving to India," Donald says. "That certainly makes Channing Institute seem tame by comparison."

Richard nods but says nothing. I raise my eyebrows in a silent question. When no response comes, I say, "Well, let's get settled and then see about those horses. Then I add to Donald, "There's nothing tame about psychiatry at Channing, I'll wager. It's just that the surroundings are a bit more serene." I wonder if he wishes for more adventure.

We've halted our horses for a rest. Richard says, "Elinor, Donald has told me that he thinks that most of our motives and actions are instinctive and irrational and that the reasons we give for them are largely attempts to rationalize something deeper. What do you think?"

I have no idea what prompted that statement. But with Richard, known in the family as a 'thinker,' there's bound to be a connection to some larger topic. He graduated from Harvard Law and has been a labor lawyer, a private assistant to our sister Faith's husband Farwell Bemis, a teacher, and always a scholar. He's very interested in the teachings of Gandhi. Most recently he's been farming. So Donald's clue that Richard is thinking of going to India doesn't surprise me.

Giving an answer I think Donald will appreciate, I say, "Hmmm. Tell me more about that."

Richard laughs, knowing I'm kidding with them both. "Maybe later," he says.

I laugh as well and move into the lead on our trailride. It's such a treat being with these interesting, jolly men, my brothers. If Alan were here, it would be even better, but he and his Eleanor are living in France where he works for the medical division of the Rockefeller Foundation.

Richard's question sets me thinking about my reasons for being in this new job. If Donald is correct, then my choice has less to do with wanting to help improve the health care for the Indians than with my own instincts for variety and adventure and being of service to others. Hmmm indeed! Why not both, my instincts and the rational wish to help the Indians? I'll take that subject up with them at dinner.

Where two or more of us are gathered together. . .the phrase from the scriptures could be amended for Washington, I think. It would say, "Where two or more of us are gathered together, politics ensues." In the short time I've been back here from my first field visit, I've learned something of the history of the Indian Bureau. It's 100 years old this year, starting in the War Department in 1824 and moving to the Interior Department in 1849. With every change of Commissioner, usually with every change of President, new influences have come to bear. So much of what has been done to and for the Indians has been, at least in part, to benefit the personal interests of people who want the land or other resources of the tribes. And that's politics. That's not to say that there aren't many people who are genuinely interested in the welfare of the Indian, but there has been so much to complicate efforts on their behalf.

In addition to the official representatives of the government—the Army, Indian Office, state governments and various advisory committees—churches, Women's Clubs, several Indian Associations comprised of interested citizens, the YWCA, the American Red Cross, and who knows how many others all have interests to pursue in regard to the Indians. It's probably just as well that I didn't study the "Indian situation" before I took the Red Cross position at Rosebud. If I had, I might have only been able to see an unmanageable forest rather than the individual trees. However, I've decided that the trees I intend to focus on are the health needs of the Indians and the use of field nurses, and for the present, field matrons, to meet those needs. And I intend to stay out of politics.

I compose that little speech and deliver it to myself mainly because the more I learn about the job, the easier it is to be confused. But, confusing or not, it's a most interesting whirl.

I adjust my hat and I'm out the door. More of the whirl! I'm dining this evening with Miss Minnegerode, Lucy she says to call her. She's Supervisor of Nurses for the U.S. Public Health Service. Although at 38 I'm hardly a youngster, she's taken me under her wing—in a helpful way. She's been in Federal service since she was chosen to organize the nurse Corps for the USPHS in 1919 so she qualifies as a Washington veteran by now. Her distinguished Virginia family has included several in elected or appointed office. So she has a good background for understanding both the forest and trees in her line of work.

"Now that the Congressional budget hearings are over, perhaps I can get some of the work done in the office," I mention while reading the menu.

"It mounts up, doesn't it?" she responds. I notice her eyeing the other diners. She'll probably soon begin her usual commentary on her observations, most of which will make me laugh. I'm surprised when she turns her gaze to me and asks, "Are you still outside of Dr. Newberne's staff, reporting directly to the commissioner?"

"Yes, it's clear Newberne wants the Medical Division to have nothing to do with me. I appreciated your advice to leave that battle unfought. And I've about mastered a method of getting cooperation on ideas I want to put over. I start with a draft of a letter to the commissioner on the subject and then take it personally to get the thoughts of each person who might be involved in approving it."

"Without actually asking them to approve it, right?" she asks.

I nod, "Just getting their thoughts. While that takes more time, it suits me because I don't like to sit still at my desk for long at a time. It also results in some good additional ideas."

"Have you developed any plans for attracting nurses for the field positions?" Miss Minnegerode asks. I begin to answer, but she's turned to charm the young waiter into bringing extra rolls and butter. He leaves, laughing at her joking manner and then her attention is back to me.

"In general, I'll try to make as much information about the Indian Service as widespread among nurses as possible. I know there must be some who'll be attracted by the adventure and the freedom of the work. One thing I'll do is try to get an article in the *American Journal of Nursing.* Another is to visit at any school of nursing along my route while I'm on field trips and a third is that I'll attend as many meetings of nursing organizations as I can. I'll have the same message in each place—the work is important, the patients will be interesting, and adventure abounds. Of course, I'll also have to try to help them understand the Civil Service appointment process. The paperwork moves so slowly that it often takes months for an interested nurse to receive an official job offer from the Commissioner."

"Tell me again, how many positions do you have open?"

"That depends on how you look at it. Since the idea is to convert the field matron positions to field nurses, then eventually to fill only those current positions would require fifty-four. But I cannot eliminate those field matrons until I have some nurses. So, while I have only a few actual field nurse positions now, I need all the nurses I can recruit—and then I can put them to work. Besides that we want to increase the number of positions overall. It's quite a jigsaw puzzle because I also must learn from the agency superintendents just where there are poor field matrons who should be replaced. That's where they are most likely to make good use of the nurses. With ninety-five different agencies, some responsible for several reservations, in twenty-four different states, just making some sense of all the individual personalities is a challenge. That ninety-five doesn't include the other units such as the twenty large boarding schools. I made a start, but only a start, with my first field trip. By the way, did you notice how quickly I came up with those numbers? I've been doing some studying in my spare time. There are something over two hundred forty thousand Indians in government care, which doesn't include those who are citizens and who live away from reservation lands. Let's see, and there are eighty-five hospitals among the reservations. *The Indian Problem*, just published in nineteen twenty-four, is the source of that information." I'm quiet for a bit, distracted by my dinner.

"I think it will be far more difficult for you to recruit than it has been for me. The salaries at the USPHS are better and the working conditions are, by comparison, perhaps less exciting, but less strenuous. And I have the benefit of some assistance. You, on the other hand, are a one-woman show without even a secretary to call your own" She shakes her head.

"My mother told me before I went to Rosebud that I have the courage of ignorance. I suppose she's right. I always assume that you don't know what you can do until you try."

"You mentioned attending nursing meetings. That's a good idea. I also think you should be involved, visibly, in the ANA's government section. Later, after you've gotten settled in a bit, maybe I can put you up for office in that section." She waves her hand in a grand gesture and continues. "Then you can begin to get your nurses involved, after you've recruited them and thoroughly worn them out with working seven days a week on a reservation in some wild part of the country." I know she's joking, but she's correct. I'll need to find ways to help the remote nurses feel connected to other nurses or eventually they will fare no better than Lottie Rasch.

"I guess I'll need to shop for a new hat and suit for meetings and I'll have to forget about sleeping," I joke in response. "Otherwise I'll never get all my reports written. I've been delinquent at least once already and notified, in writing, that I must mend my ways."

Over dessert I mention what I expect will be a continuing frustration. "Is there no way to cut through government red tape?"

"What! And do hundreds of civil servants out of the job of creating delays? I doubt that we'll ever be without regulations that generate red tape. After all, without ponderous machinery, how would supervisors be kept from acting rashly?" She feigns solemnness.

"I had what I thought was a perfectly good idea back in October when I was at the Crow Agency in Montana." I shake my head as I recall. "All the superintendents I'd visited agreed that a different field matron's report along the same lines as the one used by the district farmers would give them, and me, a clearer idea of the nature and amount of work the matrons are doing. So, I created a revised form and asked that each matron draw three up by hand and use them for three months in order to have data to decide about a final revised form. I knew that with fifteen thousand copies of the current form in stock, no one would approve printing up an immediate change. Less than a month later I received a letter from Washington telling me to have the matrons go back to the prior form and to submit any changes I want to propose to the Department of Interior for approval. I felt the rap on the knuckles. Besides that, the field matrons surely will think I'm not much of a Supervisor if I first give a direction and then rescind it less than a month later. But apparently for Washington, it's more important to follow the rules than to have data to make decisions."

"Did you do it?" Lucy asks.

"What?"

"Tell them to return to the other forms."

Giving a little laugh I reply, "Actually, I had them do both and hold the completed new forms for me until I return. The letter didn't specify not to do that. But, I shouldn't have to be devious to get my job done."

"I prefer to think of such actions as practical, not devious," she says with a wink.

"One good tangible thing did come out of my trip. As a result of the report we submitted after the Rosebud Conference, Mr. McGregor has approval to convert one field matron position to a field nurse. That's in addition to the Red Cross replacement for me."

"Mark that down. There'll be days you'll need to have a tally to remind you that you've accomplished anything," Miss M. advises.

Making my way back to my room through the streets of Washington, I miss the night sounds at Rosebud.

Errand girl. That's what I first thought when Commissioner Burke sent me here to Milwaukee. But that was probably because of travel fatigue. I had been in the field from February of '25 until mid-June making a swing from the Haskell Indian School in Kansas through the Southwest to California and back again. Oh yes, I nearly forgot—before I got to Haskell I stopped in Pittsburgh, St. Louis, and Kansas City to talk at nursing schools and anywhere else they'd listen to me. This current trip began in mid-August and was to take me to Wisconsin, Minnesota, South Dakota, Montana, Idaho, Washington, New Mexico, Arizona, California, Oregon, and back to Washington, D.C.

That's all changed now. I'm here in Milwaukee to investigate a problem with 'Indian Girls.' It seems this all started because some earnest young woman working in a social service agency was disturbed by the loose morals of a few young Indian women who came to the city to live. She urged a few influential men to write to the commissioner asking for action.

I've spent nearly two weeks here investigating who said what to whom and what services are available for young Indian women. I am convinced it is a local problem that could be handled through local social services, just as would be the case with white girls. Is there some reason to expect a higher moral standard of the whole of Indian young womanhood than of white? Surely some of any race go astray regardless of what services are available or what rules are applied. But those are my thoughts and I am here to report to the Commissioner, not to prescribe an answer.

The upshot of all the investigating was that I decided to call a meeting of interested parties from social service agencies to discuss how to proceed. After what seemed like endless talking, they came to a conclusion—it's a local problem that they should attempt to deal with through local services!

Now I'm packing again and trying to decide what I learned from this experience. First, this whole episode had nothing to do with my real job. But as a traveling agent of the Indian Service I can probably expect some side missions of this sort to crop up when I'm in the vicinity of a problem. I should be adaptable, consider them a test of my skills. In this case, I think I passed the test. The skills I used were analyzing a situation based on gathering information from many sources; applying knowledge of community organization and social service methods; appreciating the influence of social status and wealth on the ability to have influence; conversing capably with people of both genders and of all levels of society; conducting a meeting in such a way as to encourage cooperation among those present; and writing a clear report. Come to think of it, perhaps the commissioner sent me here because I am a woman. He asked Mrs. Seymour of the Board of Indian Commissioners and Miss Dabbs of the YWCA to come out during this time as well. Maybe he thought that women would handle this best. Whether that's correct or not, I do think he trusts me.

So, as we used to say at the Infant Hospital, that baby's washed! Allowing a little chance to simmer down, the situation here should cause no further difficulty. I'm ready to be off to Winnebago, Nebraska and the rest of my original itinerary.

A foolish expenditure of time, I'll admit. But lying in bed and reading a novel this morning is just what I need. I've been jaunting about with Service people for the other six days of the week and feel like a little solitude. January here in Albuquerque is beautiful. With the bright sun, the cold is not noticeable. Among my ruminations in this little spot of time alone is this-all of the reports, the home visiting, the Ford-traveling, amount to little—two straws on the stack. The real point in this job is to try in a short stay to leave something to make the day-to-day problems get increased interest on the part of the existing group of employees—superintendent, doctors, nurses, and teachers. Has it taken me over a year to learn that? Maybe I knew it in a vague way, but now it's clearer. Holding that little nugget of insight, I allow myself to drift into a nap.

In preparation for my vacation (35 days, hurrah!) I'm making a strong last-ditch effort to clear my desk. The Annual Report that I hold in my hand, I'll date tomorrow, August 27th, 1926. If it falls like a bomb I won't be here to suffer the concussion and the dust will have cleared before I return. Writing it was a good exercise because it required reflecting, identifying accomplishments and specifying continuing problems. Overall, I've accomplished more than I realized. I was on 50 reservations in the course of the year and made hundreds of home visits with matrons and nurses. And I have heard from many of them that my being there was a help to them. But back in March when I was in Arizona, I was at low ebb. I was sick and tired of all the moving and moving and moving. I wrote Mother that three years would be all I could stand before I was ready to settle down forever and grow cabbages. Of course, that didn't last long. Perhaps all I needed was to have a tirade—even if only in written form.

It helped my attitude a lot that Dr. Guthrie arrived from the Public Health Service on long-term loan to head the Medical Division. No one knew what to expect after Dr. Newberne died. The division has been reorganized so that the reservation physicians report to Dr. Guthrie through District Medical Supervisors, not to the local superintendents. As it should be, I think. I now am part of the Medical Division and Dr. Guthrie is making it hum. I got more accomplished in two half morning sessions toward putting the field nursing on the map than I did in all the time under Newberne. Lord what a relief!

I'm rereading this report just once more to be sure I've emphasized the main points.

I point to lack of success in recruiting nurses and mention the Civil Service process as a factor. I propose a solution. I try never to identify a problem without suggesting a remedy. I particularly like these paragraphs.

"During the past year the Supervisor of Field Nurses had advised some fifty nurses of the proper channels (Civil Service papers were sent to such applicants) for entering the Indian Service nursing service. None of these women have received appointments. This indicates that our methods of securing personnel are not satisfactory to the nurse. Knowing nurses, it is thought that two important points are being neglected. First, the nurse has almost no knowledge of our service from the Civil Service information sheet. We should have an Indian Service Circular of Information to be sent by the supervisor with a form letter together with the Civil Service papers. Nurses deal with superintendents of nurses in relation to securing positions. Most of them would be somewhat wary of contracting service entirely by mail with either laymen or doctors. They feel more sure of the conditions of work when dealing with a woman. This may be a foolish condition, worthy of being broken up, but the fact remains that all hospital and government services have acceded to this prejudice, if such it be."

Now here's another I like. "The other factor is the time element. Nurses, notoriously, sail close to the economic wind." That's a nice turn of phrase, if I do say so myself. There's more, but I am suddenly weary. I place the report on the desk, face down, and close my eyes. I'm not going to read this again. I've done my best so I'll leave it be.

I wonder how many times this year I've packed this bag. This time the packing is different. I'm smiling as I do it! I'm looking forward to September 1 more than I'd expected I would. Now that I don't live with Mother, I enjoy my time with her more. She's less likely to be critical and seems to have accepted that I am doing something of value in my work. I've never doubted her love. But I've felt she never expected me to amount to much beyond being a nice person, able to support myself—less than she expected my brothers and sisters would accomplish. Maybe that's not fair. She's not been critical only of me. Marjorie's received her share as well. Anyway, that doesn't matter. She's our Mother and I want her late years to be as happy and include as much luxury as she will allow, given her long-standing habit of frugality. This trip to France will be a treat for her as well as a vacation for me. She'll get to see Alan and Eleanor and to see their two children for the first time. We'll enjoy shipboard amusements en route and pretend to be ladies of leisure. Everything is arranged. Unlike my voyage during the war, this one should have no submarines lurking. I can foresee nothing to mar a wonderful holiday for us both.

A PLACE TO HANG MY HAT

"I KNOW, MOTHER, THAT YOU PROBABLY consider this handbag an unnecessary extravagance. And under other circumstances I might, as well. You'd probably like it better if I'd bought it at a second-hand store in Boston. I thought of pretending I had. But the truth is, you'd know better. I've never been good at dissembling. I'm sure you had much to do with that. I do think that you'll approve of my other decision though."

If there were other passengers near the rail, they'd probably wonder about the conversation I seem to be having with myself. The wind is cool off the ocean and this ship is quite fast, making the breezy transatlantic passage in under seven days. I'm glad I have on my light coat, both for the breeze and to make my carrying a handbag look a bit less odd. Smiling, I realize that if there were someone near, they'd soon see I'm addressing my remarks to the handbag. And they'd probably call for the ship's doctor.

Sailing west, following the sun, the days seem to last forever. I've waited until now, halfway home, near sunset, when the light is the kindest. It's a beautiful, peaceful time of day. I think everyone would approve.

We'd been having a grand time in Paris. The vacation was just the way I'd hoped for her—sightseeing, shopping, playing with Alan and Eleanor's two children, enjoying herself without the need to be responsible for anything. She had a wonderful three weeks and then she died. A stroke relieved her of ever becoming feeble and infirm. She had 74 very full years. A minister's wife with all that entails plus seven children, she'd seldom seen an idle day. If I have a choice, I'll go the same way, relatively capable one day, gone the next.

We thought that cremation was the best decision and I agreed to make a proper disposition of the remains. Her ashes are in this handbag. I'm giving her a burial at sea. Her frugal soul will appreciate that both the service and the 'plot' are free. As I hold the bag over the rail, I say, "Be at peace. We all loved you in our own ways." And then I let it go.

Nothing seems to have moved from my desk in my absence. However, there is a new mountain of unread mail. I've had lots to do since my return to the States dealing with the aftereffects of Mother's death without even thinking of the work here in Washington. Mother left her belongings to me and Marjorie. She also left some cash and an annuity that provides a small monthly income for each of us. I suppose that's what one does for spinster daughters. Now I have several pieces of her furniture and household items. I guess it's time to think of having a house for them—at least a place to hang my hat when I'm here.

No time for daydreaming, as I've learned I'm now clearly marked as the one responsible for recruiting all nurses for both the field service and the hospitals. In addition, Dr. Guthrie wants me to see to the organization of the nursing services in the hospitals. A tall order, but I'll give it my best try. I am pleasantly surprised that the plan of work I wrote for field nurses before I left on vacation met no opposition. Now the trick will be to help the nurses see how to put it into action. So much depends on their being able to get cooperation from the local physician and superintendent. That's no mean chore since many of the doctors are put off by the fact that the nurses are better educated in prevention than they are.

I've allowed my thoughts to drift, I realize, as I'm reading 'information copies' of the Commissioner's mail related to health received in my absence. Here's a name I've heard before—John Collier. He's the National Executive Secretary for the American Indian Defense Association, its says with his signature. I recall he was connected earlier with the Federated Women's Clubs in their efforts on behalf of Indians. His letter says the Indian Service attempted to dispossess an elderly man of his property in Santo Domingo Pueblo in order to build a house for the Red Cross field nurse. I wonder how that's been resolved? And I wonder about Mr. Collier and his method. The tone of the letter is rather confrontational. Either he believes he's right, and is righteously indignant on behalf of the old Indian man or agitation is his style whether he's right or not. I'm tempted to react defensively to criticism of the Service, now that I'm a part of it. That's exactly the attitude I should avoid. Smacks of the provincialism I was critical of myself before I "enlisted." It's easy to develop a thin skin when those outside who push for change do so in an accusatory tone. I suppose that inside or out, we always see our own position as the most reasonable one on any issue. I shall consider this a cautionary tale!

Now back to work. I must clear the backlog and plan for my next trip to the field. And before I get away I want to look for a little house somewhere nearby. It's a fine omen that Faith, "my niece the architect" I call her, is interested in helping. We've talked about finding a small house that's in need of some repair but is in a decent neighborhood and not too expensive. She's agreed to do the architectural work for remodeling. I'm so proud of her for going ahead with her education as an architect. She could have chosen art instead and never have had to deal with prejudice against women in her line of work. But she knew what she wanted and Faith encouraged her as only a devoted mother can.

At times I think it's foolish to bother with having a house, gone as much as I am. But I'll consider it an investment, much the way Mother did those houses she bought in Colorado Springs. When I'm ready to move on, I'll rent or sell. Besides it will be nice to be able to have some things of my own around me when I'm here. Lord knows I have little enough when I travel. When I do find a house, I must be sure to put in a sink large enough to wash out more than one shirt at a time. It's not possible to launder on the trains and my accommodations in the field seldom approach sumptuous! With trains and government Fords as my main conveyances and hotels or hospital rooms as my domiciles, I've learned to travel light.

"A home-cooked meal is truly a luxury for me. It was so good of you and Mrs. Townsend to invite me to supper," I say to Dr. Townsend. "I'll see you tomorrow in the office and we'll continue our scheming on a model service for Indian health here in the Northwest." I laugh as I put on my coat to leave.

"I do believe it's a definite possibility that the second district will be a model, Elinor," Dr. Townsend says in his soft southern accent. "I'm pleased that the USPHS sent me to the Indian Service here in Pendleton. Oregon and the entire Northwest are beautiful. And the work is truly unique. We have the opportunity to put all aspects of health care into alignment here—hospital, home bedside care and public health. Once we get the plans and the personnel put together, I believe we'll see results," he assures me.

He's just what we need a hundred of, doctors who understand prevention and who appreciate and are willing to cooperate with nurses. "Ow, that hurt!" I complain to the bedpost I just ran into with my stockinged foot. I should pay better attention to my surroundings. I could easily break a toe. But there's so much to think about—work, family, washing out my silk shirt in Lux—that I become preoccupied. That bed caster surely brought me back to the present in this hotel room in Oregon.

Now where was I? Somewhere between Dr. Townsend in Pendleton and my brother Donald. And the connection was? Nurses. I was composing my thoughts to write a letter to Donald. He's giving a talk and plans to discuss ideas on nursing education as a part of it. Surely he can benefit from my opinion! I want to warn him against siding with those who are against college education for nurses. There's enough debate among nurses themselves on that subject without having physicians lining up to take sides. Seems to me there's a need for nurses to have as much knowledge as possible, but also an increase in wisdom. I think some doctors fear that the nurse with higher education will always question or want to make all her own decisions. I am more concerned that all nurses, no matter what the basic education, should probably need to take 3-4 months of observation and part-time duty work as post-graduates every three years. There's so much knowledge, increasing so rapidly, that there should be ways to assure nurses remain competent and up to date. I make a note to myself of those ideas. I'll write the letter tomorrow.

Now back to Dr. Townsend. It all seems so easy when there's willingness to collaborate. But that's always more likely when there are common elements between those working together. In this case, we have in common a background in public health. That means we value prevention, good records and statistics and we have similar ideas about the roles of doctors and nurses. It amazed me when he told me what a good idea he thought it was to have standing orders for the field nurses, while also agreeing that under more desirable conditions we wouldn't expect a nurse to have to diagnose. But in the Indian Service it's often the nurse or no one. The best thing of all, so far, is that he's already contacted the National Tuberculosis Association for help in setting up a TB survey in the district.

Before long, if I can get approval, I hope to have assistant nursing superintendents in each of the four districts. My visiting once every year or two and writing official letters is not the nursing supervision and support that the staff requires. Standards will only rise when leadership is visible and consistent. This is definitely not a one-person job.

"It's hard to say if Mr. Burke knew what to expect from the survey of the Indian Service by the Brookings Institution. When Hubert Work, Secretary of the Interior, commissioned the study in nineteen twenty-six, Burke had already begun to try reorganization in hopes of improving the Service and the conditions of the Indians. But Lucy, from what I have read of the report so far—and I haven't yet finished—it's rather critical," I say, speaking from the kitchen. "I can't imagine he's not feeling under fire. What are you hearing?" I ask my mentor.

"Mark my words, it won't be long before another shakeup, maybe at the top. I hear that some of the Indian Associations, or at least one of them, think that report out of Brookings, they're calling it the Merriam Report, doesn't go near far enough. They're going to want Mr. Burke out. You're right about trying to stay out of the politics inside the Indian Service. Part of the credibility you've gained is because you've been tending to your own knitting. But it's a good idea to keep your eyes and ears open because your job could be affected if there's a change of Commissioner. Even though your position, like mine, is a couple of rungs down the bureaucratic ladder, a new Commissioner could make big changes," Miss Minnegerode says. Switching subjects in her interested-in-everything way, she says, "This house is just going to be perfect. I'm so pleased for you. Your niece did a wonderful job of the remodeling design."

Returning from the kitchen with a tray, I say, "Yes, I think she did a really fine job. Lucy, would you like some rum to strengthen that tea? Before you ask, no I didn't make the rum in my bathtub. It was a gift I couldn't graciously refuse." She nods and laughs. I serve the strong tea for both of us. Looking around my nearly finished house here on O Street, I smile, "I'm quite pleased. It should be shipshape very soon. I'm glad you don't mind visiting me in this current disarray.

"Going back to the Merriam Report, there are some complimentary statements about the current administration in regard to health work. It mentions that bringing in the USPHS doctors to help in reorganization and moving the medical division out of the educational division were good choices. It also says that creating my position was important and recommends adding at least one position to do planning and development work in nursing, free of administrative duties. Wouldn't that be a treat! And in another section, there's mention of adding four district nursing supervisors. Throughout the parts I've read, what they criticize is exactly the same things I've pointed to since my days at Rosebud. The education system, the school children's diet, the salaries of personnel, housing for staff, the quality of staff, the need to work in cooperation with other agencies, the need to accelerate the development of a real system of preventive medicine and public health—I could go on for hours. They're all the same problems that I've told you about. So, I won't repeat myself. Perhaps a real shakeup would make a difference, although my impression is that after the dust settles, it's the steady day-to-day grind of real work that tells if a difference is made. Policies do need change and we desperately need good quality personnel and more of them, not just in the medical services but throughout. I really cannot disagree with what the report says. I don't envy Mr. Burke his position. Even though he's trying to make improvements, the critical parts could weigh heavily against him. However, any rational person could see that the current situation has developed over a span of a hundred years, not just on Burke's watch."

As Lucy sips her tea, I notice her attention has shifted to the Indian basket in the corner. "I have to ask, since I can't figure it out. What are you planning to do with the rocks in that basket?"

Several wisecrack replies come to mind, but I opt for the truth. "That's one of the few things I collect. I choose one stone somewhere on each trip I take to help me recall the places I've been. They connect me to the places and from there to the people and events. It's a basket of memories."

"Some women collect dried corsages, dance cards and marriage proposals. You collect stones. No wonder the men you work with like you. Rocks are far more solid than dried corsages and you are far more solidly logical and direct than most women. Another thing, those rocks certainly make a better doorstop than a batch of old dance cards would," she says, laughing.

"I wouldn't be averse to having the corsages and all the rest. It just seems that many of us who went through the Great War unmarried came back to find that a lot of the young men we might have married were buried on foreign soil. And we had more on our minds than keeping house and raising children when we recovered from our exhaustion after the War. I'm over generalizing, I imagine, but that's how it's seemed to me," I reflect.

"You've described a lot of us, I think," agrees Miss M. "Oh, I intended to ask, have you requested permission to be at the American Nurses Association convention in Louisville in June? You're going to be selected the next chairman of the Government Section, you know." Her smile says she's pleased she accomplished that.

"Yes, it's in my next itinerary. I only hope I can live up to the example set by the current chairman," I joke with her, the current officeholder.

"I must be off now. Thank you for the tea and conversation. Do be in touch before you head out to the hinterlands again," Lucy says. She's quickly up and near the door. "We must work out just how our Government Section of the ANA can continue to help improve the conditions of work for nurses in the government services. That's something you can think about on those long train rides across the prairies!"

"Why thank you. I was wondering how I might occupy myself." I laugh as I wave goodbye. She's right. Working to improve job conditions for all government nurses is a contribution we can make beyond the confines of our own positions. The professional associations in nursing are an excellent way to accomplish goals for the good of the whole group. The negative side is that there's a tendency for organizations to be a breeding ground for internal conflict. Just look at the arguing among us about what is the proper education for a nurse. There's a fine line between dialogue to expose and refine ideas and plain old wrangling just to be contrary.

Polite applause welcomes me to the platform. Lucy has just introduced me as the next Chairman of the Government Section of the American Nurses Association at this convention in Louisville. My hands are still clammy from my earlier call to report briefly on the Indian Nursing Service. As I'm the only Indian Service nurse present, I feel an anxiety not typical of me. I want to do an excellent job of representing our service before these women who are our peers from the Army, Navy, US Public Health Service, and Veterans' Bureau. "Take a deep breath," I advise myself. I make a few general remarks and ask if there is interest in developing a newsletter to keep us in touch between these biennial meetings. I ask because I want to begin involving the group as participants, not just as listeners. Then I make the main point I want to emphasize. "I have not got a program of money raising or a program of relief or a program of this or that that will have a tendency to weld us together and make us all work for one special thing. The one special thing, and it is rather a far distant thing, but I want you to all realize it clearer and clearer because I have seen so much evil in it, the one thing we do want to work for is better and better conditions of work, organization of our services, the quality of our services for the United States Government." My anxiety is forgotten as I hear applause again and see many nods. Not the most coherent statement I ever made, but it seemed to get their attention.

"Well done, Elinor." Julia Stimson and I were congratulating ourselves for having put you up for Chairman. "You'll do well," Lucy says.

"If I do, it will be in large part due to having good teachers such as the two of you. It is exciting to be a part of a group that can influence the working lives of so many women. You've made an opportunity for me here. I want you to know I appreciate it," I say.

"Is there much talk among the Section members about the new entry standards that have been approved for PHS, Veterans, and Indian Service nurses? We've all worked uphill to get the requirements for employment to include two years of high school prior to nursing school, graduation from a school with a hospital with a daily average of fifty beds or more, and two years of private duty or one of institutional work. I hope people realize that long-term this will benefit our patients and elevate the standards of our Services. Without these changes and eventually even higher standards, nurses are destined to forever be classed as 'sub-professional' by the Civil Service system and their pay will always remain low." I pause for breath and notice Lucy is silent and smiling. "Am I amusing you with my rhetoric?" I ask, a bit embarrassed.

"Not at all. I'm watching you prove what I already knew—that you are a leader," she replies.

"If that's the case, then I must get in the crowd and encourage discussion. A leader must be visible, mustn't she?"

"That, among many other things," retorts Lucy, having the last word.

Out among the members of the section, I enjoy encouraging them to tell of situations in their own jobs that need improvement. I recall for one group the story of the reams of paper that were expended in 1927 in seeking improved meals and suitable prices for them for Indian Service nurses. We learned that nurses were paying $15.00 per month for the same food that lower paid employees were paying $5.00 for. In fact, it was probably only worth $5.00, if that. The only meat was beef (if you can call the parts they serve beef); there were very few vegetables; there was seldom an egg; no fresh fruit; and the only coffee was the green government brew. As a result, the nurses were buying additional food to supplement this fare and often were also providing for their Indian assistant. In doing so, they were paying more for the food than some of their fellow workers and then spending an additional part of their salary to try to bring their diet up to a livable standard. I worked on both problems with some small success, mainly in equalizing the costs of meals served to all employees. The quality of food remains a problem both for the Indians in hospitals and in boarding schools and for the employees who work with them.

As I tell the story, I realize how easy it would be to become hopeless about the many problems in the Indian Service. I create an adage on the spot: 'It is by recalling small successes that we can measure progress.' Yes, I believe my father would have liked that.

I returned from my most recent sojourn the end of September 1928. While on the road, I received the Annual Report of the Secretary of the Interior covering the period from July 1, 1927 to June 30, 1928. It was gratifying to see in print the fact that we have 12 new field nurse positions and 21 new hospital nurses, but need more. Even with all our work, the year saw a high incidence of measles and flu on several reservations and a resulting increase in the number of tuberculosis cases breaking down. I was also somewhat amazed that our population of Indians in the States is estimated at 355,901.

Soon after his annual report was issued, Secretary Work resigned and was replaced by Mr. West. But if the election goes as rumored, he may not be with us long, as Herbert Hoover, likely to be our next President, will probably name his own appointee. And Mr. Burke is still under fire. I understand that Mr. John Collier is stirring the embers, criticizing in particular the policies that restrict Indian religious practices. He's chosen a point on which Mr. Burke feels strongly, I think, if his support of the missionaries is any evidence. There's also controversy about his wanting to protect the oil lands of Indians in Oklahoma from developers that puts him in opposition to Senator Pine of Oklahoma. He also has encountered resistance to his efforts to make education compulsory for the children in the Southwest Pueblos. It's a pity that the good he has done in reorganizing education and medical service is dwarfed by these other problems.

Even his well-intentioned efforts in regard to field nursing may come back to haunt him. The Senate Subcommittee that is now conducting hearings on the 'Indian Conditions' (to finish off the year with a bang, I suppose) has scheduled Miss Florence Patterson to testify about the report she wrote back in 1924. That was the study of Indian health conditions she did for the Red Cross, at Mr. Burke's request. Apparently, it is the fact that the study showed poor conditions and was never published by Burke that the Committee will use against him. With all that's going on and Mr. Hoover taking office, I believe Lucy was correct in her prediction. Changes are about to occur. As for me, I'm happy to be here in my cozy house on O Street waiting for my dinner visitors.

JULY 14,1966—ALBUQUERQUE AND SANTA FE

"A PICNIC! WHAT A GOOD IDEA, ALICE. AND YOU did all the work. I feel pampered," Melody said as she spread a quilt under a cottonwood tree. "There's just enough breeze to keep the flies away." Settling comfortably on the quilt, she said, "Look at the river. The Rio Grande is lazy this time of year." They'd picked a spot on the east side not far from the riverbank. Two families with small children were picnicking across the river. One of the little girls waved to Alice and Melody.

"I thought this would be relaxing for us both rather than eating our sandwiches in the car. We have a little extra time today so I thought we could treat ourselves well," Alice said as she unwrapped the thick sandwiches. "I hope you like whole wheat bread."

"Always," Melody answered. "I need all the B vitamins I can consume." They munched the tuna sandwiches and carrot sticks for several minutes without talking, watching the river and the families across the way. "It's hard for me to relax without feeling I should be studying or getting home or something," Melody said. "But I do need to rest a little more, the doctor said, since I've started having some edema. Can you tell from looking at my feet?"

"Is your blood pressure okay?" Alice asked. Realizing she hadn't answered Melody's question, she said, "No, I can't see any edema, but you can probably feel it before it's visible—and isn't it more in the late afternoon after you've been on your feet all day?"

Yes, and yes, my b.p. is okay, too. I see you paid attention in O.B. class," Melody laughed.

"Anyway, it's a good excuse to be still. I haven't seen you all week except across the room in class. How's everything going at home?" Alice asked.

"Very calm. No arguments, no door slamming, no staying in the garage all evening. Brice took the baby out to play in the yard for a long time yesterday afternoon. He vacuumed the house on Sunday while I was cooking. I told him that he didn't have to, that I was going to do it, but he said he didn't mind—said I could use some rest. It's hard to tell what he's thinking, so I decided to take what he does at face value. He's being helpful, period. Otherwise, I'll start thinking that maybe he's showing me I'm such a bad wife that these things aren't getting done, so he has to do them—or some other paranoid ideas. I realize that by being pleasant like I have, I haven't told him how I feel about his tantrum. Maybe I'm taking the coward's way by avoiding it. But there's a difference this time. I'm being pleasant, and I went to the funeral, and I don't intend to forget what happened. If it continues and there's a pattern, I'll deal with that however I need to. If it doesn't, then that's good. That makes me happy too and it's good for both of us."

"Been working on your commitment to yourself?"

"I have. All that thinking is probably what's made me tired. I told you I'm not in the habit of letting myself think about how I feel about personal problems. I usually just see a problem and try to find a way to fix it—a way that will make everyone happy. No, not true. I find a way that will make Brice, or my parents, or even Baby Brice happy. My way has been, if they're happy, then I'm happy. Do you think I can actually change that? Or am I kidding myself?"

"I don't know, but I know you'll try. And I think it's good for you. Remind me in a minute to tell you about what I've been reading. But first, let me describe my week. I've been taking small steps, but I feel like they've been leaps because they made me feel so good." A sneeze exploded and she laughed. "That was a surprise! It's the cottonwood. See the seeds drifting in their little cotton parachutes. They're so beautiful I don't mind that they make me sneeze." She sneezed again as Melody laughed and offered her napkin. "Now, back to my little steps. First, I reread the Peace Corps information. It still interests me, a lot. It's so easy to imagine going to another country, being of real help. Next step. I wrote for more information about application. And, I wrote Eileen to tell her I want an appointment when they come back to campus in August or September.

"I also told Carlos that I definitely want to delay the wedding until after I graduate."

"How did he take it? More important, how did you feel?"

"Before I told him, I was so tense I thought I'd vomit. I actually was nauseated and my chest felt all tight. I was a mess. I'd asked him to come over so we could talk, so we were at my apartment. I think he sensed what I was going to say, because he didn't hug me when he came in or call me Chica like he usually does. I'd rehearsed about a dozen different versions of what I'd say, ranging from apologetic to very direct. Then I said to myself, 'Let it go. Just say what you feel and then be quiet.' I said, 'Carlos, I want us to delay the wedding until after I graduate. It's important to me to finish school before we get married.' Then I stopped. I was about to list reasons why, apologize for not realizing all this before—all of that. But before I could, and now I'm glad I didn't, he stood up and started talking. Told me it was impossible, that he had it all planned how we'd start out. We'd both work part-time between September and next May and since we'd be married and no longer have to have two apartments, that would save money. Then when I'm out of school, I'd go to work full-time, preferably on three to eleven or eleven to seven to get shift differential pay. He'd work the summer at some job, he hopes in a law firm, then off to law school he goes in the Fall. This continues for three years. He's a full-time student, works only during vacation so he can dedicate himself to studying. He said, 'You know law school is very demanding.' And then—get this—as soon as he graduates and has a good job, I can quit work and we can have a family.

"I was amazed. He wasn't angry as much as he was just oblivious. His point was, 'It's just not possible to delay. That means we continue spending more money for living expenses by being separate and besides, everyone expects us to be married by the first of the year.'

"We'd discussed the idea of saving money so he could be a full-time student and I'm fine with that. But the whole thing about my quitting work and staying home when he graduates was never a topic of conversation. I had this vision of me in a kitchen, like my mother, baking, cleaning, smiling that vague, dismayed-looking smile, waiting for the children to come in from school and Carlos to arrive from work. I had this strange smothering sensation. I knew I was breathing, but," her left hand moved to her neck in a choking gesture, "I felt I couldn't breathe."

"Did you say anything?"

Alice nodded, "Yes, I said, 'I understand you're upset about this. We can talk about the money, the other details now or later. But I'm not ready to be married until I graduate, Carlos. I love you and I hope you love me enough to understand. I need to have this extra time.' I wouldn't have been surprised if he'd demanded his ring back and left for good. But he didn't. He was quiet for a while and I was too. He said he understood and that we could talk later about setting a date. Before long he left for a study group meeting. On Sunday night we went to dinner and a movie and he didn't mention anything. Neither did I. One step; I'd promised myself."

"Wow! I'm impressed that you were able to be so calm. And for that matter, impressed that he was too," Melody said.

"He may not stay so calm when I bring up the next step."

"What's that going to be?"

"The whole idea of his plan- I work in a hospital to get evening or night pay. I may not want to work in a hospital. I may prefer public health. The plan that I'll quit work to have a family. Where did he get the idea I'd want that, or that he could decide that without me?" she asked, shaking her head in disbelief. "What did I ever say or do that suggested I want to be my mother?"

"Maybe you didn't say or do anything. Maybe he assumed it. Maybe he believes that's what a woman really wants—to be able not to work outside her home and devote herself to her family," Melody said.

"You know, I think you may be right. I'll tell you about what I just read that might be related. This book is called *The Feminine Mystique* by Betty Friedan. It came out in nineteen sixty-three. She says that there is in the culture of this country a belief, a mystique she calls it, regarding the proper role of women. That belief, the feminine mystique, says that the highest value and commitment for women is the fulfillment of their own femininity. And femininity is equated with being passive, male dominated, and nurturing. She says that the mystique pressures women into a role that is so unsatisfying that large number of women are unhappy, depressed, and—or physically sick. That is the 'problem with no name' that American women suffer from, she says.

"She goes into detail about how this mystique has been at least partly the result of the pressure of the media and of advertisers whose goal is to sell products related to the home. Her ideas come from research she's done and it's pretty convincing.

"Compare women of our mothers' age with Aunt El and her generation. The early feminist movement had won the right for women to vote and to be recognized as human and equal under law. From the early nineteen hundreds until the forties, the idea of a woman working and if she had the means, being educated, was accepted as being a legitimate choice. According to Friedan, gradually this has been eroded, encouraged by many psychologists and social scientists who used Freud's work as their basis. The idea was that women who didn't want a traditional feminine role had a sexual problem and needed to be helped to adjust. At the same time our mothers were growing up, the pressure was increasing in the media and in advertising to glorify the woman who finds housework a medium of expression for her femininity and individuality. Early marriage was encouraged and even for those women who did go to college, the main emphasis for many of them was finding a husband while there."

"Do you think your mother had a problem with being a homemaker?" Melody asked.

"I do, but I think if I asked her she wouldn't be able to see it. She's always had some sort of minor illness—headaches, backaches, female trouble—since I can remember. And then there's the way she's so finicky about the house and so overprotective of her children. I wouldn't say she's unhappy, just never quite happy and frequently ill. That fits with the description Friedan gives of the 'problem with no name.' What about your mother?"

Melody answered, "She's the perfect housewife. Busy all day doing cleaning, cooking, mending, gardening, PTA, church, non-stop. I'm pretty sure I learned from watching her that a good woman never relaxes. I really never thought about whether she's happy or not."

"See. Carlos' mother is about their age. Plus, she has the added pressure of having traditional Hispanic parents. The woman's role is very definitely home and family for them."

"So you think that Carlos assumes this is what a woman really wants because of the example of his mother and the culture in general?" Melody asked.

"Either what a woman wants or what a woman should want. That book gave me a lot to consider. I think you should read it, too. We might be able to weave it into our project report in some way."

"Okay, I'll read it. But tell me, does the author think this is something that can or should be changed?" Melody asked.

Laughing, Alice said, "I hate to give away the ending. But yes, she does. Wait a sec and I'll get it and read you a quote." She trotted to the car.

"I'm jealous of your being able to run. I'd tip over for sure," Melody said when Alice returned.

"You'll run again. For certain with Brice Junior and the new baby, you'll run from one to the other non-stop. Here's the quote. It's on page three hundred sixty-four. 'We need a drastic reshaping of the cultural image of femininity that will permit women to reach maturity, identify completeness of self, without conflict with sexual fulfillment. A massive attempt must be made by educators and parents—and ministers, magazine editors, manipulators, guidance counselors—to stop the early marriage movement, stop girls from growing up wanting to be "just a housewife," stop it by insisting, with the same attention from childhood on that parents and educators give to boys, that girls develop the resources of self, goals that will permit them to find their own identity.' What do you think of that?"

Melody raised an eyebrow. "You know, as you were reading that, I remembered something my mother said to me when I told her I was going to finish school after we got married. She said, 'Since you're going to nursing school, anything you learn, you'll be able to use raising your family, so I suppose it's not a bad idea.' I'm not sure exactly why that came back to me, but it seems related. That message sounds now, as I recall it, as if it meant that education is okay as long as your only real work is your family. No wonder I'm confused. For a while I though it was only from hanging round with you. Yes, thanks I'll have that oatmeal cookie," she said to Alice who was waving one just out of her reach. "You'd better give me that. Hell hath no fury like a hungry pregnant woman!"

"Okay, into the car. We have miles to go," Alice said.

Heading north toward Santa Fe, Alice drove slower than usual. She broke the pleasant silence after about 15 miles. "I hate to spoil our post-picnic high with school talk. But we need to decide what else we need to do to complete our project. Do you have the guidelines there in your notebook?"

"I do," Melody said, patting her bookbag. Retrieving two sheets of paper, she said, "Professor Orr is nothing if not explicit."

"One thing you can say about our faculty, you never wonder what they expect. Let's see. We have four more visits with Aunt El, including today. We have to turn the project in on Friday, August twelfth. So we'd have time to put the report together between the fifth and the twelfth. I can't imagine being able to describe what we've learned before we've finished our visits. Can you?"

"No, and I don't want to try to force what we do to fit the report," Alice replied. "So, what I need to do is just relax and let this unfold."

"Aunt El, I see a lot of pill bottles here. Are you not feeling well?" Melody asked.

"Oh no, no, I'm feeling my usual—strong in the head, a bit weak in the hoof. But for my age, I think I'm well. These are vitamins. Both my brother Richard and I are great believers in vitamins. I also give myself B-twelve by injection each month. Richard tries to get his vitamins by eating a special diet but he supplements, as well," Elinor answered. "Are you taking prenatal vitamins Melody?"

"Oh, yes, and eating a proper diet. Too much of the right things, maybe, but the right things." Melody laughed. "Aunt El, I was interested in your memory of how you were helped by the other women who were heads of the government nursing services. It sounded as if Lucy Minnegerode, in particular, was a big support to you."

"Certainly Lucy was both a friend and a mentor. She helped me understand how things worked in the government and the bureaucracy. The others were helpful as well and were quick to cooperate. When we wanted to improve the salaries and working and living conditions for nurses we were a coordinated force, bringing forward the necessary proposals in each of our own services and seeking outside support from nursing organizations and other groups and individuals.

"Lucy emphasized using organizations such as the ANA Government Section to impress members of Congress and the people in our own services of the broader issue of how treatment of nurses affected the quality of care.

"Women working together in that way was not uncommon in those days. Some examples are the YWCA, the Women's Clubs, and the early Suffragettes. They used the influence, the money, and the social position of their members to accomplish their aims by working through their organizations. Often the women had both family position and wealth and had married wealth and position. When they had a goal they could be a powerful force. Their goals often had to do with improving social and health conditions for those less fortunate. For example, some of the Women's Clubs worked on Indian projects. The YWCA did, as well. Although I've often been impatient with voluntary organizations because of internal bickering, overall, group action is an important way to accomplish goals. It's far stronger than individuals working alone."

"Would you say that women were encouraged to be involved in life outside their homes at that time?" Alice asked.

"I don't know if I'd say encouraged, but there were certainly lots of women who were." She paused. "I've never really thought much about women being unable to do whatever they chose to do. I've always known and had friends who were women who worked or even if they didn't have jobs, were involved in activities outside their home and family, so my view is probably not typical of all women. Certainly I know that there are fields of work where there was and perhaps still is prejudice against women and where it is difficult for them to succeed. Nursing, fortunately, is not one of those fields. But it's also true that nursing and other fields in which women predominate have always been poorly paid, so that may be another form of discrimination.

"Back to your point about women working together. Another factor that I believe was important is that working women, such as those of us in the government services, joined not only with our peers but also with women of other social classes. It's easy to feel more comfortable joining only with those who are most like us. But that can be a form of snobbery that reduces our effectiveness. I learned that people with different motivations can work effectively toward the same goal."

"What do you mean by different motivations?" Melody asked.

"Here's an example. A socially well-placed woman, member of a women's club, might feel an obligation to help those less fortunate because of her religious or moral background. She chose to work for aid to Indians. My position in the Indian Service defined improving conditions for Indians as part of my job responsibility. We might have had some differences in our motivation. At least in part, mine was job-related. But we could work together, particularly if we valued and understood each other as humans; weren't snobs who valued only those of our own type.

"Lucy was accomplished at working with people of different backgrounds and social classes. She had the manners and family position of the upper class, but also knew the life of a working woman and could speak the language of both. I learned a great deal from her example. But I must say, the ability to work across boundaries of class, race, income, gender or economic status springs first from the attitude that all humans are of value and worthy of respect.

"I imagine I'm preaching to the choir when I say that to you. After all, that's an attitude basic to nursing. But sometimes it's easier to feel comfortable working with those most like us than with those in social or economic or other circumstances different from ours—either more or less advantaged." Elinor stopped, silent, smiling comfortably at the girls who were deep in thought.

"I wanted to ask you about being the first to set up nursing in the Indian Service," Melody said. She stopped to follow Aunt El's gesture as she pointed to a Steller's Jay outside the window. The bird was peering at them from a perch on a juniper. He appeared to be interested in the conversation. "When a person is the first, is actually building from the ground up, where do you begin, and more important, how do you know if you're doing the job correctly?"

"If you mean where do you find a pattern, I can only answer by telling you what I did. I used all I'd learned in other situations—in my administration course, my public health education, in the jobs I'd had, in life in general. I tried to extract principles from those, ideas about nursing and about organization and about people, particularly people at work, that seemed to hold true across many settings. For example, it's necessary to have a structure; it's important to have policy and procedure; you have to identify standards of quality; goals must be defined; plans must be developed; communication is vital and must be clear and concise; people should be involved in developing plans they will be responsible for carrying out—principles like that. I picked the brains of other people who'd had some similar experiences. Lucy was one. She'd started the USPHS nursing service, so I asked her counsel frequently and that of many others.

"Another important thing in being the one to place the first bricks is, I think, to have an attitude of openness to change, to know that whatever you do will be a basis for the future, not a permanent fixture. Some degree of self-confidence and humility help too. You must know you'll make mistakes that will be laughable and that few mistakes are terminal. Another important part of being the one developing a new service is to know you won't be there forever and won't be the last so you must find the best people you can to work with you, to eventually replace you, to carry on. You help them find the best in themselves by encouraging and supporting them."

As they left Santa Fe, Alice asked, "Do you remember in that last tape when she told about her niece Faith studying architecture, the one who helped her remodel her house on O Street? Did you know that's the niece she's living with now? That's her house we've been visiting."

"No, I didn't make the connection. I feel nosey enough just asking about her life. I didn't consider asking about her living arrangement. Are you certain?" Melody asked.

"Yes, I am and when we get back to campus, I have a surprise for you that will explain how I know," Alice said, looking pleased with her secret.

"Not till we get to campus?" Melody asked.

"Nope. Now let's listen to the next tape on our way back. Don't forget to put *The Feminine Mystique* with your books. I want you to read it so we can discuss it. Why don't you scoot the seat back so you can put your feet up?"

"Yes, nurse," Melody said, laughing.

PRESIDENT HOOVER APPOINTED HIS QUAKER friend (is that redundant?) Charles Rhoads as the Commissioner of Indian Affairs in April while I was in the field again. Part of the package was Mr. Scattergood who is officially the Assistant. Although that's his title, his desk is in the same office beside Mr. Rhoads and they seem to operate as one. The Commissioner's Annual Report for 1929 that I've just received now in July states this administration's aim very clearly. "The fundamental aim of the Indian Service will be to make the Indian a self-supporting and self-respecting citizen as soon as this can be brought about. He will be considered a potential citizen instead of the ward of the government." Farther on, it says, "Problems of health and education should, as soon as possible, become responsibilities of the various states. Pending that change, vigorous emphasis will be placed upon the two factors in seeking Federal appropriations." Mr. Rhoads took the position of Commissioner only after Mr. Hoover assured him of support to implement the recommendations of the Merriam Report. If that's the case, I need to do more than dream about how and where to use new nursing positions. I must have the plans ready and must redouble my efforts in recruitment.

In this optimistic new environment in the Indian Service, I'm filled with eagerness. Planning my next trip to the field competes for my attention with developing a position description for an assistant nursing supervisor. I plan to be *ready* when opportunity knocks. I'll have plans and alternate plans ready in my desk drawer.

Three months in our nation's capitol and I'm back on the train. After a few days in Minneapolis at the District headquarters, I'll be heading south to Kansas, Iowa, and Oklahoma before returning to D.C. in December.

If this train arrives in Minneapolis on time, I'll be able to check in, freshen up and have supper before this evening's "performance." Since I'll be the performer, I believe a nap is a good choice of activity for the next hour.

"Close your eyes, if you will," I ask my audience of graduate nurses and senior nursing students. I notice that they comply. I'm beginning one of the speeches I make at every opportunity along my itinerary. Even with the snail's pace of the Civil Service appointment process, several nurses have joined the Indian Service as a result of these talks. Tonight I'm trying something new.

"Now open them just a slit—enough to let in light and just to barely see me," I pause for effect. "I'm not asking you to alter your vision because I'll look better if seen dimly." I hear some laughter. "No, keep them just that way for a few minutes. It will be uncomfortable. And that's what I want you to experience—how it is to have vision limited by trachoma." A murmur spreads among those assembled. Perhaps this is just the attention-getter I hoped it would be. "Now I want you to use your imagination. Add to the limited vision some degree of pain and irritation in your eyes, as if you had sand under the lids. That's how it feels to have trachoma and to have the scars on the conjunctiva that it causes. Imagine that when you sleep, there is discharge from your eyes that adheres your eyelashes. You're unable to open them at all when you first waken. As you are imagining this, realize that trachoma is endemic in several Indian tribes and that eradication of this disease will require a number of things. But one thing that is vital is good nursing—for education about hygiene and for follow-up of treatment. You could, as a nurse in the Indian Service, mean the difference between vision and blindness for many people.

"Trachoma is not the only reason that the Indian Service needs nurses. I will tell you more about the Service and its opportunities for you before I leave this evening. But now, I'll tell you a bit more about this blinding disease that affects so many Indians.

"You've been looking at me through slits for several minutes now. Can you imagine how it is to be unable to open your eyes much wider than that? One of the more radical treatments, tarsectomy, removes the eyelid's cartilage plate and the result can be inability to fully elevate the lids, just as you feel now. Aside from complete enucleation, tarsectomy is the most radical treatment for disease of long standing. The disease begins with irritation and infection of the conjunctiva. Initial treatment has been the daily instillation of various medications such as one percent silver nitrate, Argyol twenty-five percent, or Mercurochrome one percent. This often fails because the patients dislike using the drops. When that has failed, grattage has been a common treatment. This procedure involves vigorous scrubbing of the conjunctiva to express infected material from the tissue. I've seen the scrubbing performed with a variety of tools—a special metal roller, a gauze-wrapped finger, and even a toothbrush. The treatment may seem worse than the disease. And for that reason, some may wait too long for treatment. None of these is a comfortable procedure.

"Why, you might ask, isn't the disease prevented, so that these uncomfortable or radical procedures are not necessary? Trachoma is certainly spread from person to person and by common use of towels and by generally unsanitary conditions. In the past three years, work by the USPHS scientists has provided more knowledge about the pathology and bacteriology of the disease. New emphasis is being placed in the Indian Service on using the more radical procedures of treatment only when all else fails, in short, to be gentle in treatment. Children with trachoma are being moved to schools where the disease will be contained, separated from non-infected students, and where treatment can be supervised and administered regularly. An attempt is being made to eliminate this disease and the disability it causes. Indian Service nurses are involved at every stage. Field nurses find cases, teach prevention, and follow up treated cases. Nurses work in hospitals where surgical cases are treated. School nurses care for trachomatous children and emphasize hygiene in living quarters and in school. And there are special nurses who travel with and assist the special eye physicians. There in a capsule you have a picture of just one of the important goals that nurses in Indian Health are vital in helping to meet.

"Now open your eyes! I will now make you uncomfortable with your eyes open, by telling you that in the Indian Service you would do this important work in primitive conditions, with few colleagues nearby. Your hours would be long and the hardship frequent. In the tribes where trachoma is not endemic, you would have plenty of other challenges, such as tuberculosis, maternal and infant mortality problems, and general resistance to medical care, to mention a few. I could continue, at length. But I will stop and say that working as a nurse in the Indian Service is not for everyone. It is only for those who relish the uncommon, who have the skill and confidence to practice nursing with little support and who are committed to making a difference in the health of this country's native people. I'm now open to questions and I hope that you have many."

I am gratified that there are many questions and requests for application materials. Why didn't I think before to dramatize my remarks? I use the question and answer period to get across the same information I always include in my speeches. A similar presentation using our other major disease, tuberculosis, as the theme could work also. Although, a room full of coughing nurses might be a difficult audience.

Marjorie would be proud of me, I'm sure. She always engineered plays with roles for each of us when we were children. And to this day she never simply tells a story, she brings it all to life. My streak of indolence would make it difficult to sustain the effort to make each moment of life a drama. But it does seem that a bit of emotional involvement improves an audience's attention. Tonight's speech has also reminded me of the distance we have yet to go in dealing with trachoma.

As is often the case, my tablemates in the dining car tonight are salesmen. While I ride the rails from one reservation to another, I am often in the company of the purveyors of all manner of goods. They pass from town to town with their sample cases offering storeowners the newest in necessary and fanciful goods. In the five years I've traveled for the Indian Service, the number of salesmen seems to have increased.

"This is the last trip I'll be making on this route. Company combined it with another one and gave it to the other salesman. In fact, I won't be surprised if the company cuts my job out altogether. Notions and fabric are just not selling like they were two years ago," says the sad-faced older man sitting next to me.

A younger man directly across from him nods and says, "I may have to move back to the farm. Thought I'd never have to run a thresher again, but I may'a been wrong. Seems to me that there are fewer and fewer people in the cities with any money to spend, what with so many people having trouble keeping factory jobs. There's always work on the farm and we'd never go hungry. Arkansas may see me again 'fore long even though I swore if I ever got out, I'd never go back," he laughs. "I started selling shoes in nineteen twenty, soon as I left the farm. For the first five years, it was great. I even made enough to buy some stock—y'know, invest in th' stock market. Never much, mind you, but everythin' was lookin' good. Got married in St. Louis and bought a little house. The wife just loves it. It got so the money I was makin' in stocks was as much as what I make sellin' shoes. See, I learned about buyin' on the margin." He stops speaking to take a bite of his pork chop.

Encouraged by the pause, the other man at the table, sitting next to me, leans forward. He says, punctuating with his knife, "See, it's people like you that are the cause of all the money troubles these days. Buying on margins is spending money that's not real and getting a benefit from it. But you mark my word (the knife points again) it's all about to tumble down. I've been reading the papers, and I tell you—what happened last Thursday the twenty-fourth is just the beginning."

I can't resist asking, "What happened on Thursday?" Today is Saturday and I haven't seen a paper in three days.

"The reports aren't exactly clear about what started it, but a lot of people started selling stock, all different kinds of stocks. Maybe they began to look around and saw that no one had money to buy what those companies were manufacturing. The people at the New York Stock Exchange couldn't keep up; there were so many orders to sell. When all that selling continued, prices of the stocks fell. J.P. Morgan and some other bankers bought stock just to keep the market afloat, stop the panic. One of the papers called it Black Thursday."

"Were the bankers successful in settling it down by buying up the stock?" I ask

He shakes his head. "It did for the time being but I don't think it's over by a long shot"

Chewing his pork thoughtfully, the younger salesman says, "Looks like my wife did me a big favor."

"How's that," asks the man who has made the dire prediction.

"Last year she made me stop buyin' stock altogether. Said it was the same as gamblin', which she's dead set against, bein' a good Baptist. Didn't want me goin' to hell for ill-gotten gain. I've been tempted, though, since shoe sales've been droppin' off. Guess the price of stocks fell a lot with all that sellin' goin' on, huh?"

"Sure did. Those margin buyers won't have any profits to finish paying for what their stock cost to begin with. This is when they learn that making a down payment and planning to pay the rest off from profits only works when there's a profit. She's right, your wife. It's a gamble and what's worse, it's gambling with credit. To be fair, I have to say the papers don't attribute all the trouble with unemployment just to the stock market, or to investors. Manufacturers have put too much into producing when there's so few with money to buy what they're making. And so many have been put out of work because of machinery doing the work that people once did. If I were a betting man, I'd wager that next week will see a far darker day than Black Thursday."

We all finish our meals silently. As I leave the table, I'm thankful for two things. One, I have stock only in Bemis Bag Company. Faith's husband, Farwell's, family's business has always been sound, so it's been my only foray into investing. And I paid cash, not credit. Second, I have a job that can't be replaced by a machine. And then I think of a third. I've never had much money, so I'm not likely to suffer much if I have to do with less. If my dinner companions are correct about the economy, I'll be seeing fewer salesmen on the trains between reservations. Too bad, their talk usually makes dinner interesting.

"This is the first time since I've been with the Service that I've felt good about writing my annual report, Lucy. Although I realize that part of the reason we've been able to recruit more nurses is the general unemployment and bad economy, it's thrilling to be able to report that in fiscal year nineteen thirty we had an eight-five percent turnover rate compared to the one hundred twenty-two percent we had in nineteen twenty-seven. I recall that was the first time anyone had done a turnover study and it was such a shock to everyone to see just how bad it really was." Lucy Minnegerode and I are talking shop over coffee in my O Street living room. It's early June 1930, and spring has given way to the heat and humidity of an early summer. Lucy begins to fan herself with a copy of *Time* from the end table. I open the windows for ventilation.

"Give yourself some credit. The economy may have been a factor, but you've capitalized on every opportunity that the new Indian Service Commissioner has made available. You had a position description for an assistant supervisor proposed as soon as Mr. Rhoads arrived. You have a policy now for promotion for faithful and efficient service. You've worked diligently to reduce the number of situations where nurses have twenty-four-hour-a-day duty," Lucy says, holding up a hand and ticking the items off on her fingers.

Before she can continue I say, "Yes, you're correct. Now only twenty-three are in that deplorable situation rather than the ninety-six there were last year. But, to be honest, without a difficult economy, I doubt I could have recruited enough nurses in this short a time to have relieved all of those nurses of sole responsibility in the small hospitals and boarding schools."

"You're incorrect if you think that what you do is ordinary. Only an excellent administrator uses data, develops plans, patiently works her plans through channels for approval, capitalizes on the positive potential of even the worst of situations, and does it all with good humor. Speaking of good humor, I need to tell you I think that the way you have handled the interim meetings of the Government Section have been just right. You've made everyone comfortable by keeping the discussions, even the disagreements, good-humored. As a result, we've made progress with the work on the government personnel system as it relates to nurses. That will pay off eventually. It's important for a new group like ours, in the larger ANA organization, to become cohesive and you've helped that to happen by encouraging everyone to see a purpose. We'd only been organized two years when you were selected chairman and you were just the right choice to follow the first chairman, who did, I might say, an excellent job." She laughs at her own joke. She was the first chairman.

"I refuse to take credit for the result of the group's work. They are a group of very competent women," I say.

"True enough. But, you've kept them on target and kept them smiling at the same time," Lucy says.

"It's made a difference that I have a bit more time when I'm here in Washington now that Sallie Jeffries is my assistant. I can't tell you how much it pleased me that you were willing for her to move from the USPHS over to the Indian Service. It's so good working with someone who's not only a colleague but also a friend. Our days in the Great War together cemented that. She's made it possible for me to accomplish more, both here and in the field. I hope soon to have an assistant for each district."

"Do you feel that you're settling in now—that you know the Service and its people well enough to have the influence you need? I recall it was about five years before I felt I'd hit my stride," Lucy says.

I nod. "It's interesting. Even though I have no direct authority in the field, it seems that most of the superintendents as well as the doctors accept my advice now. The nurses have always seemed grateful for my presence, but it's only through developing relationships over time with the doctors and the superintendents that they've come around. It's part of what makes my time in the field so valuable, working with them face to face, sharing meals, riding together in government Fords," I laugh, thinking about the Fords. "And then there's the committee work, advisory groups put together on so many topics. That's the way the commissioner operates. Tiresome as it is, it bears fruit. One of the fruits will be another reorganization of the Service, I expect. It will mostly affect the central office and should emphasize health, education and agricultural extension as being separate from matters of Indian property. Oh, and here's an interesting possibility. I hear that we may get Alaska added to our purview. Can you imagine recruiting nurses to work in the dark for six months each year?" I laugh and imagine equipping nurses with snowshoes. I've had enough difficulty trying to get decent living quarters for the ones we have now. I'll not wish for expanded territory!

The sky above the horizon to the west is the color of the dry ground below and the brown in the sky is rising higher. The odor of dust reaches me even here on the train many miles away. Riding through Nebraska and Kansas, I've seen barren fields where corn is usually ready for harvest. This drought and these dust storms can only add misery for people who are already in bad straits because of the depression. I hope that rain comes soon because the reservations will suffer along with their neighbors in these dry times. The Indians in the Southwest are accustomed to arid land and to the blowing dust. They've adapted and survived. But the Sioux of Rosebud and Pine Ridge and their brethren on the Great Plains are ill-equipped for long drought.

As I ride toward Haskell Indian School, I've been writing some preliminary ideas for a training course to help prepare Indian girls to enter schools of nursing. We've had some accepted to schools in the past few years and even have a few back working in the Service. But their chances of doing well in the training schools could be improved if they had some stronger education in their secondary course and perhaps some practical work as nursing aids. I'll begin to discuss it with some on the education side and see if some superintendents think it's worthwhile.

But the dust distracts me. I think I'll put this away and write a letter to Faith. Richard has commented that since Mother's death, Faith has seemed like the center of the family. He's correct in that. She's so good to be concerned about all of us along with her own husband and seven children. She's perpetually searching for ways to assure the best situation for everyone. Her letters keep us in touch between visits. She passes along other letters from our siblings with her own newsy notes. Her home at Louisburg Square and the farm at South Tamworth are always a haven, open to us all. I have little time to visit these days. Maybe I will get there this Christmas, 1931. Regardless, writing her assures that the whole family hears from me.

Looking out the window again, I think that the stone I collect from this particular journey will be sandstone.

"It seems that every nurse I visit on my field trips, no matter what reservation, feels you are a personal friend. They ask about your health and when you'll be out again. How have you managed to make that happen along with your supervision?" Sallie asks. She's just back from a field trip filled with supervisory visits.

"Perhaps it's because I try to know them as individuals so that I can help them build on their strengths. As we discussed when you first came here, most of these nurses are well-trained and need little actual work on procedures. What they do need is help with adjusting to reservation life and working with the physicians. And they need to know that someone understands the situations they work in and represents their interests as nurses here in Washington. So as I make home visits with them or work with them in the hospitals, I try to make sure those are the messages they hear from me," I respond, hoping that the long answer will benefit her. Although I know that she does an excellent job without tutelage.

"I think this past year has been the best yet as far as seeing progress. Do you agree?" Sallie asks.

"Definitely. Even with the problems for the Indians in the Dust Bowl states and the blizzard in the Southwest, our work has made progress. I attribute that to Mr. Rhoads' doing everything he can to implement the Merriam Report and see that we have money for positions and support. His reorganization seems to be working satisfactorily also. And of course, the economic depression has made it easier to recruit nurses. Everyone needs work. Yes, I think fiscal year nineteen thirty-two was a banner year," I say. Now that we've begun nineteen thirty-three, we can only hope that when Mr. Roosevelt arrives and Cabinet appointments are made we won't see any reversals."

Sallie nods. "What else is new since I've been away?"

"What's new is that Dr. Fellows wants me to come to Alaska as soon as possible. Since we received Alaska early last year, you know we've recruited a couple of nurses to send there for field positions. I'd thought that might be all they would want until they have the health service organized. But he wants me to help. I've done some background work and here's what I know. There are about twenty-nine thousand Indians and Eskimos. Six full-time and five part-time doctors, one traveling dentist, seven hospitals, fifteen hospital nurses, twenty-eight public health village nurses and thirty-two assorted other workers for a grand total of eighty-two health personnel serve that population. They do have access to two non-Indian Service hospitals, one in Nome and another in Anchorage plus three in Washington and Oregon that accept their cases. I believe they are correct in identifying that they need more public health nurses. Tuberculosis is a major problem there. So, I suppose I will be traveling near the Arctic Circle. But I'll not be going right away. After all, they've been working for years without any professional medical or nursing supervision until they were transferred to the Indian Service. There are more immediate concerns to attend to."

Sallie falls for it. "What? Do I need to be working on a new project?"

Sober-faced, I say, "We both do. We must decide right away what will be the best place on the route to watch the Inaugural Parade for Mr. Roosevelt. I hear there's going to be a "New Deal", and I want to see it from the start." We are both laughing as we leave the office for the day.

A NEW DEAL

I HAVE VERY LITTLE NEED TO DO ANY BANKING on any day. So, Mr. Roosevelt's four day Bank Holiday is no real concern for me. He declared it as one of his first official Presidential acts. The purpose is to begin to set the economy straight, I understand. What does concern me and many others in the Indian Service is the fact that we are going to lose Mr. Rhoads and Mr. Scattergood. Things are far from perfect but we have had four years of progress. Selfishly, I think of the effect on health services and nursing in particular. We have increases in number of positions. I have assistants for each district and recruitment has been good even though the Civil Service appointment process remains slow and tedious.

But, with this new Democrat administration, we know that President Hoover's Republican administration appointees will be replaced very soon. It is clear that many of the people in this country are suffering because of the economy. I shall never forget seeing some 20,000 veterans of the Great War—the Bonus Expeditionary Force as they called themselves—camped here in Washington last year to protest their pension benefits. Some said they were misguided, but many of us who had served with them were shocked when President Hoover sent in the Army to break up their demonstration. So perhaps the changes will be for the better, overall. And perhaps the New Deal that Mr. Roosevelt campaigned on will even be good for the Indian Service.

We hear that Mr. Ickes is to be the Secretary of the Interior. I have no opinion on that appointment. I do have an opinion on the man whose name is being bandied about as the Commissioner of Indian Affairs, John Collier. I've never met the man, but I do know that he's long been involved with various groups interested in Indian matters. And I hear that he's a favorite of Mrs. Ickes, who apparently influences Mr. Ickes in many of his decisions. Perhaps it is unfounded, but I have a suspicion of Mr. Collier because I know he was involved in causing Mr. Burke's departure. I have fond memories of Mr. Burke, my original boss here. Ah well, these are things I cannot change. So I will count them all as part of the adventure.

226 The rumors have become fact. Mr. Collier is at the helm now. Who knows where we will sail? One part of the New Deal that's not new at all is reorganization. Mr. Collier, the newly appointed commissioner, as each of his predecessors, is bent on shaping the Service to his liking. The first steps are beginning, with the appointment of committees to study what changes should occur. For the time being, the health division is unchanged. That's good because we have plenty to do without making adjustment to organizational change.

The government effort on solving unemployment has worked to our benefit. Indians can sign on with the Indian Conservation Corps and be paid to do work on soil erosion and other projects on the reservations that are actually quite useful. And there are several new hospitals being built as Public Works projects. This results in a need for even more nurses and for organization in the new hospitals. We have over 400 nurses in the Service now and around 50 more open positions.

If I could stay in the field and spend no time here in the office, my spirits would be fine. I'd see only the increased numbers of nurses and the serious work being done to improve the reservations. But when I'm here, I feel the turmoil that Mr. Collier creates. He's a brilliant man but erratic as hell. Perhaps he's not the source of my current concern, but I cannot help thinking so. Just as we were making progress by having assistant nursing supervisors for each district, it seems we'll be taking a step backward. Two of those four positions are being cut in order to satisfy budget reductions. I've campaigned hard for additional supervisory positions. We must have a revitalization of the field nursing service because we've been marking time in that area for the past three years due to expansion in hospitals. Either we move forward with new ideas, new people, new approaches or go back to routinization of existing channels of thought. My intention has been to change supervisory loads with these new positions to give time for directed effort and freedom from detailed routines. This was bad timing on my part, I suppose. I understand the overall need for some budget reductions. But why not in less essential areas, I wonder. I've not given up the idea that we will eventually be able to fully create correlated health service, a correlation of the service with community purpose as well as a correlation of illness and wellness. And the only way that can happen is to have competence in both the hospitals and in the field.

"You look a million miles away, Elinor," Lucy says. We've gotten together to plan for entertaining the members of the ANA Government Section during the 1934 convention. It will be next month, June, here in Washington. We want to make the hospitality memorable.

"Sorry Lucy. I was thinking about Mother," I reply.

"Missing her?" she asks

"Actually, I was thinking about whether to break her rule against gossiping about people," I say.

"Maybe it's not actually gossip that you are wanting to do. You see, it's only gossip if what you tell is not true or not confirmed, if it's supposed to be secret or private, or if it's only your opinion. If you talk of the facts of a situation, you're just reporting," Lucy says in didactic fashion.

Laughing, I reply, "That's a rather elaborate distinction. Sounds as if you've given it some thought."

"My mother had a similar rule. But sometimes I just must talk about what people do or I'll worry myself to death, not able to discuss it. Will it help if I swear not to tell anyone?"

Putting aside the pad I was making notes on, I draw a deep breath. "As you know, Mr. Collier, like any new Commissioner, has been busy putting his mark on the Service, by making personnel changes, reorganizing, and starting new projects. He's also pressing for the legislation that's officially known as the Wheeler-Howard Act. I've wondered if I'm paranoid about what I'm going to tell you. You see, he's employed a woman by the name of Sallie Lucas Jean. She's a nurse who has made her name in what she calls health education. She's said to have invented that idea. He created a position called Supervisor of Health Education and declares she will organize a health education program under the joint auspices of the divisions of health and education. She's a nice enough person and I'm not blaming this on her. But what I don't understand is why Collier hired her first and then told us we're to cooperate with whatever she develops."

As I pause, Lucy asks, "Are you thinking this cuts into your territory; that she might be affecting your programs and the staff in the field?"

"She's done nothing to indicate she's interested in actual nursing. So, I'm not too concerned about that. I'd be untruthful if I said I hadn't considered how her position might affect me. But my more immediate concern is why Collier would spend the money for her and whatever programs she develops when we have so many needs for nurses in the existing operations." I feel my face reddening. Lucy's right. I do need to get this off my chest.

"This week topped it, though. Miss Jean has developed a request that's to be sent to the Rockefeller Foundation to set up a program with the Navajos. The idea is to have a short course, an institute she calls it, to train some Navajo girls to be nurse aids of a sort. This is on the assumption that they'll be able to influence the Indians to accept the hospitals, help them acculturate, it says. There's lots more to the proposal. But the point is that she had the proposal all developed and *then* the medical division was told to develop the budget to include in it. Just like that (I snap my fingers) with no input at all.

"I was so put out that I wrote and told Alan about it. I'm not sure it was an ethical thing to do—to tell him my thoughts which are in opposition to what the commissioner and Miss Jean are proposing in their request. He's my brother. I can tell him my thoughts on any subject because of that. But he also works for the Rockefeller Foundation and if I were a good soldier, I wouldn't have told him anything that could have endangered the request. Fine time to have an attack of conscience, after I've done the deed, isn't it?"

"I can understand your reaction," Lucy says. "But, isn't it fair to say that your brother will make his own decisions rather than be influenced entirely by your view?"

I'm calmer now that I've told my story. "Yes, that's a good point. Alan is certainly his own person as far as making decisions." After a few moments of consideration, I say, "I'm not entirely sure what about Collier bothers me so much. I can't say he's not trying to get money for additional positions for nursing. He had me put together a memo telling some horror stories to illustrate the needs. He attached it to an appeal to Secretary Ickes."

"What stories did you tell?" she asks.

"As you know, I have no lack of material to illustrate distressing conditions. Every field trip increases my repertoire. I wrote about the nurse on twenty-four hour duty in a school hospital. She had a little girl dying in an upstairs ward with tubercular meningitis, having severe convulsions every half hour or so. Her lips and tongue were swollen and bleeding because of her having bitten them. Downstairs there was a boy having been ill with typhoid fever. He had hemorrhaged twice and was disoriented. He was not wildly delirious but his mind wandered so that when left alone he tried to get up. The single nurse had slept, or tried to sleep, in the hall where she could hear both of these cases. The answer to my query about getting another nurse was, 'No funds.' When I insisted that something must be done, the superintendent hired an old man to sit with the boy and call the nurse. The Indians have contempt for this sort of care provided by the government.

"Another situation was this. In a sixty-bed hospital, filled to capacity, we found one nurse on night duty. She had among the sixty patients two new obstetrical cases, one newly-operated gallstones with drainage, one boy with seven feet of intestines removed five days before and barely on the living side of the balance, two bed cases of tuberculosis, and we expected her to handle this and be in the receiving ward for any automobile accidents that were brought in.

"Last summer, I found one nurse caring day and night for a gonorrheal infection of the eyes, a second stage case of syphilitic ulcers, an advanced tuberculosis, and two newly delivered obstetrical cases. If the obstetrical case or the baby developed gonorrhea or syphilis, was the nurse to blame? There were fifteen other patients under her care.

"I told several other equally distressing tales to illustrate the point. What I didn't say was that the current situation is a vast improvement over the past. But we must not stop now. We have a very long way to go." Realizing I was shaking a clenched fist in the air, I stopped, embarrassed. "I probably shouldn't allow myself to get so worked up."

"It's important to be passionate about your work. You just need to let off steam sometimes. And no, I won't tell anyone." Lucy assures me.

Knowing that the legislative process is neither within my control nor my influence, I've spent no time speculating about the Wheeler-Howard Act that Commissioner Collier is so dedicated to. Even now, as 1935 approaches and it has become law, I understand it only in general, because I have been too busy to concern myself with the details. The main effects of the new law have to do with property, repealing the General Allotment Act of 1887 (the Dawes Severalty Act). It is based on an ideal of giving Indian tribes the authority to incorporate and to govern themselves. To all who will listen, Mr. Collier explains this is an important part of spiritual rehabilitation to remedy the inferiority produced by arbitrary supervision of the Indians. It could be a very good idea. But there's always such a distance between the ideal and the actual. It's clear there will be lots of activity by those attempting to implement the new law. And there will probably be an equal amount of effort expended resisting the change. At this time there's no major implication for the medical service. We do hear that there will be a push to eliminate boarding schools in favor of day schools and the use of local public schools. That also could be beneficial. So much depends on the funding and on the follow-through. The devil is in the details.

Collier also is adding anthropologists to the Service and seems to be discouraging the missionaries. That probably has to do with some grander plan that will all be revealed in time.

I've managed this past year to avoid tangling with the commissioner by making field visits and tending to my own mountain of bureaucratic red tape. My placement in the Medical Division, not reporting directly to the commissioner, has the advantage of buffering me from regular direct contact with him. Except, that is, for one occasion, back in April. He called me in and asked if nurses were prepared to teach birth control to Indian women. It seems he'd written to a physician at Columbia University seeking his opinion about the notion that nurses could be of great service to the Indians by teaching some method of birth control. I'm not certain what the physician's reply was and I have nothing against birth control. But the idea of agents of the government "selling" birth control to wards of the government is fraught with thorns.

If the Indians wanted birth control it would certainly take more than the occasional efforts of a field nurse to do the job properly. And the nurses have more than enough to say grace over without that. My answer was clear and direct. That incident shook what small amount of faith I might have had in Mr. Collier's administrative wisdom. But I've heard nothing more about birth control, so maybe it was a whim.

This trip to Alaska could help. Nothing invigorates me more than new places. Thus far 1935 has been both busy and sad for me. Lucy Minnegerode died in March. As the death of someone close often does, her passing made me realize how precious and how short life is. The enormous administrative load of recruiting, supervising, and endless bureaucratic paperwork leaves me weary, wondering if work is all I want of this short life. I know that it's grief and fatigue giving me that attitude because there's much more to my life than work. I have family, friends, and interesting experiences.

One satisfying new experience has been developing the training program for Indian nurse assistants at Fort Sill. Representative Johnson from Oklahoma wanted us to set up a school for practical nurses at the reservation hospital there. I thought it would be better to train nursing assistants. In that way they can enter schools of nursing and become graduate nurses if they like the work they learn as assistants. This will avoid limiting them to the secondary practical nurse category. And they will be directly employable in the Indian Service with their basic attendant training, if this is their choice. While I'm concerned about the graduate nurses having time and supplies for teaching, I think the plan is sound. And everyone has agreed to it. I'll be even more gratified when we can have large numbers of registered nurses from among the tribes and some system of preference in hiring if they choose to enter the Indian Service. That's a long-term project, but one that I know is sound.

Back to packing. What does one wear for Alaskan adventure?

Galoshes. That would have been a good idea. As it is, I have none with me. So, I have been carried, with as much dignity as could be mustered, between ship and shore and between shore and airplane. This expedition has included travel on the North Star, the Indian Service supply ship; pontoon plane; narrow gauge train; and even automobile. Because it's summer, we've missed dog-sled travel but I did get a taste of what it's like when I was dressed in a full winter outfit, fur lined parka and all, and posed behind a team and sled. Today we will leave aboard a larger twin engine plane.

Everyone here is so glad for visitors that I've been treated like royalty. They've shown me everything they could think of. All the oddities of

Alaskan existence have been spread before me. I've seen Eskimo and Indian families living in tents and sod houses. The children are a delight; so cunning and friendly. People have fed me fried bread cooked in walrus oil, reindeer tongue stew and some excellent salmon along with vegetables that flourish in the short but sun-drenched summer. Giant cabbages!

The Eskimos are similar in appearance to the Navajos. And their hard-scrabble existence is also similar in some ways, although colder. There's no Dustbowl here, just miles of vast expanse that will soon be covered with snow and ice.

The nurses in Alaska are a hardy lot. They look fit, probably from spending time outdoors and doing hard work. The tales that the village nurses tell of dog-sled travel in winter make anything I did at Rosebud seem tame by comparison. Of course, they need help and support. I must appoint an assistant supervisor for Alaska as soon as there is money. And I will send Sallie out here soon as a follow-up to my visit.

Thinking of what the public health nurses here do, much of which is medical treatment, I wonder if we should accept this as a special kind of nursing with special training, rather than winking and saying it's only because there's no doctor. After all, this is not the only situation where nurses are the only people available to provide care. The Red Cross Delano Nurses in Appalachia and elsewhere, the nurses of the Frontier Nursing Service in Kentucky, and the field nurses on some of the reservations in the states all are in similar situations. Everything in my training, in standards for public health nursing, says to leave medicine to the doctors. But there's midwifery—always a gray area—and there's this work in areas where the physicians are so few. I don't know.

I've been in Alaska since August 14th. It's now October 1, 1935, and we must get out today before the "freeze up." Otherwise I'll be here until the thaw without galoshes.

Certainly my photography is inexpert, but the movies I've taken on this trip will give an idea of the vastness and of the tremendous adventure that nursing in Alaska can be. I hope to use the film for recruitment. One day I'll have time to improve my skills as a photographer. But for now I must pack again. Ah, here's the stone I chose for this trip. I must pack it in my stockings for safe-keeping; these flecks could be gold.

The feeling I have today is a strange one. Elated, as I make my report to the ANA Government Section meeting here in Los Angeles. I'm thrilled to tell of steady improvement in Indian Service nursing. Yet there's a tinge of melancholy. Perhaps it's that I realized that this year, 1936 marks ten years I've been with the Service. I believe the name of this feeling is ambivalence. All the indicators of size support a conclusion that progress is being made. We have more nurses, more hospitals, and almost no remaining field matrons. There's progress also in programs. We're collaborating with the State Health Department in Florida to bring public health nursing to the Seminoles. Similar joint efforts are working in Minnesota and in Oklahoma. There's the consultation by the National League for Nursing Education about our developing education program in Oklahoma and about quality of nursing as it relates to ratios of nurses to patients. We have three nurses away at the Phipps Institute in Philadelphia to work on tuberculosis nursing. Bertha Tiler has been appointed as Assistant Nursing Supervisor in Alaska. We expect soon to be able to have assistant supervisors again in each of the districts. A real coup is the initiation of a small fund for research and studies that should result in stimulation of interest in our work. Approximately fifteen percent of our graduate nurses are of Indian ancestry. Yes, these are signs of progress. Why am I only partly elated?

I wonder if it's my natural restlessness. When I came to Washington, I seldom sat still at my desk more than an hour and a half. Even now, when I'm there, I must be up and moving. Could that part of my personality be chafing at ten years in one place? Or is it the constant red tape and endless regulation, tons of paperwork and never-ending requirement to move slowly and indirectly through channels to arrive at a goal? Could be it's none of the above—or all of them. But I'm aware that even the sunniest personality has cloudy days. So, I'm not ready to abandon useful work for—who knows what. I've heard it said the devil you know is better than the devil you don't know. So, I'll stick with this devil.

The woman who just entered this elevator with me is giving me a long look. Finally, she speaks, "You're from Boston, aren't you?"

I smile and say, "No."

"But you do live in Boston, don't you?" she says.

"What makes you think that?" I ask.

"Your hat's from Boston." Her tone implies a slight accusation.

"You're correct," I say as I the elevator arrives on my floor. "The hat's from Boston. But I'm from Washington." Leaving her wondering if I stole the hat, I laugh as I go down the hall to my room. I must tell Faith that her hand-me-down hat nearly got me in trouble. I know if I can laugh at such silliness, I'm not too morose.

Expressing my frustrations last year after the convention, I told Faith of my ambivalence. Now, a year later, I see things a bit differently. Finally, after all these years, some headway is being made with trachoma and perhaps even with tuberculosis. I attribute it as much to adequate personnel for follow-up, those being field nurses, as to the treatments themselves. Trachoma among school children can be arrested. The special intensive treatment at the Roosevelt Trachoma School on Fort Apache Reservation has demonstrated this. Tuberculosis vaccine is being administered to children with intensive follow-up and record keeping by the field nurses. And some physicians are trying pneumothorax on the affected lungs of selected cases. Collapsing a tuberculous lung to rest it seems to allow the body to fight the infection. Only the fact that more Indians are willing to use the sanitoria makes such radical treatment possible.

Several nurses have shown their initiative and commitment by taking unpaid leave to receive special instruction in tuberculosis care and epidemiology. Even though we still have high turnover, these nurses make me proud.

Mr. Roosevelt began his second term as President this year, in 1937. So I suppose we'll be in for more of Mr. Collier. I can't say I look forward to that. Although I'm more hopeful than last year, my restlessness has been visiting me frequently in the few odd moments when I'm not occupied with the details of bureaucracy.

Faith's recent suggestion probably has a lot to do with that. She thinks I work too hard and should quit. Knowing her, she's been ruminating on this since last year when we had that conversation. Has it all worked out, she says. She'll buy annuities to supply a modest income for me and help me with a place to live. No one could ask for a more generous sister. She's helped Marjorie and wants to do this for me. My reason for hesitating is not because of concern for her finances. Farwell was very successful and his death last year left her well situated. Even if that weren't the case, it's her nature to want to take care of us all.

There are some days when I'm tempted to agree to her offer. I've imagined myself doing things I haven't time for with all the office work and travel. Putting aside the stack of official Indian Service correspondence I've been tackling, I smile as I picture myself raising pigeons as Alan does; gardening in more than a desultory way; camping in the mountains; and riding horseback. I'd find volunteering to do and if all that became commonplace, I'd take a job. It's easy to visualize and it's attractive. But there are so many things yet to accomplish here. That's why I hesitate. I see my secretary looking at me questioningly. That's why I'd better quit hesitating and get back to work!

JULY 14 AND 15, 1966—ALBUQUERQUE

"WHAT'S THE SURPRISE YOU HAD FOR ME? YOU promised it when we got back to Albuquerque," Melody said as they drove to the campus parking lot.

"There it is," said Alice pointing to Zimmerman Library.

"What do you mean? There's a surprise at the library?" Melody asked, puzzled.

"No, the surprise is the library. I found out that Aunt El's niece is married to John Gaw Meem. He's the architect who designed the library, our favorite building on campus. It was one of those Public Works projects done during the Depression. I think it's such a beautiful building. It fits so well, reflects both the Hispanic and the Indian cultures of the Southwest. It's a peaceful place for me. I always hate to leave when I'm there."

Melody nodded agreement and said, "You're quite a detective."

"Not really. I just happened to think about the name of her niece, the one we met the first day we visited Aunt El. Faith Meem. I recalled Aunt El said she was an architect and the name Meem sounded so familiar. So I asked some questions at just the right place, the reference desk at the Zimmerman Library. Some detective work, ha! I just fell into it, but I thought it was a good surprise."

Staring at the library, Melody said, "It's amazing the different ways that people leave their mark—on the landscape, on people, on the things we believe."

"It is," Alice agreed, watching her friend's serious gaze.

"Take the things Aunt El was talking about on this last tape. So many of those things she worked on in the Indian Service left a mark on people's lives. You know we're so lucky to have her as our subject," Melody said, slowly turning away from the library to face Alice. "I have some errands I have to do now, but I wonder if we can get together tomorrow to talk about this tape. I'll have time in the morning about eleven." She consulted a small calendar she always carried.

Laughing, Alice said, "Your list has a blank spot? Amazing!"

"I'd like to throw this list away sometime and just float along for a few days. But there's a lot I need to stay up with—school, home, you know. By the way, I want to thank you again for the picnic today. It was really nice to have a break like that."

"You're welcome. Okay, I'll meet you here tomorrow at eleven," she said as she pulled her red hair into a ponytail to cool her neck.

Melody started toward her car with a backward wave to Alice. As she traversed the parking lot, she wore a small frown. It disappeared after she sat down in the car and took two deep breaths. "Braxton-Hicks, you can't scare me," she said aloud to herself as she started the car.

"I'm on my way, just about to walk out the door. Some little contractions this morning slowed me down," Melody said. "I'm sorry you were so worried that you called. I'll be right there."

Alice hung up the receiver of the pay phone. She thought, "I'm going to make her go to the doctor if she has one more contraction."

"Hi. I'm ready to work. No, before you ask, I'm not feeling bad. Those were just Braxton-Hicks contractions. You know they can happen when the uterus starts enlarging and they don't affect dilatation or effacement," she said, patting her round belly with her right hand. This little girl's just moving around, stirring things up."

"You think it's a girl?" Alice asked.

"I do. I hope so, because she'll be the last."

"Do you mean you aren't planning to have any more children?" Alice asked.

"Right. And this time I'm planning on no more accidents."

"Just for the sake of curiosity, what's it going to be—a tubal ligation or The Pill?" Alice asked.

"Or a vasectomy—don't forget that possibility," Melody said, laughing. "I'm going to discuss it with Brice soon. If he's not willing yet for one of us to do something irreversible, I'll take pills. Regardless, two babies are enough for us. Enough for me." After a few seconds of silence, she said, "I'm ready to talk about this book," holding out *The Feminine Mystique* to Alice.

"You've already read it?" Alice said, surprised.

Melody nodded. "I couldn't go to sleep until early this morning because of the contractions and feeling jittery. So I read."

"What did you think?"

"I think she's probably correct that there are a lot of women of our mothers' age who are dissatisfied and don't know why. I only say that from inference, not from any intelligent questions I've ever asked Mother or any of her friends. But Friedan's description fits her to a tee. I don't know enough about psychology to know if she's right about blaming a lot of this on distortions of Freud's theories. The part about education treating women differently from men seems true to me, even now—forget about just when mother was growing up.

"And I was really stopped short by what she wrote about women's magazines and advertising emphasizing how women can feel important by being executives in the home. To think that part of the reason for that is to sell appliances and other products. That seems so. . .dishonest is the only word I can think of. But I guess it's naïve not to realize that advertising is a type of manipulation. Certainly makes me want to be more critical when I look at advertising. After I read that part, I got out a couple of magazines and really studied the ads. If you ask yourself what the underlying message is, it's easy to find examples of appeals to a woman's desire to be the perfect homemaker. Also quite a few indicate that the buyer will be more sexually attractive. Check out the hair product ads for that. Come to think of it, I'll probably go beyond critical to cynical.

"Aren't you sorry you gave me that book, I'm lecturing. There's more! I realized that I've probably 'bought' the 'housewife as executive' belief. Down deep, I know I feel that I'm better than Brice at doing anything related to cleaning, cooking, decorating, or child care. I'm sure I'm more efficient and that I do everything more thoroughly. No wonder I wear myself out. Somewhere I learned I'm really the best and at the same time, somewhere, he probably learned that's true. So we have perfect division of labor. I'm the perfect housewife-executive and do the all such work better than he does. He agrees. Therefore, he stands back and let's me do it. In fact, even when he tries to help I don't encourage him. Dumb, dumb, dumb! Tell me nurse, do you think I can be cured?"

Laughing, Alice said, "Maybe not cured, but possibly arrested like a case of tuberculosis."

"What did you think of the book, besides what you mentioned yesterday?" Melody asked.

"For one thing, I agree with you that she's described my mother and a lot of her friends. Who knows if she's correct about all the reasons? But even if her reasons aren't absolutely accurate, her recommendations make sense on their own. There'd surely be no harm and possibly lots of good to come from changing the expectations society has of girls. What bad could come from expecting a woman to become a person before she marries? I know lots of people our age who feel that in order to have a purpose, like a career, or want to develop a talent, like art, that they'd have to give up the idea of having marriage and a family. I also know a lot of girls here on campus whose primary goal is to find a husband before they graduate."

"I wonder if I'd read these ideas when I was eighteen it would have made a difference to me," Melody said. "Probably not. I was so sure that I wanted to be married right then. I was just as sure that I could go on to college after being married. I could have children. I could do it all. And I guess I can, but some days it's not easy. According to what she writes about housewife types, I'm closest to the balanced homemaker. I have some interests outside the home but want to do the housekeeping efficiently and perfectly. Primary target of the advertising manipulators." Suddenly she laughed. "It's good I'm an executive housewife. Otherwise I'd never be able to get it all done."

"It occurred to me after I read the book that if I were married now, I wouldn't be as free to decide about so many things I haven't tried out yet. Where to live, what kind of car to drive, the kind of food I like, what color I want my hair..." Alice stopped talking to watch Melody adjust the waistband of her maternity pants. "Are you okay?" Melody nodded in response.

"Seriously, it makes me even more certain that I'm not ready to be married." The look on Alice's face was a mixture of sadness and resolve.

"That doesn't surprise me. But you know, don't you, that no matter how long you wait to be married, you'll never know what you think or feel about everything. What I think is important is to have the confidence that what you think about anything is important—that your opinion, your desires could be important enough to be, well, selfish about. Like we were discussing with Aunt El a few weeks ago. I didn't know that before I married. And I wish I had. I'm having to learn it now, maybe a little late," Melody said.

They both stopped talking as a young man opened the door to the study room. "Oh, sorry. I thought this room was empty. You about through?" Alice smiled a bright smile in his direction. "No, we've just begun." Melody stifled a laugh as he left.

Still smiling her high-wattage smile, Alice said, "Enough about us. Let's talk about this last tape of Aunt El's.

"It sounded to me like she had increasing frustration as the number of nurses increased, as the Service grew and the number of programs they developed increased. Remember, she said all the indicators were positive but she was ambivalent. I wonder if that was because she was less and less able to be involved with doing direct nursing. I hear nurses today saying that as soon as they do a good job they are promoted away from the patient into management. They're ambivalent, too."

"But there's the possibility that having administrative authority makes it possible for you to set up systems, develop programs, help people develop so that the ones giving direct care can do a good job," Melody said.

"Sounds like you've thought about administrative work."

Melody nodded. "I have. I realize I have very little experience to base my ideas on. But I also think it's a mistake to promote excellent nurses away from direct care. They should be able to get better pay and recognition without losing the ability to do what they do best. At the same time those who have the ability and interest to develop programs and people and to lead should be encouraged to get additional education to do that, to do it in nursing. Some of those people who are excellent nurses might want to do administration, but not everyone should have to. In a way, promoting them may actually be punishing them. It's like saying, 'Do really well at this job and we'll reward you by giving you a different job you're not as good at, but we'll pay you better'. No wonder they're ambivalent."

"So how should they be rewarded?" Alice asked.

"For one thing, there could be a chance to get pay increases that are significant while still being a direct care nurse. Some system of promotion among staff that recognizes experience and excellence, not just time on the job. And it shouldn't be that the only way to get significantly more money or better schedules, like more weekends off, is to be a head nurse or some other type of manager," Melody said.

"What do you think about those graduate programs for clinical specialists?" Alice asked.

"They're rather new, so I don't know any more than what I've read. But I do think that having those clinical specialist jobs available as one form of possible advancement would be another way to improve care and reward nurses who do it. As far as I know, right now there aren't many jobs for clinical specialists that use their knowledge and still keep them in patient care. See, what is needed is well prepared, strong administrative nurses who would create jobs for those well prepared clinical specialists. So, both are needed," Melody said.

"Do you plan to go to graduate school?" Alice asked.

"I'm not sure yet. I need some real experience to find out what I'm best at. But I do know I'm good at organizing and at helping people work together."

"When Aunt El was talking about the medicine those nurses did, in Alaska and on the reservations, I thought about a program I read of at Colorado. It's a new thing. As part of a nursing Master's degree program they're teaching primary care pediatric medicine to nurses. They'll work with pediatricians. They say that these Nurse Practitioners, as they call them, will be able to care for about seventy percent of the types of patient problems that come to a pediatrician's office. They expect that because of their nursing knowledge, they'll be better at doing the preventive aspects of care than the doctors are. If they also took care of adults, that would have been the perfect type of special education for those Indian Service field nurses. Of course they'd also have to be able to drive a dogsled." Alice laughed.

"There's so much about nursing, about health care that has changed since the days Aunt El is remembering. Antibiotics, for example. Think of how much easier it would have been to treat trachoma if there'd been an antibiotic. Or tuberculosis. Can you imagine inducing pneumothorax in order to rest the lung! I know tuberculosis is still a problem, but antibiotics have made a big difference. At the same time, there's so much in nursing that's the same—teaching about prevention and treatment, encouraging people to see good health as a possibility, helping people in pain, working with parents to promote healthy child development." Melody stopped speaking, looking thoughtful.

"What?" Alice asked.

"I just realized that until we met Aunt El, I'd never really thought much about what I want to accomplish in nursing. I just knew I wanted to be a nurse. Figured it would come to me as I go along, what I want to do, I mean. And I don't want to make a lot of specific goals because that might cause me to miss opportunities that come up. But thinking about what I value in nursing and what would be important to make the best use of my personality and my skills is a good thing and one I've not done before. What about you? Had you thought about these ideas before?"

Alice shook her head. "Nope, never!"

HOME IS WHERE...

THE FRIENDLY FACE OF MY NEW TRAVELING clock, given to me by the Washington office staff, almost reproaches me saying every morning 'Tempus Fugit' as well as 9 a.m. What better Sunday achievement than to write a letter of thanks to them?

When I look at the gift card, all kinds of pleasant memories crowd through my mind. Glimpses of them waiting for the elevator, greetings at lunch, telephone conversations, jokes and arguments, agreement, disagreement and compromise, rewrites and the filing system, the long horizontal journeys and the open doors of the old Interior Office, the reverberating Dictaphones and creaking floors of the Tempo building, the vertical elevatorless excursions in the Hurley-Wright Building, the smooth expansive comfort of the present all holding the daily exchange and the occasional sharp recall of 'The Field' in that guarded look of 'Mebbe so' on the faces of visiting tribal counselors and their better halves. "Enough, Elinor. You've resigned and now you have the rest of your life to live," I scold myself.

I guess I actually decided in 1937, but didn't tender my resignation until Fall, 1938, effective with the end of the year. I made that decision carefully, and I don't regret it.

Nursing in the Indian Service had reached a point where new ideas could energize and move it forward. Numbers increased during my tenure from about 16 nurses to more than 600. Structure and policies were in place to support their practice. A new type of position was created for nurses with no public health experience in which they would receive intensive supervised experience for six months and an Experience Center was created to support that new type of position. If the USPHS at some time acquired responsibility for the Indian Service health care, these nurses would fit into that new arrangement. If that transfer continued to be blocked by Mr. Collier, this structure and these nurses would be the basis for continuing improvement within the Indian Service. I left it better than I found it.

My sister Faith urged my decision in two ways. She promised some financial support and she encouraged that I live near her daughter Faith who now has a daughter, Nancy. That cinched it.

After my resignation was announced, I did receive one plaintive letter that gave me pause. Looking at that letter now, I feel much as I did when I first received it; both a bit sad and very gratified.

The last paragraph is the one that tugs at me the most. "You have a much bigger family that needs you. I am one of that latter family and I can speak in assurance for myself and many others. Don't leave us hanging in mid-air. We want you who thinks of each of us as an individual person with an understanding interest that is humanly genuine and not someone else to whom we can only be part of the cold spokes in a wheel. Please!"

"What are you doing sister o'mine?" asks Alan cheerily as he enters the room.

"About to get maudlin, I'm afraid. Trying to write a thank you for this clock. I made the mistake of re-reading a few letters from some of the nurses," I say.

"Read some to me," he says.

I look at his face to see if the request is a joke, but it shows real interest. I read from one by a nurse in Muskogee. "This same mail brings to you, from all of us, your Oklahoma nurses, a gift which is quite insignificant compared with the real love and abundance of good wishes that accompanies it.

"If this could be an expression in each nurse's own words of her appreciation of all you mean to her—it would be not just a letter, but instead as many volumes of books as there are nurses in the Oklahoma Indian Service. It is much as Miss Meredith says, 'Miss Gregg is the Indian Service.' And it is true that you are the spirit of our Nursing Service.

"After all is said and done you have stood for all that is fine and true in and for our service, and the deepest affection and respect of the whole group reaches out wishing for you ever increasing joy and happiness in the years now directly ahead, those years which are the best in one's life."

I stop and look at Alan who is smiling in his dear, sweet way. "Read me another."

"Just one more and then we'll have dinner. This one is from a New York Indian nurse. 'I'm sure that every Indian Nurse that has ever come in contact with you feels the same as I, at least I hope they do. We have lost a very great friend, a great loss, that perhaps some of us shall never know just what you have done toward helping us establish ourselves after we have struggled through our training. With your wise and thoughtful guidance many of us have gone much farther than we would ever have had we not had your help.

"I have often marveled at your patience and your understanding when some of us made horrible mistakes. Did you chastise us? No! Merely showed us the right way and said, 'Try again'."

I skip to the end because there's a catch in my voice. "We shall miss you Elinor Gregg. You have been a brave and a faithful worker among my people, so don't go too far away." I keep my eyes on the letter as I fold it and return it to the stack. When I'm sure of my composure, I smile at Alan and say, "Harder to leave than I thought it would be. But I'm looking forward to moving West. It's difficult to say if Faith really thinks that her daughter needs some support there with the baby and John or if its just her way of taking care of me.

"Regardless, I'm eager for Santa Fe. When it's built, my house will sit on a place where I'll have room for small animals and a garden. I can spend as much time as I like outdoors. And I'll be just a short walk from Faith and John's door." Pausing, I think of just how I want to explain my earlier feelings. "Alan, I want to correct something. Earlier I said I was being maudlin. That's not the correct word. Grateful and probably undeserving are better descriptions. And thinking of that brought me near to tears. But, as you know, even emotion must give way to hunger. Shall I call in the children for dinner?"

"Even though I know you're eager to be in your own place when it's finished, I'm glad you're able to be here to help with the children while Eleanor's in California taking care of her mother. I'd be at sea without you," Alan says as we enter the dining room.

"I'm happy to be here as long as I'm needed. I've not spent enough time with these children because of my traveling. I'm enjoying them more than you can know. I intend to specialize in parenthood-by-proxy with all my nieces and nephews. Spoil them and then leave them for their parents to repair," I say, laughing.

"You can't kid me. I've watched you. You make a special connection with a child. You provide something a parent can't—an adult who takes them seriously and knows just the kind of encouragement they need," Alan says.

"Perhaps. But I think I'm the one benefiting in this situation. I've never had this kind of responsibility for managing a house with four children before. It's a learning experience for me. It's sure to come in handy at some point."

"Sunshine, you are such a silly girl. That moth is gone. It left through the crack in the floor and all your looking won't bring it back. I suppose you'd like to go tell Socrates about your adventure. You're such a flirt with all that wiggling and kissing his big face. Come here, we'll go over to see Portia and Charlotte and you can visit Socrates." I take the cocker pup in my arms and head down the aspen lined trail toward the center of the camp. Music wafts from the practice studio. Charlotte and Portia have operated the Perry-Mansfield Camp here in Steamboat Springs, Colorado since they founded it in 1913. The combination of drama, dance, horseback riding, tennis, swimming, music, and art are perfect to bring out the talents in the campers. All the girls must take different activities, not just concentrate on one. That balances their creative activities with outdoor exercise. As the camp nurse I tend mostly to bumps and bruises, headaches, stomach aches, cuts, slivers, colds, and fatigue. Most of the kids get overtired the first ten days. Nursing here seems tame compared to work on the reservations. No tuberculosis, no trachoma, no malnourished mothers with frail infants. I remind myself that the needs of these privileged girls are important to their development into responsible adults, even if nothing is life threatening.

"That Great Dane could snap you with one bite, but he loves all the attention," I tell Sunshine as we return to our cabin. She's a very comforting bundle of warmth in my arms.

I peer into the mirror on the back of the closet door. These new teeth will take a bit of getting used to. The appearance is fairly natural and the shape of my mouth isn't changed. Over a period of three weeks, back in Washington before I headed west, I sat in the dentist's chair at least a dozen times. It's fortunate that the gastric muscles take over the function of the teeth to some degree because I'm still not chewing as handily as with the 'originals.'

Sunshine and I averaged 500 miles a day and a total mileage of 2,050 miles on our way out. I kept it to about 50 m.p.h. until I struck Kansas when the roads were so straight and flat that I worked up to 60 and 65 without knowing it. The pup was much admired everywhere we stopped. A good traveling companion now, she'll be even better when she acquires a vocabulary!

The howling coyotes sing accompaniment tonight for the northern lights as they play ecstatically against the clear sky. Coming here was a good choice. The days have sped by. I can hardly believe it's already July 31, 1939. Concentrating on vitamins and exercise for these past two months has given me more pep. I'll need it when I get into setting up my new house in Santa Fe. John designed a simple, beautiful and functional house that is just perfect for me. The best part is the portal where I'll be able to sit outdoors in shade and shelter almost year round. Although I don't foresee much sitting with all the plans that crowd my list. As soon as I move in, I intend to build a goat pen and get some goats for milk. The milk should be good for Nancy. I may try my hand at cheese-making, too. And I'll buy or borrow a billy so there'll be kids in the spring. The ticking clock reminds me that I should try to sleep. A four-day horseback trip into the Yampa Canyon begins in the morning.

"I'd probably be a better foster mother for girls than for boys, don't you think?" I ask Faith and John.

"Aunt El, you'd do fine with either, but if you prefer to have girls, we'll make that our request. Boys for us and girls for you. None may actually come, but as long as we're making ourselves available to take in British children during this war, we may as well express our preference," Faith says. "But are you certain you want to do this? You know what a lot of work children can be. And you've only just begun to get some time for yourself after all those years of travel and of supervising so many people."

"I think it will be good for me and it's a way to help," I respond. I think without saying that it's time I help someone else, I've felt quite self-indulgent for the past several months. One major reason is that I have this wonderful house in a place I love. It feels like home in a way the O Street house in Washington never did. Maybe it's because I have more time to make it mine. I'm making a darkroom in one of the utility areas and I'm thinking of a greenhouse. Since I could never repay Faith for making it possible for me to be here, I can be certain I do some good for others.

Although the camp nursing was useful to others, even that seemed vacation-like compared to the Indian Service. An example of sheer indulgence—I treated myself to a trip with Marjorie through Navajo country and the Grand Canyon. Six days and 1600 miles. A mirage on the desert nearly sent her into ecstasy. Spending our nights in sleeping bags created an adventurous air. The eastern branch of the family will hear, in detail, of every mile of the trip, I'm sure. Nobody tells a story quite like sister Marj. We had the best time together than I can recall. We have seldom ever enjoyed one another's company for long stretches of time. It's not a matter of hostilities, just a difference in temperament. One or both of us must be improving because we both enjoyed her time here.

She went with me to begin my camp nursing job at Perry-Mansfield this year as she was on her way back to New Hampshire. On the way we visited Regina Dodge and her sister Carolyn Bailey near Denver. They've decided to build here in Santa Fe. So, there'll be more of the old Colorado Springs crowd within arms reach.

More indulgence. Alan and Eleanor's daughter, Nancy, was a P-M camper this year. A bit of pride, most inappropriate in an aunt, crept in as I heard her counselor report that Nancy was responsive and responsible with initiative and was a pace-maker in the group.

Thinking of camp, I ask Faith, "Did I tell you about the error I made in nursing care at camp?" We're sitting on the portal listening to one of the beautiful recordings Alan gave me for my birthday.

"No, what sort of mistake?" she says.

Struggling to stay serious-sounding, I begin the report. "One of the campers was feeling a bit low and came to me with a succession of complaints—finally with 'knots in her back', so I gave her a good massage with oil of wintergreen. The second night the knots were in a new place lower down. Again, I gave a massage, but this time I inadvertently rubbed her back with Sunshine's louse oil. It helped too." I laugh recalling my surprise when I realized my mistake. "When I reported it to Charlotte, she thought it was so funny she wrote a little poem about it. No one told the camper. Her health had improved. And she had no lice, either!"

"Welcome Stuart. Welcome Michael. I'm Elinor Gregg. Call me Aunt El. Was your train trip fun? I thought it would be an adventure for you to come on your own."

"Oh, yes ma'am. It was indeed, thank you. Is this Santa Fe?" Michael asks, eyes wide, as he looks around the train depot in Lamy.

"Oh, no. We're twenty miles from Santa Fe. But this is the nearest train depot. Let's get your baggage so we can start for home. The girls are eager to meet you. They wanted to come along, but I told them they'd just have to wait." I notice Michael, age nine, silently mouth the words 'girls, yuk' to his 14 year old brother Stuart. Just what I'd hoped. I know boys of Michael's age usually 'hate' girls.

Both boys are neat, clean, rather pale and clearly ready to be off the train after their trip from the east coast through Chicago and out to New Mexico. On the voyage from England to the U.S., they were accompanied by Pam Milligan, the daughter of a relative of their father. She and the four girls will arrive here before long. She plans to join her fiancé, Deric, here in the Southwest. It's definitely safer here than England now that the Germans have stepped up the war.

"Best laid plans," was my only response when we were informed that we'd receive four girls and two boys as our wartime charges. We quickly concluded that I would take the two boys and Faith and John and Nancy would welcome the girls. My ersatz sons and I complete the drive to Santa Fe in short order. Their heads turn eagerly, taking in the mountain scenery as we make our way uphill. Their silence is understandable. This looks little like their home in Stratford-upon-Avon. What are they thinking? I wonder. I'll know soon enough, I'm sure. For now, I'll just let them take it all in.

"Meet the girls," I say as Sunshine and Tiddler rush from the house to welcome our new housemates.

"These are the girls?" Michael says with delight as the dogs lick him with their version of a proper greeting.

"They are," I laugh. "Were you worried?"

They both nod and laugh as they absorb the sights. Their parents had written that Stuart has a mechanical mind, is ready for high school, and should be a help in looking after his brother Michael. The younger one was described as full of fun and very good at school with the ability to learn anything. The father hopes he'll become a doctor. He'd also hopes I might find bicycles for them.

I show them to their rooms and think, so far, so good!

"Tell me Elinor, how your life differs now from a year ago. The changes must be enormous for you," Carolyn says.

That's an understatement, I think. Carolyn Bailey and her sister, Regina Dodge, live near us. My visits are one of the afternoon diversions Carolyn arranges for her near-invalid sister. "We could count the ways," I respond with a laugh. "For example, in August, nineteen-forty, I had two dogs. The household, as of now, October, nineteen forty-one, includes forty-five rabbits, ten pigeons, nine dogs (six are puppies that arrived last night after I served as midwife to Tiddler for five hours), two goldfish, two tadpoles, one kitten, two boys and myself. Goats will join us soon. My main chore is to remember the feeding schedule.

"Being busy isn't different, because I enjoy having lots to do and will always find a project if free time weighs on me. And responsibility is not new to me. But parental responsibility is in a class of its own. You know, there's concern about who their friends are, where they are, whether they're learning how to become good men. Those are continuous concerns that a parent must have." I stop and laugh at myself. "Listen to me. Behaving as if I knew parenting inside out.

"I do think that the boys are in much better shape as to psychology this Fall. Needless to say, I see lots of chuck-holes that have filled in and though new patterns have new weak spots, still the gains are appreciable.

"My most difficult and yet enlightening situation was brought out by an X-ray of Stuart's chest. He began school with a miserable hay fever cold that ran down into his chest and sprung an asthmatic wheeze. After that cleared up I asked the M.D. for an X-ray, thinking there might be a spot or two on the chest that would account for the susceptibility to colds, general fatigue, and high pulse rate. The film showed a clear chest and a heart one and one-half inches smaller than it should be and very elongated. That explained the fatigue and inertia. Now I'm asking Alan's advice on managing the situation and his thoughts on next year's school situation. Of course, I've written his parents, also, but I haven't heard from them yet."

"Joys of parenthood. Has all this changed you?" Regina asks.

"Changed? I'm not sure. I certainly feel an additional sense of purpose. I also occasionally feel unsure I'm doing all the right things. But the four months at Alan and Eleanor's learning about running a family helped me enormously. I sucked up an awful lot more than I realized until I had to use it. I feel much more kin to all mamas and papas than I ever have before. Another two years of this and I'll become a quite possessive maiden Aunt, I fear," I answer.

"You think they'll be here two more years?"

"I don't expect the war in Europe to be over by nineteen forty-three. Do you?" When they both silently agree, I continue, "What a colossal stupidity it all seems. These people that must be hammering hard on other people in order to feel sure of their importance get me down."

Carolyn says in a serious tone, "I won't be surprised if the U.S. enters it soon. But, let's not talk more about war."

I agree. Almost any subject suits me better. "Do you want a puppy? There are six to choose from."

A crisp January day finds me knee deep in household duties. I stop to rest here on the portal and decide I'll list my day's activity. Faith may find it an interesting account in the letter I'll write her this evening. That is, if I don't fall asleep in my chair.

Santa Fe has thrown itself into the war effort since Pearl Harbor last month. There's Bundles for Britain in which our English children are enthusiastic participants. Community preparedness activities abound. We're encouraged to garden and raise small livestock for food, conserve fuel and collect scrap metal. Everyone seems to bend to their tasks with determination and industry. We all listen nightly to the radio for news of the war.

I also listen to *One Man's Family*. I've thought the Gregg family could provide plenty of material for a similar saga. The ingredients are all there—strong family ties, interesting characters, complicated intertwined plots. Faith Mary is the beautiful, wealthy matriarch who tends to the lives of her own seven children and her six siblings with equal enthusiasm and generosity.

Our elder brother, James, is the kindly minister who spent several years as president of Hampton Institute where he worked to help elevate Negro education. Donald, until his death two years ago from cancer, was a psychiatrist with a wealthy clientele in Massachusetts. Richard, educated as a lawyer, has traveled the world, is a passionate pacifist who has studied with Gandhi and who believes strongly in bio-dynamic farming. He's certain no one in the family really understands him but knows we all love him.

Alan would be one of the stars of the show, just as he is in the family. Like Donald, he's also a physician. But he works for the Rockefeller Foundation placing dollars into projects that can have broad results rather than practicing medicine directly. Alan is respected by all his siblings as a wise man, even though he's the youngest. And the family has not one, but two spinster sisters, as different from each other as night and day. (That's Marjorie True Gregg and her sister, yours truly.)

Quite a cast. But that's not all. There are spouses; four remaining since Faith's Farwell died in 1936. And children. Faith has seven, James four, and Alan four. Several children have spouses and children. *Radio Guide* would have to carry a family tree to accompany the program.

As for plot, there's never a lull. Someone has something going on at all times. For example, at the moment, Marjorie is working herself into a nervous state about, well, one never knows exactly. But, typical of her, she's involved totally and completely and utterly, body and soul in whatever concerns her. For the past several years, she's focused on religion. It's offered numerous opportunities for both elation and despair. Faith's last letter identified the object of Marjorie's current distress. It's her dog.

I smile as I think of how the children of The Reverend and Mrs. Gregg might entertain America. Even without transmission on the airwaves, they entertain me. They also give me strength and support.

The past three years run like a movie reel in my mind. The background music for the feature film sounds like the classical records that play constantly on my living room Capehart.

"This darkroom needs tidying up, Stuart. My, that's a beautiful photo of the dogs. Your technique with enlargements is far better than mine." I say.

"You're a good teacher," he replies as he begins the cleanup.

"Here's the broken radio I found at the second hand store. Michael, you and Harlow can use it for parts for what you're building."

"Great, thanks, Aunt El," Michael says.

"But if you want supper, you'll have to move it off the table and take it to your room. Be sure you put my pliers back in the cabinet when you're through," I remind him.

"Your nose is bloody and there's a bruise on your chin. Michael, are you all right?" I ask

"Oh, I'm fine, just a dust up on the way from school with some gang fellows," he replies calmly and perhaps a bit proudly.

I lift his chin to see if I agree with his assessment. No major damage apparent. "Well, then, clean up and see to your pigeons. Remember you promised the chef at La Fonda you'd deliver a half-dozen squab this afternoon."

"Stuart, if anyone should ask, just say you're sixteen-going-on-seventeen," I advise.

"But, should I be learning to drive before I have a license?" he asks.

"Definitely. Regardless, you couldn't get a license now at fifteen unless you lived on a ranch. Just go ahead now. You can do it," I urge as he squints down the street in every direction before accelerating. "Can you see that stop sign?" I ask.

"What sign?"

"Have you ever worn glasses?" I ask.

He shakes his head no, without looking at me. Concentrating, his hands are tight on the wheel and he's moving cautiously ahead.

"We'll get you to the eye doctor. Glasses will help you a lot," I assure him.

"Still hungry, Michael?" I ask.

"Yes, Aunt El. Could you make more tomato toast please?"

"Hold up a minute. Did you boys feed the animals?"

"Yes, Aunt El. We must go now or we'll be late for school," Michael says, always eager to get to his friends.

"Stuart, I'm going to get you some dancing lessons. Everyone should know how to dance. You may want to take a girl to a dance this year," I say.

"I don't think I'll be much good at it."

"Doesn't matter. You still need to know how."

"Michael, I'm sending you to boarding school next term because a boy of your age needs a male influence, not just your old maid aunt. That's what you'd be doing if you were home in England. Los Alamos isn't far away and you'll be coming home for holidays and some weekends."

The music stops and I'm back to the present in 1943. These boys have really gotten next to me. And now Stuart's ready to go, waiting for the train. I knew it would eventually happen, but I didn't realize I'd feel so attached. "I know you're aching to join the RAF, so you must go and try. But when you get to Canada, if the military doctors say there's any problem with your heart, just turn around and come back here," I tell him.

"I will. You'll hear from me, I promise," he says with a quick hug for me. Then he's on the train and gone. Seventeen seems so young.

"Well, Michael, it's just us now until you go to Dallas for school."

"Great fun," he says. A few miles pass. We both avoid speaking. As Santa Fe comes into view, Michael begins singing, "You are my sunshine, my only sunshine."

I join in, "You make me happy when skies are gray."

"Your parents will be so glad to see you. Your mother wrote in April that Stuart came home on a seven-day leave and they were both thrilled. Think of how happy they'll be that you're back for keeps." I'm busying myself straightening his tie.

He's frowning. "Perhaps, but I'll miss you terribly."

"And I'll miss you Michael. You Cooke boys have been a treasure for me," I assure him. And I think, "You've also been an education."

"Aunt El, would you hand me that mending basket? I'll stitch while we talk," Faith says. "I wonder how much longer this war will continue. It's been five years in Europe and nearly three since Pearl Harbor. It seems it will never end."

I nod. "Peace seems hard to come by." I'm watching Faith who is intent on her sewing. "It will certainly be peaceful here with the English children gone. Is Nancy missing the girls?" I ask. I think Faith also misses the busyness of the full house.

"Oh yes. And you? Is it too quiet without the boys and their friends?" she asks.

"Although I enjoy the time to myself, sometimes the quiet surprises me."

"Amazing how children adjust to changes. They all did seem to feel at home here," Faith says.

I nod. "Home can be wherever you feel loved."

DO SOME GOOD

"A STROKE OF GENIUS IS WHAT I'D CALL IT, Faith, when your Maternal Health Clinic group decided not to call itself a birth control clinic. You received valuable information and assistance from Margaret Sanger and the Planned Parenthood group when you started in nineteen thirty-seven. But, those people from New York didn't appreciate the differences between a small town like this with a largely Catholic population and New York City. Your choice recognized the facts of life in Santa Fe, not just the 'facts of life'." Faith was one of the founding members of the clinic. The Center is our topic of discussion because I recently agreed to be a member of the Center's Board.

"Aunt El, everyone is so happy you're going to be on the board. You have what we need; knowledge of how a clinic should operate, ability to teach volunteers to assist in clinic, and willingness to volunteer," she says.

"It's true I can do those things and I'll be pleased also to be clinic assistant for some sessions regularly. It'll keep me off the streets." I laugh. "There's one other way I think I can help."

What's that?" asks my niece.

"A lot of the women who are on the Board and other volunteers are what we called "Uplifters" in the Indian Service."

"Uplifters?"

"Yes, they are people with good intentions who believe their way of life is the best way. They wanted to change the values and customs of the Indians, or in this case, the Spanish American poor, to be like theirs. They truly believe that it's the only way to improve their lives—to uplift them. They don't understand or appreciate the first thing about any culture other than their own.

"This clinic serves proud people whose heritage is important to them. Most of them speak Spanish and have little money. They happen to have in common with us a desire for their children to be healthy. It's important that we respect them and that we deal with them in a way that shows that respect. I can try to help the volunteers know how to do that."

She nods her understanding. "Some of us are probably better suited to use our good intentions to raise funds for the clinic rather than make home visits, I agree."

Faith is such a good soul, never a harsh judgment. She wants to preserve good will among everyone. I hope my blunt ways won't prove an embarrassment for her.

"We've made good progress, I think," she continues. Three years ago when we opened, the Catholic Archbishop of Santa Fe told his flock, from the pulpit on Christmas Eve, they shouldn't have anything to do with us. He was sure we'd be making them all want birth control. Now, we have women bringing their children in for care. And we're making slow steps with getting more mothers to have some prenatal care.

"I may already have told you that one of the reasons we started the clinic was because we learned that Santa Fe County had the fifth highest infant death rate in the nation. There were one hundred and four infant deaths in every thousand live births."

I shake my head sadly and recall similar situations on some of the reservations. "Birth control information may be part of an answer to that.

But even if we never provide a single diaphragm or condom, we can be a source of care that can help the mothers and their babies stay healthy."

"I move that we empower the Cookie Sale Committee to select the bakery based on the price and quality." My motion is my first of the meeting but not likely the last.

A question, "Do you mean the committee will decide without coming back to the board?"

"Yes, this motion would allow them to decide so that they can move quickly before the next board meeting with plans for this fund raiser. I make the motion because I trust the committee's judgment," I say with a smile.

The questioner seconds the motion, to my surprise. The motion passes. Mentally, I dust my hands; another step in the direction of efficiency of operation. That's one of the reasons I think the Girl Scouts invited me to join their board. I volunteered to work with a troop soon after I got settled here in Santa Fe last year. They were very happy to have me. Right away they asked me to join the board. Moving them along is my specialty.

Last weekend our troop rode about six miles and had a cookout. We're the only mounted Troop around, as far as I know. Having that distinction gives the girls a bit of extra pride in the troop and a way to practice their horsemanship. Gives me a good excuse to be outdoors and to ride. The girls are not really any trouble. I treat them as if they had good sense and usually they do.

"Happy birthday to me, happy birthday to me, happy sixtieth birthday, old girl, happy birthday to me," I sing to myself, hitting and holding a high note at the end. There's a rainbow in my soul today and lightness in my step. I pause in my sashay around the kitchen. The portal calls me for a "sit down," an early morning celebration of this beautiful place. Coffee in hand, I let the dogs precede me. As they frolic, I breathe in deeply. There's a scent of pinion in the air, so strong it's almost a flavor.

As is my habit, I begin to construct a list for the day. The last item, "write Richard," holds my attention. Richard has had a hard year. The time had come, around the first of the year, that he had to decide what to do about his wife. She'd become progressively deteriorated, mentally, over the past couple of years. He was expending almost all of his energy either caring for her or worrying about her. All that plus attempting to maintain his teaching at Putney was almost enough to put him under. I went east in February to help.

My contributions were: a) to relieve Richard of the burden of asking other people to sit with her while he was away in the evening twice a week; b) to give him an understanding wink when the fantasy was too gorgeous; c) to stoke the furnace mid-morning, mid-afternoon, and mid-evening; d) to build Nonie a simple dress that he could force her into (she was stinking dirty); e) to begin to go over her things in the storeroom—17 trunks, boxes, and hampers; and f) to talk over the various strategies and tactics which he must evolve in order to get her to give him voluntary guardianship over her affairs and to get her into a sanitarium.

The hours and hours that we talked reminded me that I am far more pragmatic than he. Philosopher and gentle soul that he is, he had to come at his own pace to the difficult realization that she's getting worse and never will be better. He needed to talk through the issues of quality of care in the state sanatarium, decency, compassion, coercion, love, money, commitment, integrity, and I don't recall what all else.

One of the alternatives we discussed was his leaving his job and bringing her to Santa Fe so that I could help him care for her. He was much relieved to know that was a possibility. She's more cooperative with me than with him. She doesn't know exactly who he is any longer. Calls him "That man I sleep with."

I'm glad that my being there helped him move from thinking to action. I'm even gladder that he's now accomplished her move to a sanatorium and will be able to leave his teaching position. Now he can do what his heart tells him he should be doing-writing his book about non-violence.

The dogs return to notify me that it's feeding time. "Up and at 'em, Elinor. There are goats to milk and much good to do before this birthday's over."

"Aunt El, tell us what you've been doing since we've been gone. All we've talked about is us," Michael says. I've been here in England a week. Mr. and Mrs. Cooke have introduced me to all their friends as Michael and Stuart's Aunt El from Santa Fe. We've seen all the nearby sights and after the whirl of activity, I'm happy to be still, just talking with the boys. It's 1948 and the years have made a great difference. They're young men now.

"You recall that I was working with the Maternal Health Center when you were there. Well, I've continued that. I do home visiting, clinic assisting, and have continued as a board member. Those activities let me see the full spectrum. On the one end are the actual patients we serve, women and children with many health and social needs and little or no money. At the other end of the scale are the members of the board, who have money and social position and a desire to help in the community. It's a continuing education for me as well as a way to be useful. Sometimes it's also great fun. There are women on that Board who have the most interesting ideas about ways to raise money."

"Do you mean other than by contributing or asking others to donate?" Stuart asks.

"Oh, my, yes. Of course there's a regular appeal by mail to those who've contributed before. They receive the annual report and personal stories about some especially touching cases that have been helped. But besides that they have these interesting parties, teas, and dances as benefits. At one all the guests wore headdresses or hats that told a story or conveyed a theme. It became quite the costume affair. Uncle Sam, Miss Liberty, royalty in tiaras and top hats, a fruit basket—you name it, someone had it on their head. The proceeds from the tickets benefited the center; the newspaper covered the events with many movers and shakers of the town getting personal mention; and everyone had fun," I laugh, recalling it.

"It sounds as if you're very involved with the center," Stuart says.

"I get great satisfaction watching it grow and help so many. We got some young people from Scouts involved with another fund raising activity, Tag Day. Doing service of that sort can help them see how they can be working for the larger community when they become adults."

"What is Tag Day?" Michael asks.

"Adult volunteers and the Scouts are positioned at strategic intersections downtown, particularly near the Plaza. They have small printed tags that say 'I Support the Maternal Health Center of Santa Fe.' Each tag has a tiny piece of diaper pinned on it to make it noticeable. The volunteers ask each passerby to wear one of the tags. If the pedestrian agrees, the volunteer tells about the fund drive as she pins the tag on their lapel. Getting people all over town wearing these tags is the kickoff for the annual fund drive. The tags raise awareness in all segments of the city," I relate.

"Too bad, isn't it, that good works must at some level always be about money," Mrs. Cooke says, who has just entered the room as I was explaining.

"True. I'm just glad that there are some people with money who are willing to help those without. And I'm glad that there are those both with and without money who are willing to give their time and effort. Makes for an interesting mix and some lively times for me." I smile as I gratefully take the tea she offers.

"Summer, nineteen fifty, is nearly over. Santa Fe's been missing you and so have your friends," Carolyn says. "It's almost time for the symphony broadcast, but until then you must fill me in on your mission of mercy."

"Where to begin. You know that the reason I went to Ohio was to help Jim, my nephew. Since his father died in nineteen forty-six, we've been his next of kin. Jim's in the midst of an upheaval caused by a divorce. It's a messy, uncivil situation complicated by questionable lawyers and judges. I won't belabor the details of all that. But, the call for aid came from Mr. Merrill, a minister there in Portsmouth who wrote my sister Faith with a plea to convince me to come and help.

"Jim and his wife, Dell, have four children. During the divorce proceedings the children were living with Jim with regular visits to their mother. Now, here's the reason for the emergency. Mrs. Stillman, the father's helper he employs, took ill. Marie, that's her name, required immediate relief. Mr. Merrill's letter described her as being 'utterly worn with fatigue and nervous outpouring of herself.' Marie had decided that I would be perfect to take over while she had a furlough.

"I'd planned to go there in July to be with Jim and the children for a while anyway. Instead, off I went in late June."

"To the rescue!" Carolyn says, laughing.

"I'll get to that part of the tale in a minute. First, we need more strong tea."

Returning with tea, rum and ashtrays, I pause at the door. The late afternoon light casts a peaceful glow across the scene; portal in foreground, mountains in back. Sure beats Ohio, I think.

"When we left 'Our Gal Elinor,' she was journeying across country, responding to a call for aid." Carolyn mimics a radio announcer.

"You've listened to one too many soap operas, I'm afraid." I smile. "No surprise to me, when I arrived, Marie was in bed, issuing orders to Leona, the cook. Marie's plans were to stay in bed a week there and my plans were to move her out pronto. Luck was with me. She got a wire from friends in Tennessee saying they'd meet her in Nashville two days later at three p.m.

"I packed her clothes and Jim drove her to Cincinnati, leaving at five-thirty a.m. on the day she was to be there. I heaved a sigh of relief and set to work cleaning up the welter. She's a pack rat like myself. I recognize the species. Six cartons of stuff went to the attic before there was a space for my things."

"So there's a cook and the father. What was your special function?" Carolyn asks.

"Organizing and encouraging. Jim was befuddled by the whole situation. He was barely able to round himself up to get to work. He sleeps poorly and worries about everything. At sea and in a fog," I answer. "His relief was immediate when Marie left. After a few days he took some initiative about building a playhouse and getting a wading pool for the children. I think it's important for the children that they have some fun during the times with their father.

"The children are my greatest concern. Jim's an adult. He'd eventually figure out how to take care of himself. But, the acrimony of the divorce and the shuttling between parents can damage children. No one wants that to happen," I say.

"What was the situation when you left?" Carolyn asks.

"Marjorie came out in July. We got Jim to see a doctor; I met with one of the attorneys to get an objective view of what to expect in the suit, thinking I might help Jim plan for the possibilities; and I made several new friends in the neighborhood and in town. Without the nervousness and instability of Marie, the household settled down to a more regular routine. Then the divorce suit decision came down. July twentieth, I believe was the date. Immediately, the children were taken by their mother who gained custody.

"Now begins an appeal, not on the issue of custody, because Ohio seldom gives fathers custody, but on the basis of the money awards in the judge's order.

"Marj and I agreed that if need be we can take turns helping out there until things are more settled. We also agreed that my car needed a new engine before I trekked back out West. For the four days required to install the engine, I rested. My final mission was to pass through Nashville and visit Marie.

"In the two nights and one day that I stayed with her, I spoke to her like a 'Dutch Onkle.' She does have high blood pressure and angina pectoris and I know she had reason to be difficult to live with. But, with all the turmoil of the divorce and its effect on Jim, they don't need her there making it worse. I took the blame for her hurt feelings about our shipping her clothes to her. She'd felt 'kicked out-like a cur,' she told me. There's no way of knowing what she made of it all after I left, but I intended for her to know that for at least the next six months, she should stay away and take care of herself. Jim's family will help him.

"Then I got in the car, made a sharp right turn, headed west and here I am in the Land of Enchantment, once again. Just in time to start my term as president of the Maternal Health Center."

The second most beautiful month of the year in Santa Fe? I'll nominate September. Today is one of the reasons. Pleasant temperature, clear bright blue sky, shades of green in every direction, mountain guarding the entire scene, beautiful shadows in the long rays of fall sunlight. First place is reserved for October. All the same conditions will be present, double plus! Standing still, surveying my little corner of this scene, I'm smiling. The addition of this one-person apartment completes my territory. Renting the apartment when I'm gone so there will be someone to care for the plants and animals will work fine until the Ohio situation settles out. My greenhouse now sports its own water line. We buried it only 18 inches because the ground was so hard this summer—driest and hottest on record. We filled the trench above the line with sawdust to prevent freeze-up in the winter. I delight in having the greenhouse to start my plants. The dogs sniff suspiciously in the new apartment. They'll soon adjust and own it as they do the rest of the place.

I'm going to walk over to Faith's and show her these pictures I just finished developing. Carolyn and I visited the Lunts at their 4-O Ranch in Wheatland, Wyoming last month. These photos and the stone I selected are the loot I brought back from that journey.

"Aunt El, these are beautiful photos of this valley," Faith says.

"That valley runs north and south at the confluence of Sturgeon Creek and the North Laramie River. The week before we arrived a flood came down the river and brought with it a lot of debris from ranches thirty miles away. Fortunately all the heifers turned up. The greatest loss was the concrete dam for the swimming pool and the hired man's bunk house," I point to the next picture. "See, here, the cabin was lifted off its foundation and tossed high above the bank behind those two cottonwood trees. The hired man who is stone deaf heard the roar of the rising water and escaped with his life and his violin but left behind his rubber boots and false teeth. Amazingly, both were found in the mud as the water receded." I shake my head recalling the tale.

"And is this the main house?" she asks, pointing to another photo.

I nod. "Yes, it was filled with muddy water to a depth of about four inches. For two days, we scrubbed out dry silt. They'd shoveled out the first layer before we arrived so we did the polishing off. Enough exercise for two old workhorses. It was a good vacation. Carolyn needed the time away. She's worked hard taking care of Regina and I was ready for some relaxation, as well."

"Before you ask, yes, everything went fine at the center while you were gone. You've put so much of yourself into it, I know you think about it when you're gone," Faith says.

"I do. And I've been thinking that perhaps I should go off the board when my term as president is up next June."

"Oh, I hope not. You've made such a difference. Setting up the Policy Committee to establish written policies and revitalizing the Advisory Board were things that no one else had realized we needed to do. Your experience has kept us out of more than one disaster. That business with the nurse who fabricated reports; the issue of potential for malpractice concerns with the baby that was placed for foster care; and no one can communicate with the doctors on the level that you do. They'd never deal with lay people with the respect they show you. I know that being President is a big job. But when you complete your term, some of the load will lessen." Faith puts her hand on mine. "Don't make a final decision just yet, please."

"All right, I won't decide now," I reply. How could anyone refuse a request from that good, kind woman?

JULY 18, 1966—ALBUQUERQUE

"CAN YOU CHANGE OUR TIME TO WORK ON gerontology on Thursday from morning to afternoon? My parents are coming this afternoon on their way back down to Silver City. They'll stay here until around nine on Thursday morning. So, afternoon would be lots better for me," Melody says.

Alice looked at her friend and noted with satisfaction that her color was no longer pale and her eyes and smile were bright. "Are they going back to visit the aunt and uncle whose son died in Viet Nam?" Alice asked.

"Uh huh." Melody nodded. "Uncle Junior and Aunt Lou are having a very hard time. So much grief and anger. My parents are concerned they'll get sick. Aunt Lou's a diabetic and Junior had a heart attack about two years ago. So Mother and Dad are going to be with them for a few days."

"That's really kind of your parents."

"I think so too. It makes me proud they're my parents. Some people see a situation like that and send a card or make a condolence call. Probably would think that their daughter Shirley can take care of them. But Mother and Dad know that Shirley's got her own grief for her brother and they believe that having caring people beside you can help with the burden."

"To answer your question, sure we can change the time. Would Friday be better than Thursday afternoon?" Alice asked.

Glancing at her watch, Melody shook her head, "No, Thursday afternoon will be fine. Library at one okay with you?"

"Sure. Are you in a hurry right now?" Alice asked.

"I need to do some grocery shopping on the way home. Brice is going to pick up the baby early so we'll all be home when they get here. Why?"

"Nothing urgent. See you Thursday," Alice said. She watched Melody walk toward the parking area, moving as quickly as a pregnant woman could. Walking slowly Alice lectured herself silently, "Go on Alice. You've procrastinated long enough. Go directly to your mother's house, tell her, do not pass go, do not collect two hundred dollars." Chiding herself, she says, "It's time to tell her. In fact, it's past time."

You've done what!" Evelyn Fryer nearly shouted. Her eyes widened, then narrowed as her cheeks flushed. "I cannot believe you told Carlos you were delaying the wedding. I won't be one bit surprised if he breaks the engagement. What ever possessed you?"

Before Alice could answer, her mother continued, "No, don't try to explain. There's not a reason you could give that would make any sense. You've done some embarrassing things before, but this tops the list."

"Embarrassing?" Alice responded. "I'm not embarrassed."

"You should be. I certainly am. Everyone expects you to be setting a December date," her mother said.

"Who's everyone?"

"Don't do that!"

"Do what?"

"That. Arguing with me, picking at the words I use to avoid the point." Her mother stood up abruptly and walked away a few feet with her back to Alice.

Alice took a deep breath and moved around to face her mother. "I'll start again. I'm sorry that you're upset. And I'm sorry if you'll be embarrassed in front of your friends. But I thought carefully about this. I want to at least finish school before I get married."

"But you had it all planned, except for the date."

"Actually, I didn't have it all planned. You had made a lot of plans. I had never agreed to them."

Her mother dabbed at her eyes and sniffled. "So now it's all my fault?"

"Please don't cry. There's no fault. Nothing bad has happened. Just listen to me. It's important to me that you hear what I've been thinking. I'm not asking you to agree, but to try to understand."

The look on her mother's face said she was resisting, but she didn't speak. Alice plunged ahead. "Setting a date now makes it too soon and too definite. I've realized that I want to be certain I'm ready to make marriage my first priority whenever I do get married. I'm sure that I'll feel I missed too much if I settle down now. Or worse yet, I might not really know myself well enough to be a real partner in a marriage."

Her mother looked puzzled. "What can you possibly have missed? You've had every opportunity—camp, trips, all kinds of extracurricular activities in high school and the same in college. You're nearly through with your degree. Marriage is the next step."

"Next step toward what, Mother?"

Silence filled the space between them. Finally, her mother spoke, "Toward. . .well, being a grown woman."

"Getting married is one possible part of growing up. But mother, it's not the only part. And it's not necessarily what's next for me," Alice said quietly.

"Do you mean you might break the engagement?" her mother asked. She looked stricken at the thought.

"I don't know. I love Carlos, but I do know I'm not ready to have a wedding in December. And I may not be ready in June either. It wouldn't be fair to marry him if I'm not ready. One or both of us would be miserable," Alice spoke softly, hoping to keep the conversation calm.

"What will you do?"

Alice was tempted to ask, "What do you mean, what will I do?" But she knew that would start her mother crying again. She composed her thoughts, then said, "I'll live each day as it comes. I'll finish school. I'll find work. If it's right, I may marry then. If not, then I won't. I'll think about what I want to accomplish in my life. I'll be a good person. I'll live a good life, Mother."

"I don't understand."

"I guess you don't. But, I hope you'll just trust me. I know this is right for me." Neither spoke for what seemed to Alice several minutes. She noticed her mother studying her, as if she were a specimen of a strange species. "Can I ask you a question, Mother?"

Evelyn Fryer nodded, dabbing again at her eyes.

"Have you ever felt you married too young, that maybe you missed something?"

Her mother recoiled. "Is that what you think? That I regret marrying your father. That I don't love you children?"

"No, that's not what I mean. I've never doubted you love us all. What I mean is, have you ever wished you'd known more about yourself before you married, that it might have made a difference to you?"

"No, never," her mother responded, her lips in a tight, thin line. She'd stopped sniffling and dabbing.

"That's where we're different, Mother. I'm not sure. So, I'm going to try not to do what might be wrong for me. Try to see it from my point of view," Alice said.

"I don't understand," Evelyn repeated, shaking her head.

Alice tried to keep the sigh she felt in her chest from sounding in her voice, "Then think about this. You won't have all the worries of a wedding to plan before December. That should be a big relief."

"School's fine. No, actually, school's good. I'm taking a very interesting class in gerontology. Alice and I have a really interesting person we're interviewing. Really getting to know her." Melody sat and patted the place next to her on the couch. "Sit down here, Mother. Let's talk."

"Isn't there something I can help with? Dinner? Laundry?" Her mother glanced around the room. Melody wondered if she was looking for dust or cobwebs to whisk away.

"No, everything's fine. Do you mind if I ask you a question, a personal question?"

Her mother's focus turned to Melody. "What's the question?"

"Have you always been happy being married and having children? No, wait, that's not exactly my question," she said, trying to find the right words. "What I mean is, were there things you dreamed of doing but didn't because you had responsibilities for your family?"

Martha Colgate frowned at her daughter. "What makes you ask a question like that? Are you unhappy?"

Melody shook her head. "No, it's something I read that made me ask. It's about women being sort of programmed to put themselves in second place, behind the needs of husband and children. I'm interested in whether women I know feel that's what's happened in their lives."

"I've never given that any thought. And I'm not sure you should be either. Is that what college does for you? Makes you unhappy with your life?" she asked, a worried look on her face.

"Actually, this wasn't something I read for school. So, now that you do think about the question?" Melody prodded gently.

"I don't recall ever wanting to do anything but be married and have a family. I think I've done a good job as a wife and mother. I always felt I was fortunate not to have to have a job and that I could be a full-time homemaker. Being involved with you children, your school, church work, and helping friends when they need it have all been plenty for me to do along with running the house. Your father's always seemed happy with that arrangement. Said he liked having a full-time wife. So, I guess the answer to your question is no, I haven't missed out on anything I dreamed of."

Melody paused before venturing another question. "If you and Daddy disagree about something, do you discuss it, argue it out?"

"Melody, you lived in the house all your life. You know we don't disagree very often."

"But if you do?"

"I've never liked disagreements, the tension in the house. Don't you remember how I never let you kids argue?" her mother responded.

Melody nodded, thinking but not saying, "And I learned that's what a good wife does, by watching."

"Now I'll repeat my question to you, Melody. Are you and Brice getting along?"

"Most of the time." Melody looked directly at her mother as she answered.

"I don't want you to be unhappy. Pregnancy is difficult enough without other problems. Is school causing trouble between you?"

"Not really. I'm fine. We're fine." Knowing her mother really would rather not hear about unpleasant things, she changed the subject. "I'm glad you're able to go to Silver City and be with Aunt Lou and Uncle Junior. I feel sad for them"

"I hope we'll be able to help." Martha began scanning the room again. "Speaking of help, isn't there something we need to be doing? The men will be ready for supper soon. Just tell me what I can do to help you get it ready. Or is there some laundry that needs to be done?"

Melody put the baby in his bed, pulled up his light blanket and stepped across the hall to the bedroom where Brice was taking off his boots. She closed the door and began undressing. Speaking to Brice's reflection in the mirror, she said, "Brice, I've been thinking about something."

"What?" he asked without looking up.

"We need to decide about birth control," she said.

"A little late, isn't it?" Brice responded.

Melody laughed, thinking he was joking. "I mean after this baby's born. Two babies are plenty, don't you think?"

"Why are you bringing this up now?" His tone was no longer jocular.

Melody ignored the warning his tone conveyed. "It's been on my mind and I thought we should talk about it now instead of later. One reason is if I'm going to have a tubal, it could be done right after the baby's born." She tried to ignore the rapid pulse she felt at her throat. "Or if you have a vasectomy, it could be done and over with by the time the baby comes." She saw that he was staring hard at her. She turned to face him.

He muttered, "I don't know what's going on with you. Why are you so concerned about birth control anyway? If we need it, I'll use rubbers."

"Condoms don't seem to be too reliable for us. Do you mean you think we should have more children?" She tried to keep her expression bland.

"Maybe, maybe not. It'll depend on how I get along with starting my own business when I get my contractor's license. Who knows, you might actually want more children when you don't have to work," Brice said.

Melody stood still, quietly thinking about small steps. Brice stepped near to her and said in a lowered voice, "We're not going to discuss this now, especially with your parents in the house."

JULY 21, 1966—ALBUQUERQUE

"ANY MORE CONTRACTIONS?" ALICE'S ABRUPT greeting showed her concern.

"No, I'm fine. I'll be carrying this girl around until October. I took it easy for the last few days," Melody said. A smile crossed her lips, "Strike that. I took it easy, physically."

With a long look, Alice appraised her friend as she considered Melody's careful wording. Melody's color was good and her movements were lively. "Okay, I'll buy that." She knew Melody was taking her measure as well. She waited for the pronouncement.

"You, on the other hand, haven't had enough sleep lately," Melody stated. She saw the dark circles under Alice's eyes and noticed that her freckles seemed to stand out against a pale background. "Shall we talk about the tapes first or about life?" Melody playfully poked at Alice with an index finger.

Alice dodged, smiling. "The tapes, definitely. I don't know if I'm up to life yet. You first."

Melody nodded. "I'm looking forward to putting our report together. It's going to be a good report because we have the best subject. Have you thought about how we should present it, a paper or some other type of presentation?"

"I did. We should ask for class time for a presentation. That'll mean we have to have it ready for the last class day at the latest, but what we'll have will be worth people hearing, I think," Alice said.

"Good. I thought the same. We have photographs that we could turn into slides, also. We'll ace this. Thanks to Aunt El. This last tape answered a question for me. I was wondering what Aunt El did after she quit the Indian Service. I thought maybe she just quit being a nurse. Was I ever wrong! All the things she's remembering show that she didn't stop. She changed her focus. But she continued using her skills."

Alice nodded. "There are so many ways to use the knowledge that makes up nursing and administration. I was impressed by her ability to work with all kinds of people. Women at the Maternal Health Center, girls at the camp. By the way, I wonder if that camp's still in business. It sounds like the perfect summer job." A thoughtful expression settled on her face. "She's never said this in any of these tapes, but I noticed almost all the work she did was in situations where there was not much structure. She worked out what needed to be done to provide care rather than working where there were clear routines."

"What about all the bureaucratic government rules and routines?" Melody pointed out.

"Those were in place to operate the Indian Service not for actually providing nursing care. She's the one who developed the structure for care. At the camp, she was there to do whatever needed to be done. No structure, no routines. Then with her brother's wife—same thing. The real care she provided there was not only for the wife, but also for Richard, helping him decide on a course of action and helping him move on his decision. Gently."

"Now that you mention it, I see how her volunteer work used her administrative background. Remember, she said her specialty on the Girl Scout Board was 'moving things along'," Melody noted. "She recognized when structure and routine were necessary, though. For example, one of the first things she did as president of the Maternal Health Center Board was to set the policy committee to work." She paused to scan her notes.

"This is an entirely different topic, but have you noticed how close her family was, or is? Always ready to help one another and staying in touch with letters and visits. Their parents must have been proud of them."

Alice took a deep breath and put her head in her hands for a second. When she looked up, she said, "Speaking of parents, I have one who's not too proud of me right now."

"You told your mother?"

Alice rolled her eyes and nodded.

"What was her reaction?" Melody asked.

"Predictable. Upset. 'He may break the engagement. Why are you doing this?' But the best was 'This is so embarrassing.' Why should she be embarrassed if I'm not? Don't answer that. I know. She's been telling all her friends how hard she was going to work, how much of a strain she's under. Et cetera, ad nauseum," Alice said.

"Your mother speaks Latin?" Melody tried to lighten the mood.

It worked. Alice smiled. "It was pretty tense but she didn't have a hysterical fit or anything."

"Are you relieved that step is over with?"

"Yes, I dreaded it almost as much as telling Carlos. I'm glad I did it and got it over with, though. And I did learn something while I was there. I asked if she'd ever felt she missed anything by marrying when she did. Absolutely not. She seemed to take the question as an accusation. 'So you're saying this is my fault?' Maybe it was the wedding business that had her upset so she wouldn't answer any other way, but she denied any possibility that marrying young was in any way a problem," Alice said.

"How old was she when she was married?"

"Twenty. She'd been to college nearly two years. You should see the wedding pictures. It's no wonder she thinks I should have a big production. She had three attendants and a long white dress, even though it was during World War Two. She just kept saying to me 'I don't understand.' And, you know, I guess she doesn't. It occurred to me later that Friedan didn't say much about the effect that the war might have had on that generation as part of the reason for marrying early. She discussed that women went to work and then back home when the war was over and that many of them were dissatisfied by the return. But thinking about my mother, I wonder if some women of her age married young in wartime as a way of subconsciously expressing hope for the future."

"That's an interesting idea." She paused to consider it more. "When was it that you told your mother about the wedding delay?" Melody asked.

"I went there just after class on Tuesday."

"Is that what kept you from sleeping since then?" Melody asked.

"No."

"Well."

"I've been upset about something else," Alice said.

"Do you want to talk about it?"

Indecision showed in her expression. With a sigh, she began, "Carlos was supposed to come over for dinner and to watch TV last night. He called around three yesterday afternoon and said he had to study and wouldn't be able to come. I told him I'd already made his favorite, lasagna, so why not come and eat and then go and study. I knew something was up when he turned down home-cooked lasagna. Just couldn't take the time, he said. Really important exam. I tried not to be hurt, just let it go. After all, I did delay the wedding, putting a crimp in his plans.

"We talked about his classes for a couple of minutes and then he said, 'Oh, I nearly forgot, I won't be able to see you on Friday night. My brother's girlfriend's cousin's wedding is Saturday and one of her other cousins is here from Mexico. They want me to escort her to the rehearsal dinner.' All I said was 'Fine, see you Saturday or Sunday or whenever you can fit me in!' Then, I hung up. I thought he might call back, but he didn't."

"Did you believe him?"

"No. Well, I don't know. Some of it may be true. But the point is that he's trying to pay me back, I think. Or push me to be jealous enough to change my mind or. . .I don't know." Her mouth quivered as she spoke. After a deep breath, she said, "I had to laugh because I heard myself sounding just like my mother, saying 'I don't understand'."

"Do you intend to say or do anything?"

"If you mean throw his ring at him, no. But I do intend to try to get him to talk about all of this whenever he turns up. If he turns up."

"So, it's not true what they say"

"What's not true? Who are they?" Alice knew she was being kidded.

"People who say redheads are hot-tempered and impulsive," Melody said, smiling.

Smiling in return, Alice said, "You wouldn't think that if you saw my bedroom. When I got off the phone, I was so mad I threw everything on the floor and beat on the pillows. Bits of tissue are strewn everywhere I blew my nose while I was crying. I was upset. I just didn't tell him exactly how upset. Yet."

"Will it work?"

"Trying to make me jealous? Sure, he can make me jealous by dating someone else. But that's not the way to make me change my mind. He wouldn't respect me ever, if I changed my mind because I thought I might lose him," Alice answered.

"No wonder you haven't slept much."

"Part of the problem, with sleeping I mean, is that I was imagining how I'll feel this weekend when he escorts the cousin. I was making myself miserable about something that hasn't happened yet. When I realized what I was doing, I looked in the mirror and said, 'You're a pitiful old-fashioned female. Remember this, one of the hazards of making your own choices is that other people may not like it. And they may make some choices of their own!' The redhead in the mirror laughed at me. She didn't want to hear any more of my lame lecture, so we went to bed. And now I'm okay." Alice said as she straightened in her chair and gave Melody a look that challenged her to think otherwise.

"Wow! Growing up isn't easy is it?" Melody said.

"Not doing it this way. My mother said that getting married is the next step—to being a grown-up woman. If I hadn't known she was serious, I'd have laughed," Alice said with a delicate snort.

"We were both doing interviews, I guess. I asked my mother essentially the same question. The difference was that she wasn't upset about anything when I asked," Melody said.

"What was her answer?" Alice asked.

"Same, basically, but then she wanted to know if I was unhappy. Asked if this is what college did for me—got me upset with such ideas. I said no, one of my friends, not college, had started me thinking about this."

"You didn't! And if you did, you didn't mention my name!"

Laughing, Melody said, "No, I didn't. But that told me she's still not convinced education is right for a female—at least for me. Then she started looking for laundry to do."

"I guess all we can do is love them as they are, even if we don't want to be exactly like them. We're good people, so that means they did some things right for us, whether or not they always enjoyed it," Alice said.

"There are a lot of ways I'd want to be like my mother. That way of caring about people, enough to help them when they need it even if they don't ask, is something to aspire to," Melody said.

"You're right. There's a lot to admire about my mother too, but it's easy to forget when she's pushing me."

"Do you think we'll ever really understand each other—mothers and daughters, I mean?" Melody said.

Alice's answer was a shrug. Her thought was, I wonder if I'll ever understand myself.

JULY 28, 1966—SANTA FE

MUSIC IN THE BACKGROUND, CLASSICAL. MOZART? Vivaldi? Melody cocked her head, listened more intently. "That's beautiful. Do you listen to a lot of music, Aunt El?"

"Yes, although not as much as when I lived in my own place. I played records on the Capehart almost every day, classical mostly. Our mother loved music and exposed us to it often. I guess it took." All three listened a few minutes enjoying their tea and the music. Aunt El spoke as the piece finished. "I have a tape here for you. Am I correct, this won't be your last visit even though this is the last tape?"

"We plan to come back next week if that will work for you," Alice said.

"Oh yes, I'll look forward to it. I'd like to talk with you today about a couple of things." She laughed. "More modern topics rather than my ramblings. I want to talk about you."

"About us?

Elinor smiled at their surprise. "Why yes. That seems to surprise you. For example, I am interested in your thoughts about birth control, particularly the pill."

Alice replied first, "I have no religious beliefs that preclude the use of birth control.

So, there's no conflict for me on that basis. As an unmarried female, I haven't been confronted with the question of family size or spacing children as a family concern. But I know that women often have had more children than they have money or energy to care for because their husband or partner refused to use condoms. So, for that reason I think the pill is an excellent idea." She thought further before she continued. "I still haven't sorted out all my thoughts about sex outside of marriage. But I tend to think that believing that unmarried sex is sinful is behind a lot of very bad marriages. For unmarried people, the pill also puts women in a much better position to have control over their future. My mother would hide in embarrassment if she heard me say this. Young people's hormones do affect their behavior in ways that have little to do with love or with the basis for a stable marriage."

"Your mother would be embarrassed by that idea?" Aunt El asked.

"She'd be embarrassed that I'd say it. I think she'd like me to be able to swear I'd never have sex until I'm married. She'd surely want me not to say otherwise in public, no matter what I think. Or do. Something occurs to me now, for the first time."

"What?"

"That may be part of why she's so eager for me to marry," Alice said, with a wondering look.

Melody smiled and shook her head at Alice's expression. "Don't tell us you hadn't thought of that before. You can work on how to answer that truthfully while I give my honest opinion." Elinor laughed at the girls' teasing.

"Controversy surrounds the pill, I think, because it's a much simpler form of birth control to use. The woman takes more control of reproduction than ever before. It's a decision she can make and execute on her own. The logical extension that frightens some men may be that if women decide not to have children, or so many children, what will they be doing? Running for public office? Creating art and music? Succeeding at jobs?" Melody said.

"Are you thinking it will eliminate the 'barefoot and pregnant' life for poor women?" Elinor asked.

"I don't know. Women bear children for a lot of reasons. Some have the money to provide for several children and truly love motherhood. Others see children as a way to bind their men to them. Others truly believe controlling pregnancy is against God's plan. And there are others who may not believe that, but are too intimidated by their man to use a diaphragm or to demand he use condoms or abstain. Unfortunately there are also some women who are ignorant. They have no idea how their body works. If they knew, they might want to have some choice.

"It's dangerous to assume that all women, or all women of a particular religion or a particular culture have the same opinions and beliefs about childbearing and contraception. Or for that matter, that a particular woman has the same opinion throughout her life. People change, even change their beliefs based on their experience, or learning. When they are less ignorant, they may have a different opinion. Or they might reach a point where their man's opinion is not the only factor that affects their actions.

"I'll use myself as an example. I know that neither of you will discuss this with anyone else so I'm comfortable telling you. Until recently, I probably wouldn't have taken the pill if my husband didn't specifically agree. But I've decided that I will."

"Did you discuss it?" Alice asked.

"I tried. Brought up the general subject of birth control for after this baby's born. Not the pill in particular. I listed options, including vasectomy. I'd prefer a tubal. But his response was that if we need birth control, he'll use condoms. As far as he was concerned, that was enough discussion. My opinion is that while I'd have liked for us to agree, I tried. I'll take the pill," Melody emphasized her words with a firm nod.

Alice raised her eyebrows. "That sounds like a big step."

Melody smiled. "I think of it as a small step following several other small ones. Aunt El, let me explain what that means. After listening to some of your stories, we discussed that your style of accomplishing goals seems to be one of taking small steps, steadily, rather than taking impulsive leaps. We also heard clearly when you talked about the necessity of people placing themselves and their needs high on their priority list, making a commitment to themselves. We've both learned a great deal from you."

"I'm flattered to think I've helped you," Aunt El said quietly.

"It's interesting you'd bring up birth control because we had wondered about your opinions on the subject. You had very different experiences with the Indian Service and with the Maternal Health Center," Melody said.

Elinor nodded. "I believe women should have the ability to choose. But, like you, I think the choice has to be made in light of understanding the options fully. At the time I was in the Indian Service, there were fewer options. The nurses were ill-equipped. They had neither time nor information nor, for that matter, birth control devices to be able to offer informed choices. I suspected that informed choice was not part of the agenda.

"The Maternal Health Center is different. Although the culture and religion discourages many, there are women who understand the choices. The pill is a boon for women, for all the reasons you've mentioned. Maybe they will run for public office or perhaps they'll simply live healthier and happier without spending twenty years of their lives pregnant!"

The three of them shared a companionable silence for several minutes, enjoying the view from the window. Elinor spoke first, "Tell me about your ambitions. Will you run for public office?"

Both Melody and Alice laughed in surprise. Aunt El smiled gently. "Or do you have other plans?"

Melody said, "My first goal is to have this baby and finish school. I'm focused on the immediate, I suppose because pregnancy makes me think that way—a big event, a hurdle, new responsibility. But you may be asking what my ambition in nursing is. As for that, I want to first work at a basic position and gain experience; to feel really competent as a nurse. While I'm doing that, I intend to pay close attention to the things nurses say about their work situation. I've heard lots of nurses say they love nursing, but don't like their jobs. That must mean there's something that could be improved in the way work is organized or the way the nurses are dealt with as workers. Paying attention to that, sort of like taking field notes in anthropology, may help me decide the next step I want to take.

"I'd like to think I can fit my nursing and the other parts of my life together so that there's no conflict between my family and my work. That may not be a good explanation of what I mean." She thought a minute, then said, "I want to be able to put myself fully into both. Now that I'm saying this, I think that's my ambition. I'm glad you asked."

"Working, being married, and having children must be difficult for women unless they have a very supportive husband. I've often wondered how some women manage. I'm not certain I could have done it," Elinor said. "Is your husband supportive? More importantly, is he helpful to you?"

"I'm trying to learn to let him help. Or even to occasionally ask him to. But that's not easy for me. Somewhere in the back of my mind a voice tells me I should be able to do it all. Keep house. Care for the children. Succeed in school. If I don't cure myself of that, in five years I'll be completely exhausted and entirely without ambition!" Melody said.

"Don't let her kid you. She's Superwoman. Her organization and efficiency amaze me," Alice said. "But I think she's right that she'll wear herself out if she continues as she is. I'm glad I don't hear voices."

"What about you, Alice?" Elinor asked.

"My ambition is to have an interesting, adventurous life while doing some good."

Elinor pointed to Alice's left hand. "I notice you wear an engagement ring. What does the man you're marrying think of your ambition?"

Alice gave a sharp laugh. "I don't think that's what he has in mind. But, I'm not ready to give up on the idea or on him."

"Sounds like conflict brewing," Elinor said.

"Already boiling, I think. I hope he'll be able to understand," Alice said. "But, I'll be surprised if he does. There may be some difficult choices for me to make before long."

"Do you have an idea of the type of nursing you want to do?" Elinor asked.

"I think public health. Your stories make that sound exciting to me, the perfect opportunity for adventure in the line of duty."

Elinor nodded. "It certainly can be. But adventure is as much an attitude as a place. And Melody, administration can be challenging and rewarding. You're both far ahead of where I was at your age. I had to cast about for quite a while before I found what suited me best in nursing."

"We were interested in how you continued nursing after you left the Indian Service. Camp nursing, volunteer work, helping your family all benefited from your nursing skill," Melody said.

"I thought of it as simply doing what I could, being who I am. But you know, don't you, that if you're a good nurse, you're never not a nurse," Elinor smiled and her blue eyes twinkled.

MORTAL AFTER ALL

"YOU'RE THE NURSE, NOT I. BUT I'M CONCERNED that you could do some things to improve your health. Diet makes a tremendous difference, getting the correct minerals, and rest. Will you consider taking time to attend to your own health?" Richard asks.

"I will, Richard, I promise. But, the only answer may be a number." I tease him gently.

Puzzled, he says, "A number?"

"The number is seventy-three. That's my age, you know. That may be the source of my aches and pains. But, I will try what I can to improve things." I do understand his concern. We've had three deaths in the past two years. We lost our nephew, James Gregg, our brother, Alan, and then sister, Faith, this past year. Only Richard, Marjorie and I remain of the seven children of The Reverend and Mrs. Gregg. He doesn't want me to depart prematurely nor suffer infirmity.

I'd made that promise when Richard and his second wife Evelyn visited last month. The 'Duties of Office' (that's how I think of the activity of being President of the MHC Board again, for '58–'59) kept me from doing what I promised. But now I intend to sit still and take stock. If I do decide I need to see another doctor, this will have been a useful exercise.

I've always considered myself well and strong. Friends have said I have an indolent streak in my makeup. I don't worship efficiency, and I understand the value of the Fabian policy. But I can carry a heavy load of responsibility and work hard and long hours when necessary.

"You're packing light, Aunt El. Are you certain this will be enough?" Faith asks.

"Keeping up with luggage takes energy. I've learned a bit about conserving mine in the past few years. So, yes, this will be plenty and it will fit in two bags," I say. "I expect we'll do a bit of sightseeing, but most of my time in England will probably be spent visiting with the Cookes. So my wardrobe won't be much of an issue. Seeing Michael and Stuart and their families promises to be exciting. There are so many years to catch up on." I'm eager for this trip. Fourteen years have passed since I last saw England in 1948.

In line with my recent policy of saving my strength for the essentials, I accepted the airline's offer of a wheelchair for airport transit and assistance with luggage. Arriving now in comfort, I wonder why I carried my own bags for so many years. The Cookes wave from the arrival lounge. "Aunt El, over here! How was the flight? You look well. Shall we need a wheelchair for you? We can get one easily," They all talk at once.

"No, no I'm fine, just taking advantage of airline hospitality." I laugh. To prove it, I stand and depart the airport arm-in-arm with my boys.

Notes, copies of my Indian Service field reports, drafts of paragraphs, and odd scraps of paper cover every available surface. Another good reason to live alone, I think. No one else could tolerate this mess. It's the only way I know to do the writing. I have it spread out where I can see the pieces as they develop.

William Chenery and Nicholas Roosevelt, whom I met through Alan and Eleanor, encouraged me to develop a memoir of my days with the Indian service. I intended to call it *The Courage of Ignorance* based on my mother's rather acid assessment of my choice to go to Rosebud. I was persuaded otherwise. It will be called *The Indians and The Nurse*. Writing it seemed like a good idea; a way to honor the nurses of the Service and to do something productive. Now that I'm in the midst of it, I wonder. Some days all that seems right is the title. Getting the words right is not as simple as I'd imagined.

The unwelcome thought returns, "it's time". I turn it away firmly. I'll consider it only when I've finished the manuscript and found a publisher.

Faith and John first mentioned it some time back. "You should think about moving into the house with us. There's plenty of room for you to have your own space. We'd feel more secure with you nearby. Suppose you fell at your house. We might not know for hours or even longer."

"I understand why you'd say that. And I will think about it," I'd responded. I dislike the idea of being supervised and moving from my own house. But I know the time will come.

"Having you here will be a help for us. You'll be here to watch the house and take care of things when we travel. With Nancy and her family in California, we'd like being able to visit them without worrying," Faith suggests, knowing an appeal to usefulness will be the most effective with me.

"John, it's time. Get ready. I'm coming to stay." Those were some of the hardest words I've ever had to say. But I raise my chin and firm my resolve. It is time, because my legs and balance are often unreliable. I'm going to move over there beginning today. But I'm determined not to give up my car. Yet.

Today's the day I'm meeting the nursing students. They're coming to help me reminisce. I wonder what I have left to tell.

AUGUST 4, 1966—SANTA FE

"TERMINATION. THAT'S WHAT IT WAS CALLED IN the psych-mental health course. When you bring an end to a therapeutic relationship," Alice said, then deepened her voice, sounding as if she were quoting a text. "It should be explicit and to the extent possible, mutually agreed to by those involved." She turned in the seat to view Melody's profile. "I don't like the word and I like less the idea that our visits to Aunt El are over after today." Wearing a flowered skirt and a pale yellow blouse that complimented her red hair, she was dressed both for the summer day and for a festive event. "I hope she'll like this little tea party we're bringing."

Melody had also acknowledged the special day in choosing her attire. The white middy blouse with navy blue tie and navy maternity skirt were crisp and flattering. She'd put her dark hair in a braid and tied it with a white ribbon. She said with a slight frown, "Even though you terminate the original therapeutic purpose of the relationship, you can continue to be friends, can't you?" Melody was driving. They'd agreed her air-conditioned car was more comfortable even though it was a

1963 Ford, not nearly as sporty as Alice's Karmann. A careful driver, Melody maintained a steady speed five miles per hour below the posted limit. About ten miles north of the Albuquerque city limit, traffic thinned and her posture relaxed.

Alice said, "I've been thinking about this course. I expected to learn some things in gerontology about the elderly that might help me when I have older patients. For some reason, I had the idea that old people are different in some obvious ways from younger people—that at some specific age, say sixty-five, a person becomes old. I probably just felt it more than thought it, because, if you think about it, that makes no sense." After a pause, she continued, "Now it's clearer to me that aging is not an illness, it's simply a fact and each person ages in their own unique way. If you're alive, you age each day. I suppose the fact that at some point a person has predictable declines in strength or some sensory functions makes it important to know what those are." She wasn't yet clear about what was troubling her about aging and the words she'd said didn't satisfy her.

"You mean vision changes, hearing declines, hair loss, changes in blood vessel elasticity, reaction time changes, things like that?" Melody asked. "But there's so much individual variability in when and to what extent those happen it almost seems discriminatory to assume that at a particular age, they will be present—to lump them all together and call it old age, doesn't it?"

Alice nodded, "Listing all the physical declines typical of different older age groups can be depressing. If you think about inevitably just running down with lungs, kidneys, heart, blood vessels, senses, mental functions all sort of just fizzling out, you wonder it it's not better to die at fifty while you're still in good shape."

"Go out while you're at your peak, you mean?

"Uh huh, exactly."

"Well, if that's the case, we should have quit at about eighteen or twenty. That's nearer the physical peak. But we both know there are good reasons not to think that way. Aunt El is one example. It's possible for an older person to do so much good. Partly, that's because their age has given them experiences that in some people creates wisdom. She's taught me a lot. Things a younger person couldn't have. Every age has its job. At least that's what I understood from those developmental theory lectures," Melody said.

"I really don't know enough about other cultures to know, but I believe that some actually value aging, far more than we do. We seem to value children so highly. But we don't think of it as abnormal that a child has different abilities than an adult. We compensate by carrying them until they can walk, protecting them, teaching them. The same should be true with the changes that occur with aging, whenever they occur. The key for me is that a nurse's job is to help each person, whatever their age, achieve their best possible level of function. What's possible depends on a lot of things we have no ability to influence, like a person's genetic makeup. But we can help with the things that we can affect like environment, information, and even hope," Alice said.

"Do you think we can affect a person's hope?"

"Yes, definitely. I think hope is contagious." Alice smiled. "I catch it from you quite often."

"Do you? That's a really nice thing to say. I'd like to think I have that effect. But why would you need to get hope from me? You're an optimistic person."

"Usually, but I'm losing hope for Carlos and me."

A puzzled look crossed Melody's face. "Why? Did something happen?"

Voice strained and breaking as she spoke, Alice said, "I told myself I wasn't going to let this spoil today. But yes, some things have happened. He came by on Sunday afternoon and told me, among other things, that he was taking Valencia, the cousin's cousin, out again that night. Said he just wanted me to know so I wouldn't hear it first from someone else. He didn't even pretend that he had to take her out to be polite, just said he wanted to see her again. He wanted to see my reaction, I know. And hard as I tried, I couldn't help but react. Tears, storming around, and lots of words. Things I probably shouldn't have said." She shook her head sadly and sighed. "I called him self-centered and uncaring. Told him I knew he was trying to hurt me because of the delay of the wedding. I said he didn't have respect for me or anything important to me. He argued, denied everything and that made me even worse. I told him to leave and I offered him his ring back. I had it off my hand, ready to throw in his face."

"You're wearing the ring now," Melody said.

"That's what I'm the most upset about. Part of me wanted to hurt him like he was hurting me; throw the ring; never see him again. But another part wanted to hear him say that's not what he wanted; that he understands about the delay; and that he's sorry. I wanted him to say he wouldn't take her out. A tiny part even wanted to hear him say she was ugly and boring."

"Did he?"

"Say she was ugly and boring?" Alice managed a small laugh. "No. But he said he'd break the date. He's so charming when he wants to be. He took the ring from me and put it back on my finger, very gently. Kissed my fingertips and said, 'marry me, please'. Next thing I know, I'm in his arms, feeling—feeling like I wanted to stay there forever. We're kissing. Then we're on the couch. Then we're in the bedroom. I caught myself thinking, 'Are you using sex to hold onto him?' But one second later, I wasn't concerned about motives, mine or his. I did want to hold on and not let go. For a few hours, I felt wonderful. No thought about commitment to myself, about adventure, about independence. Just feeling wanted, loved and secure."

"But now?"

"But now. Well, actually, but then. The next morning. Carlos had stayed overnight. That was only the second time we've slept together, even though we've been engaged for months. We were waiting. Living apart made that easier." She fingered the ruffles at the neck of her blouse. "I'm not upset about what we did. We both wanted it. But I'm feeling that maybe that's all we both really want, that we got engaged for the wrong reason."

"What wrong reason?" Melody asked, her eyes on the road, her mind tumbling back four years to her own decision about marriage.

"Hormones."

"You don't think love has anything to do with your feelings?" Melody asked.

"I'm sure there's love between us, but I'm not sure either one of us is ready for marriage, for the real commitment that takes."

"How will you ever know?"

"Excellent question. I don't know the answer," Alice said softly.

Melody glanced at Alice, saw her staring at the Sandias, as if an answer might be etched on some craggy surface. "Did you tell Carlos any of this?"

"No, I thought I'd taken enough steps for a while. We've seen each other for a couple of hours each night. Everything's as it was. He said on Sunday night that we'd talk in December about setting a date and I agreed. That was before I realized on Monday morning that I have no idea what I'm doing!

Melody's silent nod betrayed only acceptance of her friend.

Several miles later Alice said in a steady voice, "There's a new women's group organizing on campus. Tuesday night's the first formal meeting although several people have been working on it for a month or two. I'm going to go. You want to?"

"What's the group's purpose?" Melody asked.

"Discussion of women's concerns. That's pretty vague, but it's definitely not a social sorority. One of the organizers mentioned that they'd consider studying problems of women at the University or maybe broader women's problems like affordable child care or health care for women. The main idea is for the members to identify the topics and decide what they want the group to accomplish for women. Might be interesting. What do you think?" Alice asked.

"It does sound interesting. But I can't. Getting out at night is almost impossible for me unless it's class related. And even then. . . ." Melody's voice trailed off.

"I'll go, and I can tell you about it. But if you can manage it, I'd like us to go together," Alice said.

Melody nodded. She knew she wouldn't go because she hadn't paved the way with Brice. His typically negative reaction to any night-time activity she attended could occasionally be minimized by telling him far in advance. Even then, an evening meeting or class often prompted hours or days of surliness. No, she thought, I'm too tired to deal with that now. But I'm not too tired to tell the truth. Her face solemn, she said, "You know, it's not the children, it's Brice."

Alice looked at her friend who appeared to be intent on her driving. "I know. You don't have to explain."

Attempts to manage Brice's reaction to any change in their routine had become almost automatic to Melody. The line of least resistance was to seldom vary her routine. Stay home or go out only with him or the baby. Sometimes, even taking the baby with her was not enough to allay his sullen response. The trip to Silver City showed her that. She'd realized then that she mentally balanced any action she might take against her estimate of his reaction. No, that's not correct, the estimate was of her willingness or ability to tolerate his reaction. The price of getting along. I wonder if my mother ever had to make choices like that, she thought. "Oops, I nearly missed the turn," she said aloud.

Alice opened a plastic container of finger sandwiches and another of assorted cookies. She took out the plates of food and set them on the coffee table near Elinor's chair. From the picnic basket she produced three glasses and a thermos of iced tea flavored with citrus. The orange and lemon slices lent a nice touch to the drinks she placed on flowered paper napkins.

"Alice, you set a fine table," Aunt El said. "A tea party is just right for today."

Both girls beamed at her pleasure with their surprise. "And I brought music," Melody said, as she inserted a tape in her portable recorder. Sounds of a string quartet filled the room.

"Ah, Vivaldi. Four Seasons. Perfect background music," Elinor said as she relaxed in her chair. "I suppose you might be wondering about my thoughts and feelings after all that reminiscing," she said.

"That's exactly what we were wondering," Melody said, "but I hesitated to ask because that's very personal. Tell us only if you want to."

Alice marveled at her friend's soft, kind manner and its effect—a relaxed smile on Aunt El's face.

"Recording the memories, I felt entirely different than when I wrote the book. That involved work, searching for the right words, editing my thoughts knowing they'd be read. Even though I knew you'd listen to the tapes, this somehow felt as if I were reliving the times. It wasn't work. I enjoyed every minute." Elinor paused and both girls waited respectfully.

"Each time I completed a tape, I found myself considering the person whose life I was reviewing, almost as if I were an observer, separate. I thought about the choices I'd made, about alternate possibilities. 'What would have happened if?' Not so much second-guessing and compiling regrets as toying with the outcomes," she said.

"Could you share an example of that?" Melody asked.

"I'm happy to. I no longer have any secrets from you," Aunt El laughed. "My mother would have been happy for me to stay with her after my father died. Taking the job on the Rosebud Reservation affected the rest of my life in a very different way than staying in Boston would have. Did I shirk a duty? Some might think so. But, as I said, I was not reviewing my life as a source of regrets. I asked myself only if my decisions were carefully made, not if they were right. Because I realize that unless a question of morality is involved, right is mostly a subjective judgment. What might have happened if I'd stayed? I'd have probably taken a job in a hospital or visiting nurse service in the Boston area. Think of it! I'd have missed the adventure of Rosebud, of the West!"

"Did you feel, looking back, that choosing adventure and an independent life was worth the security you might have missed?" Alice asked.

Nodding, Elinor said, "In a way, remembering reconfirmed that for me my choices were good ones. Selfishly, I can't see that having security when I was in my thirties or even later would have been worth what it would have cost in lost opportunities. I cannot imagine being a happy person if I'd felt myself chained to a domestic life. An example—as pleased as I was to have Michael and Stuart as my 'sons' for a while, I was happy to be free of the continuous responsibility when it was time for them to go. I think I did a good job as a parent for a few years, but I realize I'm better at caring for people in times of crisis or of need than as a permanent arrangement. While I continue to love those close to my heart and never discard them or ignore a need they might have, I enjoy my solitude." She paused a moment. At the pause in conversation, her poodles, Topsy and Turvy, raised their heads but did not move from their position near her feet. "Of course, the dogs are part of my solitude, not interruptions of it," she said with a laugh.

"Your description of your preference for solitude makes me wonder. Do you think you were always that way; is that an element of your personality? Or did you become that was as a result of your choices?" Alice asked.

"You ask a very penetrating question. I don't know the answer. I've never spent much effort on remaking myself, just worked with me as I am. Warts and all," Elinor added with a laugh.

Melody sat forward in her chair and said quietly, "You mentioned losses. Did reminiscing make you sad when losses came to mind?"

"Any sadness I felt was brief. Most of the important losses were the deaths of people I loved. Many years ago I chose to believe the soul is immortal. That belief tempers the grief those losses cause." She was silent in thought for a few moments. "If anything, the memories provided some balance."

"Balance?"

"Imagine a scale. Two pans attached to ends of a beam. Every day I wake up one day older, I'm reminded of losses. Hearing, mobility, energy, independence of action all decline as years pass. Those losses are present daily. They weigh in one pan. Visiting memories of the parts of life when no such deficits were present gives weight to the other side of the scale, the positive side. Your request to reminisce was really a gift. I might not have allowed myself the luxury of detailed visits to the past and have just stayed in the present, if you hadn't asked," Elinor said. "I noticed something else. The memories from the distant past had more color, more detail to them than those nearer to the present. I wondered about that. A plausible explanation finally presented itself."

"What's that?" Alice asked.

"Incidents more recent, fresher, haven't yet been assigned a degree of importance because I don't yet know what effects they may have. But those in the past that remain as memories are there because they are important. They are signals of life's journey, like the stones I've collected. They are assigned to stay with me, so are attached to sights, sounds, smells, and tastes so that they will remain. At least, that's my theory," Elinor answered.

"Would you mind if we include that in our paper about reminiscing? That seems more than plausible to me. Perhaps Professor Orr will can look further into that for her next course," Melody said.

"For whatever it's worth, feel free to use it. I know that you told me the facts of my stories are confidential and that only the process is related in your report. But you should use anything that you think is of value, including the facts. I want you to succeed and to benefit as much as I have from this project," Aunt El said. "Alice, these cookies are really good. And Melody, the music was beautiful. Thank you for bringing all of this."

Aunt El gave each of the girls a strong hug as they said their goodbyes. They turned to wave to her as they reached the car. Flanked by her two dogs, she waved from the doorway, her smile radiant. Pausing before she opened the car door, Melody stooped. She picked up two stones and handed one to Alice. Neither spoke as they drove toward Albuquerque.

AUGUST 11 AND 12, 1966—ALBUQUERQUE

"Come on in. I'll be ready in just a few minutes. This hair needs taming before I'm fit for public viewing," Alice called from the bathroom. "You're so smart. Making an appointment for us with Professor Orr; writing an outline of the points for the paper. We'll get her reaction to our ideas for the presentation tomorrow. I'm excited about that."

Melody stood behind her in the bathroom doorway. "I don't see any of Carlos' things here. I take it he's not a permanent occupant."

"No, but it's not for lack of hints on his part. I can see the wheels turning in his mind, thinking he'll save money, or we'll save money if he moves in. But as far as I'm concerned, nothing has changed. I'm not ready to share my space." Alice stopped fussing with her hair and tucked her shirttail into her slacks. "I take that back. Something has changed. He saw the Peace Corps materials on my desk night before last. I didn't have time for his interrogation about that. In the middle of my getting ready to go to the women's group meeting, he started asking all kinds of questions about why I had those brochures. He said very little when I told him that I was getting information in order to know all the possibilities. 'You know I can't join the Peace Corps now,' he said. I had to bite my tongue to keep from saying I hadn't asked him to. Instead I said nothing. He changed the subject; talked about his American Government seminar. I told him I'd fill him in later and held the door open so he'd leave when I did. Even if it was accidental, I'm glad he saw them."

Alice circled the bedroom, picking up clothes and stacking books. "The women's group may turn out to be interesting. There were about thirty people there, some really smart women with a lot of ideas for topics and projects. We're lucky to be in nursing where most students are female. Some of them are treated badly in other schools; medical school, law school, graduate school. There's a lot of favoritism for men—in grades and assignments. And some told of outright abuse like being ridiculed by teachers and male students."

"What can the group do to change that?"

"We don't know. But nothing changes unless people are aware. That's the first step. Anyway, I intend to be part of the group. You'd be a big help if you joined. A person with your skill of organizing could help develop a focus for the work," Alice said.

"I thought more about it since last week. After the baby's born, in the fall, I'll be ready to get involved," Melody said.

"Evening's the only time people can meet. What about Brice?" Alice asked.

"I'll tackle that when the time comes. Ready to go?"

"Your outline and summary address each of the parts of the project assignment," Professor Orr said after she read the material quickly. "Combining tape-recording with personal visits to your subject is something no one else in the class has done. Very creative. With the outline and report you've just given me, I am comfortable giving the grade of A."

"Do you mean even without our presentation?" Melody asked.

That's exactly what I mean. I hope you'll still want to make a presentation, even though your grade is assured."

The girls looked briefly at one another, silently agreed and said almost in unison, "Oh, we do. We want some class time tomorrow to do the presentation, just as we had planned." Alice rose, then Melody. "Thank you, Professor Orr, for your time and for the good news. We'll go now to finish getting ready for tomorrow. See you in class," Alice said with a smile and a tiny wave.

"Thanks again," Melody added.

"Wow! That was a nice surprise," Melody said. The continued walking, nearing the library. "Do you have a portable tape recorder—so we could have two to use tomorrow?"

"Yes, why?" Alice asked as they entered the study room.

"I have a couple of ideas. Since we don't have to address every item on the list of project criteria—having our grade already aced, we can be a little more creative. We can focus the presentation on what we learned; about aging and reminiscing. We can be more artistic about how we do it," Melody answered.

"How do the tape recorders fit in?"

"On one we could play music, softly, the kind Aunt El enjoyed during our last visit, in the background as we do the presentation. If we work fast, we can get several pieces of music and put them on one tape. We've got a player and recorder I can use at home. In fact, I can ask Brice to do the recording if I get the music. He likes making tapes." Melody said.

"Okay, that's a good idea. You'll get that together?" Alice had begun making notes. "And I already had slides made of the photos she gave us when I had our copies made and I got one we took last month, with her and her dogs. We can use the classroom projector to show those. Put them up for a few minutes each, with the last one staying on while we finish the rest of the "show." This is great—the music and the pictures will be the background, setting the mood." Alice smiled, enjoying the excitement of finding ways to step outside the usual boundaries of student presentation.

"How about if I operate the equipment, and you do the talking?" Melody said.

"Are you sure that's what you want? You're a good speaker," Alice said.

"It'll run smoother if we divide it that way, I think. Now, all we have to do is decide what we'll tell. There's so much. Where to begin?" She stared into space for a bit. Alice made more notes. Melody spoke, "Oh, here's the other idea, the other tape player. We make another tape and put part of Aunt El's actual tapes on it. We could begin with her voice, as she started the first tape, then end with that cute part on the last one where she says she's meeting us and then she laughs. I love that laugh."

"That's a great idea, but you're going to be working all night to get that and the music put together."

"No, it'll be fun."

"If we can just get the key ideas down, I can write what I'll say from there and then we can split up. We'll do a quick run-through at noon tomorrow just before class. Okay?" Alice asked. Melody nodded, and Alice continued, "What did we learn about aging and reminiscence and how will it affect our practice?"

Melody looked into the same space she'd stared at before and began to speak, as if reading, "Aging is a natural part of life, not an illness. Every person does it in their own way, at their own rate. Nurses can help aging people compensate for sensory and ability changes by treating them as valued individuals and encouraging others to do the same. Helping people see the positive aspects of their past and current lives, their wisdom and experience, can balance the losses created by physical declines. Reminiscing is one way to help people appreciate those positives in their lives. That can benefit them as they do life review. And speaking of life review, it may be pronounced in the elderly, but we experienced some life review ourselves, as a result of thinking about the stories Aunt El told. So, I'd say life review is something everyone does, particularly if they are the least inclined to be introspective.

"Encouraging reminiscing is something a nurse can easily incorporate into the care she gives. The only requirements are to invite the person to recall the stories and to listen attentively, without judgment."

"You've really given this some thought. I'm impressed," Alice said. "And I agree with everything you've said."

"I learned that nursing is a career that truly is yours for life. Hearing Aunt El's stories, I learned that nursing has opportunity for adventure and excitement if you love that or for security if that's your preference.

"I learned that a woman can live a life that is full and satisfying without it fitting the traditional domestic pattern. Those things I learned by being open to the influence of an older person, by listening carefully to her reminiscence and applying lessons from those stories," Alice said.

Melody added, "I learned the benefit of solving problems one step at a time, about valuing others as unique humans and how that affects one's ability to lead, and the importance of having a commitment to oneself as a way of keeping the well from running dry."

Both of them fell silent. They looked at one another and broke into broad smiles.

Alice said, "Yes, this will be good. Even if no one else in the class appreciates it, putting this together helps me—helps me, you know, put it together." She laughed.

MAY 1, 1970

DEAR ALICE,

It's hard to believe that it's been three years since we graduated and since we've seen each other. Our days together in school, especially the summer of 1966, are so clear to me still that I sometimes expect to turn around and find you near.

First, I will tell you the sad news. As you can see from the enclosed clipping, Aunt El died just over a month ago. She was nearly 84. I had visited her once each year since we spent the summer in her company. The last time I saw her was in July last year. I felt then that she was preparing to leave. Her eyes still twinkled, but she was ill and becoming infirm. The Meems had a nurse to help her, and it was hard for her to tolerate. I know she hated losing her independence.

She always asked about you, and she had kept the postcard you sent from Guatemala. She enjoyed knowing you were having adventures. She was interested in my work and family and always seemed glad of my visits. I will miss her. Thinking of her being gone makes me cry even now.

The other enclosure is a recent photo of Brice, Jr. and little Elinor. Speaking of her, I took her to visit Aunt El, so she could know her namesake. And I intend to tell her Aunt El's stories when she's a little older. Perhaps she'll learn from them, too.

Brice's construction business is successful. He has a reputation for good work and has plenty of jobs to bid on. I've noticed he's become more self-assured and is less possessive of me, a welcome change. I'm occasionally tempted to be the perfect homemaker, but Ms. Friedan's book sits on the shelf as a silent reminder of the trap of the "mystique." When I feel the urge to "do it all," I ask Brice to watch the kids while I take a walk. Being outdoors helps me find some balance. I also have a woman come in to help with cleaning twice a month.

Brice and I share the child-ferrying responsibility, although that was not an easy situation to arrange. I had to remind myself not to take the path of least resistance (doing all the taking and picking up at child care myself). It's not unreasonable to expect we could each take part of that responsibility. Thinking that way and acting on it were small victories over my tendency to make life easy for Brice regardless of my preferences. I doubt that Brice is changing because of anything I'm doing. Instead, I think we're both appreciating each other and the life we are making together and are relaxing. We seem to be holding less to the unspoken "ideal married life" we learned in our own families and developing our own version. It's not always smooth, but it's seldom dull. I know I'm continuing to learn.

And on that subject, I've learned I'm good at supervision. My job at the Public Health Department is a treat. I enjoy the patients and the responsibility for five employees on my team. I was promoted after one year to the supervisory position. Public Health is definitely where I belong. Even though progress with patients is sometimes slow or non-existent, on the occasions when there is progress, I feel so good. An example is the fact that the immunization rate in the district I'm responsible for is now 82% of all eligible children under age 6. Compare that with 50% or less as the state average. The work it took to accomplish that was just the type that Aunt El demonstrated—persistent, small steps, never giving up on the goal. The whole team was recognized with a plaque at the state public health association meeting for that achievement.

The Director has agreed to help me work out a flexible schedule so I can attend graduate school when Elinor begins pre-school. I'll major in community health nursing. Although we had a couple of "intense discussions" about why I need more education ("You've got a good job with the degree you have. Why do you need more?"), Brice now understands that this is the next step for me. I've started a special savings account to help with expenses and I'll apply for a Federal Traineeship stipend.

Although I could go on—at length—I'll stop now to read to the children before bed. Or maybe I'll tell them a story about you, my red-haired friend, and the summer we grew up together.

Write soon.

Love,

Melody

JUNE 20, 1970

DEAR MELODY,

Your letter found me after making a couple of side trips. I am working with the Migrant Health Project in the San Luis Valley this summer. I am based here in Denver where the letter finally arrived after two forwardings by the Postal Service.

Two years in the Peace Corps were wonderful. You probably recall from earlier letters that I lived in Guatemala. I learned so much! I thought about serving a second two-year tour, but decided instead to get more education. I'll be able to do more good when I have more skills.

Last fall I entered the graduate program at the School of Nursing at the University of Colorado. Our classes are here in Denver at the medical center. I'll complete the program with a Master's Degree in nursing and will be a Nurse Practitioner. I hope to work for the USPHS on one of the Indian reservations after graduation. I don't care which reservation, but would prefer somewhere in the Southwest. My Spanish is pretty good now. Maybe I could learn Navajo, too. After working long enough to pay my college debts, I hope to return to school for a doctorate in Cultural Anthropology. Of course, I'm taking my steps one at a time. So who knows where next year actually will find me!

Thank you for the picture of your children. They are beautiful. Brice, Jr. with his missing front teeth is such a grown-up six year old and his sister Elinor looks just like you. Speaking of children, my mother forwarded a birth announcement from Carlos and Valencia not long ago. This is their second child, Carlos, Jr. There was no note in the announcement, but I imagine he is settled in his practice and proud of his family. I'm happy for him, for them, even if his wife is boring (that's a joke).

The obituary for Aunt El that you included brought tears. I wanted to think she'd live forever. But then I realized she will. She's with us both and with so many others. We can pass her spirit along.

I think of you often and hope to see you soon. If you ever need a friend to talk to or need any help, I'm at the end of the phone line. My mother will always know my number. Please do keep in touch.

Love,

Alice

P.S. In the picture I've enclosed, you'll notice a pouch in my right hand. It holds the stones I'm collecting—one for every journey.

REFERENCES

THIS SECTION CITES SOURCES FROM WHICH significant facts were drawn or from which specific segments were quoted. As often as was practicable, Elinor Gregg's own words, from letters and reports, were quoted in the context of conversation in this book. The purpose was to convey her "voice" as accurately as possible. Items cited here are not duplicated in the listing in the Resources section that follows.

I SAID I WOULD GO

p.13 "When…sorry." E. D. Gregg (interview, 1963) by John and Peg Rose, England.

p.13 "We struck wet … and came." "… by train and stage…of the pile." "… can see … and the sky." "quite sure…to have one." E. D. Gregg letter to Alice Bemis, November 15, 1922. From the Alice Bemis Thompson letter collection. K. Thompson, South Tamworth, NH.

p.14 "…like a typical "hard scrabble"…and scraped." Elinor Delight Gregg collection, Santa Fe, NM.

p.17–19 "Pa Brown…I believe him." unpublished draft manuscript pages by Elinor Gregg (nd, unnumbered) E.D. Gregg Collection Santa Fe, NM.

p.21 "A bald man…he signs them." unpublished draft manuscript pages by Elinor Gregg (nd, unnumbered) E.D. Gregg Collection Santa Fe, NM.

THE ONLY ONE

p.34 "Miss Gregg…during the war." County correspondence by our steady writers. (1922, 16 November). *Todd County Tribune*, p.1.

IN HIS MIND'S EYE

p.42 "See what you can…education." Gregg, E.D. (1965). *The Indians and the nurse*. Norman, OK: University of Oklahoma Press, p.7.

p.43 "The time has come….many things." Carroll, L. (1988 printing). *Alice in wonderland and through the looking glass*. United States: Grosset & Dunlap, p.197.

p.47 "According to the circular. . .Special Classes." Qualifications, responsibilities and duties of field matrons. Ed-Health Circular January 5, 1922 RG 75, BIA, Circulars 1904–1934.

p.48 "The message was…every good woman should know." Gregg, E.D. (1965). Op. cit. p.19.

p.28 "standpatters" Board of Indian Commissioners. (1922). *Fifty-third annual report of the Board of Indian Commissioners to the Secretary of the Interior*. Washington, DC: Government Printing Office, p.5.

WITH TIME TO SPARE

p.58 "scratching the ground". Hamilton, H.W., & Hamilton, J.T. (1971). *The Sioux of the Rosebud*. Norman, OK: University of Oklahoma Press, p.16.

JUNE 16, 1966—ALBUQUERQUE

p. 66 "Did you know…all over the world." Decades of service. Internet *www.peacecorpss.gov/images/history.html* Accessed 5/29/03.

WE CARRIED ON

p.63 "We had crossed…deck cabins." From the notebook of Mary Lathrop Wright, May, 1917 Schlesinger Library Carrie M. Hall Collection 79-M23 F.1-7 Hall, Carrie 23:4:3, Folder 3.

p. 64 "After disembarking…against the Germans." Letter from Carrie Hall to My Dear People June 6, 1917. Schlesinger Library Carrie M. Hall Collection MC 275 C Letters to Family May 1917-December 1917 Folder 3.

p. 65 "No sooner…keep warm." From the notebook of Mary Lathrop Wright, May, 1917 Schlesinger Library Carrie M. Hall Collection 79-M23 F 1-7 Hall, Carrie 23:4:3 Folder 3 p. 8.

p. 66 "The hospital's usual…bed-sacks" Letter from The Commanding Officer to Surgeon General, U.S. Army June 9, 1917 National Archives, College Park, MD RG 120 Records of the AEF WWI Base Hospital #5 File Historical Data-Base Hospital 5 Box 210.

p. 66 "We ran out…dressing." A Member of the Unit (1919) The Story of U.S. Army Base Hospital No. 5 Cambridge: The University Press p. 37.

p. 67 "The hospitals of…series of hospitals." Hatch, J. Philip (Ed)(1920). Concerning Base Hospital No. 5 Boston: Barta Press p. 17 Francis Countway Library of Medicine Harvard Medical Library Boston, MA.

p. 67–68 "Two phrases we all learned…away by evacuation." ibid. p. 17.

p. 68 "In the language…sick." Hospital Order #161 U.S. Army Base Hospital No.5 November 1,1918 RG 120 Records of the AEF WWI Base Hospital #5 Box 212 Hospital Orders 1918 #1-174 NM 92 Entry 2130.

p. 69 "Our work ran…interrupted." Hospital #10 U.S. Army Base Hospital No. June 3,1917 RG 120 Records of the AEF WWI Base Hospital #5 Box 212 Hospital Orders 1917 #1-96 NM 92 Entry 2130.

p. 69 "In June…numbers" Member of the Unit, op. cit. p.42.

p. 70 "At the end…group." ibid. p.39.

p. 70 "We hadn't…rats." ibid. p.39.

p. 70 "On August 1…rain." ibid. p.45.

p. 70 "By the end…casualties." Hatch, op. cit. p. 22.

p. 71 "I wanted to capture…shanks mare." Letter to Alan Gregg from Elinor, August 29, 1917 Alan Gregg Papers MSC 190 History of Medicine, National Library of Medicine Box 4.

p. 71–72 "since we'd arrived…just happened." Member of the Unit op. cit. p.46-47.

p. 73 "A few days later…sleep peacefully." Letter to My Dear Sara E.P. from Carrie Hall September 14, 1917 Carrie Hall Collection op. cit.

p. 73–74 "Alan had wanted…Cabot in charge." Letter to Dr. Penfield from Elinor D. Gregg, n.d.(?1952). Elinor D. Gregg Collection, Santa Fe, NM.

p.74–75 "I was night supervisor…amusing and dreadful at the same time." Letter to parents from Elinor D. Gregg reprinted in "Springs Girl Relates Exciting Experiences in U.S. Hospital in France" *The Evening Telegraph* (Colorado Springs) February 27, 1918 p.4.

p. 75 "The undercurrent…for the Allies" Member of the Unit op. cit. p 27; Hatch op. cit. p.48–49.

p. 76 "Before we'd received…flour came from." Letter to My dear folks at home from Carrie Hall November 7, 1917. Carrie Hall Collection op. cit.

p. 76–77 "By Saturday…here as workmen. Letter to Hospital Supply Service, American Red Cross, 20 Rue Troyon, Paris, France from Robt. Patterson December 19, 1917 National Archives, College Park, MD. RG 120 Records of the AEF WWI Base Hospital #5 Historical Data Box 210 ; Letter to Dear Folks at home from Carrie Hall, November 7, 1917 op. cit.

p. 77 "November seemed to be…too often." Letter to Dr. Penfield from Elinor D. Gregg op. cit.

p. 77 "Later in the month…diet." Letter to My dear Lilla from Carrie Hall December 2, 1917 Carrie Hall Collection op. cit.

p. 78 "No sooner…billeted." Return of the Nurse Corps for the month ending December 31, 1917 RG 120 AEF WWI Returns, Nurse Corps Box 210.

p. 78–79 "I was secure…in our mess." Hatch, Op. cit. p.28–29; Member of the Unit, op. cit. p.55–56.

p. 79 "In addition…accommodation." Diary of Mary Lathrop Wright op. cit.

p. 79 "That day…not mentioned." Letter to Dr. Penfield from Elinor D. Gregg op. cit.

p. 80 "But all this changed…in some of the wards." Hatch op. cit. p 29; Member of the Unit op. cit. p.59–62.

FOR THE DURATION

p. 81–83 "I left…I thought." Letter to Dearest Barbara (Mrs. Donald Gregg) from Elinor D. Gregg 1918 Elinor D. Gregg Collection Santa Fe, NM.

p. 83 "Since returning…distribute it." Hatch op. cit. p. 28.

p. 83 "As if…shell shock." Medical War Diary Base Hospital No. 5 RG 120 AEF WWI Base Hospital No. 5 Box 210.

p. 84 "Members…in the finals." Vanguard Vol. 1 #6 p 109.

p. 84 "Shortly after its resurgence…men's hut." Member of the Unit op. cit. p. 65.

p. 84 "In mid-July…our south." Hatch op. cit. p. 32–33.

p.84–85 "We had air raids…the worst." Medical War Diary op. cit.

p. 85–86 "In August…away with the goods." Letter to Dearest Alice (Forbes) from Elinor D. Gregg September 9, 1918 Elinor D. Gregg Collection Santa Fe, NM and Alice Thompson Collection South Tamworth, NH.

p. 87 "On September 25…cared for." Member of the Unit op. cit. p. 67.

p. 87–88 "For eighteen days. . .no need." Hatch, op. cit. p.46–52.

p. 88 "By October 14…Varennes." RG 120 Records of AEF WWI Box 1318 NM 92 Entry 2129 Special Orders #438 14 Oct., 1918.

p. 88–91 “Before being transferred…even more impressed.” RG 120 Records of AEF WWI Evacuation Hospital #18 Box 750 File-Historical Report.

p. 90 “The officers and nurses…Infantry.” ibid. p. 5.

p. 91 “I got back…same leave.” RG 120 Box 212 NM92 Entry 213 Special Orders 1919 #1-120 BH 5.

p. 91 “From the 17th…in the hospital.” RG 120 Box 212 Return of the Nurse Corps for month ending Jan 31,1919 RG 120 AEFWWI Returns, Nurse Corps Box 210.

p. 91 “We received orders…aboard the S.S. George Washington.” RG 120 BH 5 box 211 NM 92 Entry 213 Rosters-Personnel.

p. 91 “I reported…Boston.” Army Nurse Corps—Personal Orders Document of Elinor D. Gregg E.D. Gregg Collection, Santa Fe, NM.

INCURSION INTO BLACK PIPE

p. 97 “The Masonic Order…associated.” Letter from J. McGregor to Charles H. Burke, Commissioner of Indian Affairs Dec. 7, 1922 RG 75 CP Commissioners Chronological File 1921–1928 10/1/1921 -12/31/1922 folder 11/1/1922-12/31/1922.

p. 98 “Somehow I. . .proud of.” *Todd County Tribune* December 7, 1922 p.1.

p. 99 “Do you have. . .do next.” Gregg, E.D. (1965) op. cit. p. 22.

p. 100 “According to. . .Instruction.” Qualification, responsibilities and duties of field matrons Ed-Health Circular, January 5, 1922 RG 75, BIA, Circulars 1904–1934 National Archives.

p. 102 “As we’re getting. . .lived in Carter.” *Todd County Tribune* op. cit. p.1

p. 105 “We’ve just finished. . .serum arrives.” Gregg, E. D. op. cit. p.23

p. 105 “like Miss Stoll. . .MUD.” Report for December 1922, National Archives, College Park, MD. Record Group 200, American National Red Cross, 1917–1934. File 509.21 South Dakota Public Health Nursing, Rosebud Indian Reservation, Box 571.

A NEW LINE OF WORK

p. 106 “I thought her father…cry.” Report for December 1922, National Archives, College Park, MD. Record Group 200, American National Red Cross, 1917-1934. File 509.21 South Dakota Public Health Nursing, Rosebud Indian Reservation, Box 571.

p. 106 “to go to…coming home.” Report for December 1922, National Archives, College Park, MD. Record Group 200, American National Red Cross, 1917–1934. File 509.21 South Dakota Public Health Nursing, Rosebud Indian Reservation, Box 571.

p. 107 "detribalized…self-disciplined." Archuleta, M.L.,B. Child, & K. Lomawaima. (2000). Away from home: American Indian boarding school experiences. Phoenix, AZ: Heard Museum, p. 56.

p. 110 "Improving their nutrition…on budgets." Report for January 1923. Rosebud Reservation. Record Group 200, American National Red Cross, 1917-1934. File 509.21 South Dakota Public Health Nursing, Rosebud Indian Reservation, Box 571.

p. 110 "It will also mean a special…oil." ibid.

p. 110–111 "These students rarely…meals." ibid.

p. 111 "Only a couple of weeks…recognition by name." Report for March 1923. Boston University Special Collections. Mugar Memorial Library, Boston University, Boston, MA. Elinor D. Gregg Papers N25, Box 1, Folder 1.

p. 111 "I examine them…breathing" Gregg, E.D. (1965). *The Indians and the nurse*. Norman, OK: University of Oklahoma Press, p.14.

p. 112 "Having examined…quite plainly." Report for January 1923. Rosebud Reservation. op. cit.

p. 112–113 "It's not uncommon…dining room" County correspondence by our steady writers. (April 12, 1923) *Todd County Tribune*, p.1.

p. 113 "I'll try …talks on diet." Report for March 1923. Boston University Department of Special Collections Elinor D. Gregg Papers N25, Box 1, Folder 1.

p. 114–115 "One time Richard…corduroy pants." E. D. Gregg interview with John and Margaret (Peg) Rose, 1963.

p. 115 "I've seen so many…if I saw one." Report for January 1923. Rosebud Reservation op. cit.

p. 115 "They all imitate…do too." Report for January 1923. Rosebud Reservation op. cit.

p. 116 "Poor posture is due…Feminism." Report for January 1923. Rosebud Reservation. op. cit.

PACKED TO THE FLAPS

p. 121 "So early in April…people." Elinor D. Gregg letter to Miss Clara D. Noyes, Red Cross Headquarters, April 2, 1919. Hazel Braugh Records Center, American Red Cross, Falls Church, VA. Elinor Delight Gregg File.

p. 122 "Circuit Chautauqua…summer school." Miller, M.H. (1963). Chautauqua and the Wisconsin idea. *Wisconsin Academy of Sciences, Arts and Letters*, 52, 159.

p. 123 "In less than a month…perfect." Gregg, E.D.(1965). *The Indians and the nurse.* op. cit. p.4.
p. 124 "Sometimes when…success overseas." Staff. (August 17, 1919). "New England girls start on tour of the nation." *Boston Sunday Herald*, CXLVI(48) p.D10.
p. 124 "Proceeding… by the strength of its people." Staff. (1919, 15 August). "Red Cross nurse is coming here. *Gresham* [Nebraska] *Gazette*, (25) 18, p.8.
p. 125 "Wives and mothers…ill members." Staff. (August 15, 1919). "Red Cross nurse is coming here". *Gresham* [Nebraska] *Gazette*, (25) 18, p.8.
p. 125–126 "As a troubadour…sold to anyone except myself." Gregg, E.D.(1965) op.cit., p.5.

MY STAR DAY

p. 127 "I've never…mad horse." Gregg, E.D(1965) op. cit. p.24.
p. 128 "As soon as I utter…known for sure." Gregg, E.D. interview with John and Margaret (Peg) Rose, 1963.
p. 130 "Back at The Agency…this is our first meeting." Report for February 1923. Record Group 200. American National Red Cross 1917–1934. File 509.21 South Dakota Public Health Nursing, Rosebud Indian Reservation, Box 571.
p. 130–131 "Last month…accomplished nothing." Report for January 1923. Record Group 200. American National Red Cross 1917–1934. File 509.21 South Dakota Public Health Nursing, Rosebud Indian Reservation, Box 571.
p. 132 "organizing…lines." Gregg, E.D. (1965). *The Indians and the nurse.* op.cit, p.28.
p. 132 "too many emergencies…away." Gregg, E.D. (1965). ibid.
p. 132 "During Miss McArdle's…ideas." Report for February 1923. Record Group 200, American National Red Cross, 1917–1934. File 509.21 South Dakota Public Health Nursing, Rosebud Indian Reservation, Box 571.
p. 132 "I had put…lots of pep." Report for November 15th-30th, 1922. Record Group 200, American National Red Cross, 1917–1934. File 509.21 South Dakota Public Health Nursing, Rosebud Indian Reservation, Box 571.
P133–134 "I've been…overcome." Report for March 1923. E.D. Gregg Papers. Boston University Department of Special Collections. N 25, Box 1, Folder 1.
p. 134 "A variety…midnight." Report for February 1923 op. cit.

p. 135 "I have the usual green-carpet…War Department quick!." Report for February 1923. Record Group 200, American National Red Cross, 1917–1934. File 509.21 South Dakota Public Health Nursing, Rosebud Indian Reservation, Box 571.

p. 136 "I'm in Okreek…occasion." Report for February 1923. op. cit.

p. 136 "I have put…being printed in Dakota." Report for March 1923. E.D. Gregg Papers. Boston University Department of Special Collections. N 25, Box 1, Folder 1.

p. 136–137 "An awkward division…mentioned." Report for February 1923. op. cit.

p. 137–138 "In the midst…pan out." Report for March 1923. E.D. Gregg Papers. op. cit.

p. 138 "To leave…tomorrow." Report for February 1923. op. cit.

p. 138 "They have such a talent…as well." Report for March 1923. op. cit.

p. 138 "I may flatter myself…Indian." Report for March 1923. E.D. Gregg Papers. op. cit.

MORE THAN I CAN CHEW

p. 142 "Somehow I've missed. . .basketball going on." Report for March 1923. op. cit.

p. 143 "There are…well kept." Report on Pine Ridge Indian Reservation, S.D. by Ellen C. McArdle Nursing Field Representative October, 1922 RG 75 Records of the Bureau of Indian Affairs Rosebud Indian Agency Rosebud, South Dakota Subject Correspondence 1910–1925 M through J.A. Rennick Box a-434 HM: 1990 folder Red Cross.

p. 143–144 "Today and March will be gone…fewer cliques." Report for March 1923. op. cit.

p. 144 "Inaccurate as some…mass grave." Biolsi, T. (1992) *Organizing the Lakota*. Tucson: University of Arizona Press p.23.

p. 144–145 "My public health…around Boston." Personal Communication-Letter from Elaine Hubbard, Ed.D. Chairman, Dept. of Nursing Simmons College Boston, MA to Edwina McConnell June 5, 1973.

p. 145 "Perhaps I have been…officially." Report for April 1923. RG 200 ANRC 509.21 South Dakota Public Health Nursing Rosebud Indian Reservation Box 571.

p. 145 "There are two…which it lives." ibid.

p. 146 "I am somewhat…to build on." Report for March 1923 op. cit.

p. 147 "I am beginning…involves expenditure." Report for April 1923 op. cit.

p. 148 "In making sanitary…will suffer." ibid.

p. 148–149 "There is a territory…so much smaller." Report for March 1923. op. cit.

p. 149–150 "I find on Pine Ridge…infection of TB glands." Report for April 1923 op. cit.

p. 150 "He retorted…just won't take it." Letter from Henry Tidwell to Charles H. Burke, Commissioner May 28, 1923 RG 75 Records of BIA Pine Ridge Agency South Dakota General Records Main Decimal File 660 through 700 Box 658 Folder 660.

p. 150–151 "The children were very cunning…surgeries tomorrow." Report for May 1923 RG 200 ANRC 509.21 South Dakota Public health Nursing Rosebud Indian Reservation Box 571.

p. 151 "I'm trying to keep…energy." ibid.

p. 151 "Me and my Ford…same moment." ibid.

p. 151 "As of this week…for my work." County correspondence by our steady writers. *Todd County Tribune* June 14, 1923.

p. 151 "I have a visitor…both reservations." County correspondence by our steady writers. *Todd County Tribune* June 28, 1923.

p. 152 "Runs Reckless…he tells me." Letter from J. McGregor to John B. Payne July 2, 1923 RG 200 ANRC 1917–1934 509.21 South Dakota Public Health Nursing Rosebud Indian Reservation Box 571.

p. 152–153 "Mr. McGregor and I…pre-school children." Report for July 1923 RG 200 ANRC 1917-1934 509.21 South Dakota Public Health Nursing Rosebud Indian Reservation Box 571.

p. 153–154 "Today was a typical…Ford is almost human." Report for August 1923 RG 200 ANRC 1917–1934 509.21 South Dakota Public Health Nursing Rosebud Indian Reservation Box 571.

WHAT'S TIME WHEN YOU CONSIDER ETERNITY?

p. 155 "Since Helen…Child Welfare Bureau." County correspondence by our steady writers. *Todd County Tribune* September 27,1923; October 18, 1923.

p. 156–157 "Helen is joking…Hills land." County correspondence by our steady writers *Todd County Tribune* October 14, 1923.

p. 157–158 "He wrote it…sense of humor." Letter to Dearest Alan from Father January 8, 1922 Alan Gregg Papers, MS C 190, in the History of Medicine Division, National Library of Medicine Box 2 Father to A.G. 1921–22.

p. 158 "The next year's plan…everyone's concern." An analysis of first year of work to establish a public health nursing service on Rosebud Reservation.

RG 200 ANRC 509.21 South Dakota Public Health Nursing Rosebud Indian Reservation Box 571.

p. 158–159 "The Red Cross chapter…in development comes along." Report of October, 1923 RG 200 ANRC 1917-1934 509.21 South Dakota Public Health Nursing Rosebud Indian Reservation Box 571.

p. 160 "The government…when you consider eternity?" Report of October, 1923 op. cit.

p. 160 "My new Ford coupe…as they are concerned." Report of November, 1923 RG 200 ANRC 1917–1934 509.21 South Dakota Public Health Nursing Rosebud Indian Reservation Box 571.

p. 161 "I laughed aloud today…I wonder?" County correspondence by our steady writers. *Todd County Tribune* December 20, 1923; February 2, 1924.

p. 161–162 "Though it was a bit bold…he promises." Letter from J. McGregor to The Commissioner of Indian Affairs April 3, 1924 RG 75 Records of Bureau of Indian Affairs Rosebud Indian Agency SD Commissioner's file Chronological 1921–1927 1-1-1924-2-28-1925 Box 550 Folder 3-1-1924-4-30-1924.

p. 162–163 "All of March…cirrhosis of the liver." Report of March, 1924 RG 200 ANRC 509.21 1917-1934 South Dakota Public Health Nursing Rosebud Indian Reservation Box 571.

p. 163 "This kitten…aim for 147." Letter to Dearest Mother from Elinor Gregg June 24, 1924 E.D. Gregg Collection Santa Fe, NM.

p. 163 "On the trip back…potato for days." Report of May, 1924 E.D. Gregg Collection Santa Fe, NM.

p. 164 "I know you read…facilities for care." Report of May, 1924 op. cit.

p. 164 "but without a more…gets the glory." Report of June, 1924 Boston University Dept. Of Special Collections E.D. Gregg Papers N 25 Box 1 Folder 1.

THIS IS THE BERRIES

p. 177 "The first step…earliest convenience." Letter from Commissioner Charles Burke to Miss Elinor Delight Gregg July 9, 1924 Boston University Dept. of Special Collections E.D. Gregg Papers N-25 Box 5 Folder 20.

p. 179 "One thing…unbearable." Letter to Dear Mother from Elinor August 12, 1924 E.D. Gregg Collection Santa Fe, NM.

p. 179 "This is the berries…good fun when I do." Letter to Dear Alan and Eleanor (nd) Alan Gregg Papers, MS C 190, in the History of Medicine Division, National Library of Medicine Box 2 Elinor D. Gregg Folder.

p. 179 "The itinerary…perhaps on whim." Letter to Dear Mother August 12,1924 op. cit.

p. 179–180 "The Sioux Health…to Rosebud." Letter to Commissioner Burke from Peairs, Stevens, McGregor and Gregg August 23, 1924 BIA National Archive 48282-24 Rosebud F32 104635-1920-F32 to 48927-1914-733 Box 571 PI 163E121 HM 1998.

p. 180 "your earnest…appreciated." Letter from Inspection to Elinor D. Gregg August 1, 1924 RG 75 1924-032 Special Agent Files Box 36 #72314.

p. 181 "It might be…I reply." Letter to Dear Mother August 12, 1924 op. cit.

p. 181 "Donald has told me…something deeper." Letter to Dear Family from Richard Gregg October 4, 1924 Alan Gregg Papers, MS C 190, in the History of Medicine Division, National Library of Medicine Box 2 Richard Gregg Folder.

p. 183 "I'm dining this evening…her line of work." Gregg, E.D.(1965) *The Indians and the nurse*. op. cit. p. 82.

p. 184 "Since the idea…source of that information." Otis, J. (1924) The Indian problem. Washington, D.C.: Government Printing Office Document 149 69th Congress.

p. 185 "My mother…until you try." Elinor D. Gregg interview 1963 op. cit.

p. 185–186 "I had…knuckles." Letter to Commissioner Burke from Elinor D. Gregg October 12, 1924; Letter to Elinor D. Gregg from Commissioner Burke November 8, 1924 BIA Files #80213-24.

p. 186–187 "I had been in…back to Washington, D.C." Letter to Dearest Mother from Elinor July 30, 1925 E. D. Gregg Collection Santa Fe, NM.

p. 187 "I've spent…local services!" Letter to Commissioner Burke from Elinor D. Gregg November 16, 1925 BIA Files #80213-25.

p. 188 "But lying in bed…and teachers." Letter to Dear Mother from Elinor January 20, 1926 E.D. Gregg Collection Santa Fe, NM.

p. 189 "But back in March…cabbages." Letter to Dear Mother from Elinor March 21, 1926 E.D. Gregg Collection Santa Fe, NM.

p. 189 "It helped…a relief!" Letter to Donald (Gregg) from Elinor July 17, 1926 E.D. Gregg Collection Santa Fe, NM.

p. 189–190 "During the past…economic wind." Report to Commissioner Burke from Elinor D. Gregg August 27, 1926 RGFS Records of Bureau of Indian Affairs Records of the Inspection Division Special Agent Files 1907-48 1922-32 Special Agents Box 35 E.D. Gregg File #031 40561-1926 PI 163 entry 949.

A PLACE TO HANG MY HAT

p. 191–192 "I know…let it go." Interview of Mardi Bemis Perry by Edwina McConnell, 1998.

p. 194–195 "I was composing my thoughts…up to date." Letter to Dear Donald from Elinor March 19, 1927 E. D. Gregg Collection Santa Fe, NM.

p. 195–197 "It's hard to say…not just on Burke's watch." FY 1927 Annual Report of the Secretary of the Interior- Commissioner of Indian Affairs Washington, D.C.: United States Government Printing Office p. 251–260; The Institute for Government Research(February, 1928) *The problem of Indian administration*. Baltimore: The Johns Hopkins University Press.

p. 199 "I have not got…United States government." Proceedings of the ANA Biennial Convention 1928 , June 7, 1928 Boston University Dept. of Special Collections E.D. Gregg Papers N-25.

p. 200 "I recall…with them." Letter from E.D. Gregg to Commissioner Burke December 3, 1926; from S. Merritt to E.D, Gregg January 4, 1927; from E.D. Gregg to Commissioner Burke January 27, 1927 RG 75 Special Agent Files 1165-1927 E.D. Gregg File #160.4 Box 35 PI 163 Entry 949.

p. 200 "I returned…estimated at 355,901." Annual Report of the Secretary of the Interior for the year ending June 30, 1928 (1928) Washington, D.C.: United States Government Printing Office p.56-57.

p. 201 "And Mr. Burke…other problems." Kelly, L. (1979) Charles Henry Burke 1921-29 in Kvasnica, R. and H. Viola (Eds)(1979) *Commissioners of Indian Affairs 1824-1977* Lincoln: University of Nebraska Press.

p. 201 "The Senate Subcommittee…use against him." Committee on Indian Affairs (1929) Hearings before a subcommittee of the committee on Indian Affairs United States Senate Seventieth Congress second session ; Part 3 Washington: U.S. Government Printing Office.

JULY 14, 1966 — ALBUQUERQUE AND SANTA FE

p. 206 "This book is…products related to the home." Friedan, B.(1963) *The feminine mystique*. New York: W.W. Norton and Co., Inc.

p. 206 "housework as medium…individuality." Friedan (1963) op. cit. p.213.

p. 207–208 “It’s on page 364…own identity.” Friedan (1963) op. cit. p. 364 Quoted with permission.

AMONG FRIENDS

p. 213 “President Hoover…as one.” Kelly, L. (1979) Charles James Rhoads 1929-33 in Kvasnica R. and H. Viola (Eds) (1979) op. cit. p 263–271.

p. 213 “The fundamental…ward of the government.” Annual Report of the Secretary of the Interior for the fiscal year ending June 30, 1929. (1929) Washington, D. C.: U. S. Government Printing Office p.14.

p. 213 “Problems of health…Federal appropriations.” ibid.

p. 215 “New emphasis…be gentle.” Trachoma and its treatment. Circular #2347 July 27, 1927 RG 75 Circulars 1907-34 Box 10 PI 163 I132 HM 1995.

p. 219 “Although it’s…we had in 1927.” Report of the Board of Indian Commissioners to Secretary of the Interior (1930) Washington D. C.: U.S. Government Printing Office p. 11 note an inconsistency between this official figure in the report and that in Gregg, E.G. (1965) *The Indians and the nurse*. op. cit. p. 89.

p. 221 “One of the fruits…our purview.” Report of the Commissioner of Indian Affairs for the fiscal year ending June 30, 1931 (1931) Washington, D.C.: U. S. Government Printing Office p. 3, 12.

p. 222–223 “Perhaps it’s because…hear from me,” Gregg, E.D.(1965) *The Indians and the nurse*. op. cit. p.137.

p. 223 “There are about…problem there.” Secretary of the Interior (1933) Annual report of the Department of the Interior. Washington, D. C.: U.S. Government Printing Office p. 85.

A NEW DEAL

p. 225–226 “I shall never…demonstration.” Hanlon, M. The sad tale of the Bonus Marchers. Internet *www.worldwar1.com/dbc/bonusm.html* Accessed 4/18/03.

p. 226 “And there are several…open positions. Government Section, Proceedings of the 1934 convention of the American Nurses Association. Boston University Dept. of Special Collections American Nurses Association N8F Box 148.

P. 227 “Brilliant man…as hell.” Letter to Dear Alan from Elinor (Gregg) March 10, 1935 E. D. Gregg Collection Santa Fe, NM.

p. 227 "Two of those…correlation of illness and wellness." Elinor D. Gregg annual report for year ending June 30, 1933 Boston University Dept. of Special Collections E.D. Gregg Papers op. cit.

p. 228 "You see, he's employed…she develops." Annual report of the Commissioner of Indian Affairs for year ending June 30, 1934 Washington, D.C.: U. S. Government Printing Office p. 87.

p. 229 "I was so put out…in their request." Letter to Alan from Elinor (nd) Boston University Dept. of Special Collections E.D. Gregg Papers Op.Cit Box 5 Folder 20.

p. 229–230 "He had me put together…under her care." Memo for Secretary Ickes from Commissioner John Collier January 3, 1934 John Collier Papers 1922-1968 microfilmed from original papers at Yale University; Memo to Commissioner Collier from Elinor D. Gregg December 21, 1933 RG 48 Dept of Interior Office of Secretary Central Classified File 1907-1936 Box 1434.

p. 230 "the main effects…arbitrary supervision of the Indians." Annual report of the Commissioner of Indian Affairs (1934) op. cit.

p. 231 "It seems he'd written…it was a whim." Letter to Commissioner Collier from Haven Emerson M.D. April 18, 1934 RG 75 General Services 725-1938 30648 730-1912 32735 Box 1095; Gregg, E. D.(1965) *The Indians and the nurse*. op. cit. p.150.

p. 232 "One satisfying…is sound." Letter from Commissioner Collier to Representative J. Johnson RG 75 General Services 725-1938 30648 730-1912 32735 Box 1095.

p. 232–233 "Galoshes…freeze up." Gregg, E.D. (1965) *The Indians and the nurse*. op. cit. p.152-168.

p. 234 "Elated…Indian ancestry." Report of the Government Section Proceedings of the American Nurses Association Convention 1936. Boston University Dept. of Special Collections American Nurses Association N8F Box 148; Mountin, J. and J. Townsend (1936) Observations on Indian health problems and facilities. Public Health Bulletin 223 Washington, D.C.: U. S. Treasury Dept. Public Health Service.

p. 235 "Finally, she speaks…I'm from Washington." Interview of Mary Gregg Misch by Edwina McConnell July 10, 1998.

p. 235 "Finally, after all these…make me proud." Secretary of the Interior annual report for the fiscal year ending June 30, 1937 Washington, D.C.: U.S. Government Printing Office p. 234.

JUNE 14 and 15, 1966—ALBUQUERQUE

p. 237 "He's the architect…Southwest." Zimmerman Library. Internet *www.unm.edu/Zimmerman/history.html* accessed 5/20/03.

HOME IS WHERE. . .

p. 245 "The friendly…better halves." Letter to Staff from Elinor D. Gregg January 15, 1939. E. D. Gregg Collection Santa Fe, NM.

p. 246 "Nursing in the…better than I found it." Report of the Government Section American Nurses Association Convention 1938 Boston University Dept. of Special Collections American Nurses Association N8F Box 148; Secretary of the Interior report for the fiscal year ending June 30, 1939 Washington, D.C.: U.S. Government Printing Office p. 48.

p. 246 "Looking at that letter…Please!!" Letter to Elinor Gregg from a nurse in Eufala, January 10, 1939 E.D. Gregg Collection Santa Fe, NM.

p. 247 "If this could be…best in one's life." Letter to dear Miss Gregg from Gertrude in Muscogee December 31, 1938 E.D. Gregg Collection Santa Fe, NM.

p. 247 "I'm sure that every Indian…go too far away." Letter to Dear Miss Gregg from Johnnie (Looney) Archombane January 29, 1939 E.D. Gregg Collection Santa Fe, NM.

p. 248 "Even though…learning experience for me." Letter to Dear Elly and Alan July 31, 1939 Alan Gregg Papers op. cit. Box 2 E.D. Gregg.

p. 248–249 "Sunshine…pep." Letter to Alan and family from Elinor July 31, 1939 Alan Gregg Papers op. cit.

p. 251 "A bit of pride…no lice, either." Letter to Alan and Eleanor from Elinor July 6, 1940 Alan Gregg Papers op. cit.

p. 253–254 "For example…gets me down." Letter to Alan from Elinor October 25, 1941 Alan Gregg Papers op. cit.

p. 254 "A crisp…news of the war." Letter to Faith Mary from EDG January 11, 1942 Alan Gregg Papers op. cit. Box 2.

p. 256–258 "The past three years…also been an education." Interviews (separate) with Michael Cooke January 10, 1998, Stuart Cooke 1998, Harlow Beene January 27, 1998, and William Hudgeons, nd 1998 by Edwina McConnell.

p. 257 "Your mother wrote in April…back for keeps." Letter to Elinor Gregg from Mrs. Cooke April 30, 1944 E.D. Gregg Collection Santa Fe, NM.

DO SOME GOOD

p. 260 “Santa Fe county…live births.” Sullivan, M. (1995) Walking the line: birth control and women’s health at the Santa Fe Maternal Health Center 1937–1970. Unpublished Master’s thesis Albuquerque: University of New Mexico p. xi.

p. 262 “As is my habit…sleep with.” Letter to Alan from Elinor February 27, 1946 Alan Gregg Papers op. cit.

p. 263–264 “You recall…I relate.” Minutes of the Board of Directors of the Maternal Health Center of Santa Fe 1950–1960.

p. 264–265 “But, the call…outpouring of herself.” Letter to My Dear Mrs. Bemis from Boynton Merrill June, 1950 Mardi Bemis Perry Letter Collection Concord, MA.

p 265 “No surprise to me…my things.” Letter to Dearest Emptee-Gee from EDG June 27, 1950 Mardi Bemis Perry Letter Collection Concord, MA.

p. 266–267 “In the two nights…take care of herself.” Letter to Dearest Faith Mary from Elinor August 19, 1950 Mardi Bemis Perry Letter Collection Concord, MA.

p.267–268 ”That valley runs…relaxation, as well.” Letter from Elinor to Faith, John, and Nancy August 14 or 15, 1951. E.D. Gregg Collection Santa Fe, NM.

MORTAL AFTER ALL

p. 289 “I’ve always…when necessary.” Letter to Dear Dr. Green from Elinor Gregg (nd) 1959 Mardi Bemis Perry Letter Collection Concord, MA.

RESOURCES

THIS SECTION CONTAINS THE MOST DIRECTLY relevant of the resource materials consulted in the development of this manuscript beyond those items listed in References.

Archives

Boston University Special Collections, Mugar Memorial Library, Boston University, Boston, MA. Elinor D. Gregg Papers N25, Box 1, Folder 1.

Boston University Special Collections, Mugar Memorial Library, Boston, University, Boston, MA. Elinor Delight Gregg Collection, Box 6, Folder 21

Boston University Special Collections, Mugar Memorial Library, Boston University, Boston, MA. Elinor D. Gregg Papers N25, Box 7, Folder 30.

Harvard University Archives. Pusey Library, Cambridge, MA. Frederick Abbe materials.

Hazel Braugh Records Center, American Red Cross, Falls Church, VA. Elinor Delight Gregg File.

Elinor Delight Gregg Collection. Santa Fe, NM.

National Archives, Washington, DC. Record Group 75, Central Classified Files 1907-1939 Rosebud, 130826-1912-721 to 48327-1935-722.1. File 00-22 Rosebud 721. Box 564.

National Archives, Washington, DC. Record Group 75, Central Classified Files 1907-1939 Rosebud, 130826-1912-721 to 48327-1935-722.1. File 78771-22 Rosebud 721. Box 564.

National Archives, Washington, DC. Record Group 75, Central Classified Files 1907-1939 Rosebud, 130826-1912-721 to 48327-1935-722.1. File 95352-22 Rosebud 721. Box 564.

National Archives, Washington, DC. Record Group 75, Superintendents' Annual Narrative and Statistical Reports from Field Jurisdictions of the Bureau of Indian Affairs, 1907-1938. Microfilm Publication M1011.

National Archives Central Plains Region, Kansas City, MO. Record Group 75, Rosebud Indian Agency, Rosebud, South Dakota, Subject Correspondence 1910-1925 M thru J.A. Rennick Folder Narrative, Box A-434.

National Archives Central Plains Region, Kansas City, MO. Record Group 75, Rosebud Indian Agency, Rosebud, South Dakota, Chronological File 1921-1929, Folder 11-1-22 to 11-15-22 (1 of 2), Box A-502.

National Archives Central Plains Region, Kansas City, MO. Record Group 75, Rosebud Indian Agency, Rosebud, South Dakota, Chronological File 1921-1929, 10-16-1922 to 12-15-1922, Folder 11-16-1922 to 11-30-1922, (1 of 2), Box A-502.

National Archives Central Plains Region, Kansas City, MO. Record Group 75, Rosebud Indian Agency, Rosebud, South Dakota, Chronological File 1921-1929, 2-16-23 to 4-15-12, Folder 3-1-23 to 3-15-23 (1 of 2), Box A-504.

National Archives Central Plains Region, Kansas City, MO. Record Group 75, Rosebud Indian Agency, Rosebud, South Dakota, Chronological File 1921-1929, 2-16-1923 to 4-15-1923, Folder 2-16-1923 to 2-28-1923, 2 of 2, Box A-504.

National Archives Central Plains Region, Kansas City, MO. Record Group 75, Rosebud Indian Agency, Rosebud, South Dakota, Commissioner's Chronological File 1921-1928, 10-1-1921 to 12-31-1922 Folder 11-1-1922 to 12-31-1922, Box 548.

National Archives Central Plains Region, Kansas City, MO. Record Group 75, Rosebud Indian Agency, Rosebud, South Dakota, Commissioner's Chronological File 1921-1928, 1-31-1923 to 12-31-1923, Folder 5-1-1923 to 6-30-1923, Box 549.

National Archives Central Plains Region, Kansas City, MO. Record Group 75, Rosebud Indian Agency, Rosebud, South Dakota, Commissioner's Chronological File 1921-1928, 1-31-1923 to 12-31-1923, Folder 9-1-1923 to 10-31-1923, Box 549.

National Archives Central Plains Region, Kansas City, MO. Record Group 75, Rosebud Indian Agency, Rosebud, South Dakota, Commissioner's File, Chronological 1921-1928, 1-1-1924 to 2-28-1925 Folder 3-1-1924 to 4-30-1924, Box 550.

National Archives, College Park, MD. American Red Cross Historical and W W I Nurse Files 1918-1950. Box 70. NN3-ARC-93-001.

National Archives, College Park, MD. Record Group 120, Records of the American Expeditionary Forces-World War I, Base Hospital #4 continued, Base Hospital #5. File-Air Raid of September 4, 1912, Base Hospital 5, Box 210.

National Archives, College Park, MD. Record Group 120, Records of the American Expeditionary Forces-World War I, Base Hospital #5. File-War Diary, Base Hospital 5, Box 210.

National Archives, College Park, MD. Record Group 120, Records of the American Expeditionary Forces-World War I, Base Hospital #5. File-Historical Data, Base Hospital 5, Box 210.

National Archives, College Park, MD. Record Group 120, Records of the American Expeditionary Forces-World War I, Base Hospital #5 continued. File-Efficiency Reports-Nurses, Base Hospital 5, Box 211.

National Archives, College Park, MD. Record Group 120, Records of the American Expeditionary Forces-World War I, Base Hospital #5 continued. File-Rosters-Personnel, Base Hospital 5, Box 211.

National Archives, College Park, MD. Record Group 120, Records of the American Expeditionary Forces-World War I, Base Hospital #5 continued. File-Hospital Orders-1917, Base Hospital 5, Box 212.

National Archives, College Park, MD. Record Group 120, Records of the American Expeditionary Forces-World War I, Base Hospital #5 continued. File-Hospital Orders-1917, Base Hospital 5, Box 212.

National Archives, College Park, MD. Record Group 120, Records of the American Expeditionary Forces-World War I, Base Hospital #5 continued. File-Special Orders-1918, Base Hospital 5, Box 212.

National Archives, College Park, MD. Record Group 120, Records of the American Expeditionary Forces-World War I, Base Hospital #5 continued. File-Special Orders-1919, Base Hospital 5, Box 212.

National Archives, College Park, MD. Record Group 120, Records of the American Expeditionary Forces-World War I. File-Memoranda 1917, Base Hospital 5, Box 213.

National Archives, College Park, MD. Record Group 120, Records of the American Expeditionary Forces-World War I, Evacuation Hospital #18. File-Nurses, Box 751.

National Archives, College Park, MD. Record Group 120, Records of the American Expeditionary Forces-World War I, Evacuation Hospital #18. File-History, Box 750.

National Archives, College Park, MD. Record Group 120, Records of the American Expeditionary Forces-World War I, Evacuation Hospital #18. File-Returns, ANC, Box 750.

National Archives, College Park, MD. Record Group 120, Records of the American Expeditionary Forces-World War I, Mobile Hospital #6. File-Rosters, Mobile Hospital 6, Box 1318.

National Archives, College Park, MD. Record Group 120, Records of the American Expeditionary Forces-World War I, Mobile Hospital #6. File-Daily Reports-Changes-Personnel, Mobile Hospital 6, Box 1318.

National Archives, College Park, MD. Record Group 120, Records of the American Expeditionary Forces-World War I, Mobile Hospital #6. File-Special Orders, Mobile Hospital 6, Box 1318.

National Archives, College Park, MD. Record Group 120, Records of the American Expeditionary Forces-World War I, Mobile Hospital #6. File-Historical Data, Mobile Hospital #6, Box 1318.

National Archives, College Park, MD. Record Group 120, Records of the American Expeditionary Forces-World War I, Mobile Hospital #6. File-Hospital Orders, Mobile Hospital 6, Box 1318.

National Archives Gift Collection, College Park, MD, Record Group 200, Records of the American Red Cross, 1917-1934, Group 2, 591.1 Army Base Hospital #4-13. Box 577.

National Archives, College Park, MD. Record Group 200, American National Red Cross, File 500.003 Central File 1917-1934 (Group 2), Box 556.

National Archives, College Park, MD. Record Group 200, American National Red Cross, 1917-1934. File 509.21 New Mexico Public Health Nursing Jicarilla Indian Reservation, Box 568.

National Archives, College Park, MD. Record Group 200, American National Red Cross, 1917-1934. File 509.21 South Dakota Public Health Nursing, Rosebud Indian Reservation, Box 571.

National Library of Medicine. History of Medicine Division. Alan Gregg Papers, MS C 190, Box 4.

Mardi Bemis Perry letter collection. Concord, MA.

Alice Bemis Thompson letter collection. South Tamworth, NH.

Books

Adams, D.W. (1995). *Education for extinction—American Indians and the boarding school experience, 1875–1928*. Lawrence, KA: University of Kansas.

A member of the unit. (1919). *The story of U.S. Army Base Hospital No. 5*. Cambridge, MA: The University Press.

Archuleta, M.L., Child, B.J., & Lomawaima, K.T. (2000). *Away from home: American Indian boarding school experiences*. Phoenix, AZ: Heard Museum.

Bial. R. (1999). *Lifeways-The Sioux*. Tarrytown, NY: Benchmark Books.

Bordeaux, L. (1985). The album of native Americans. In *75 years in Mellette county*. (pp.1-8). Mellette County, SD: The Mellette County Historical Society.

Biolsi, T. (1992). *Organizing the Lakota*. Tucson, AZ: The University of Arizona Press.

Brainard, A.(1922). *The evolution of public health nursing*. Philadelphia: Sanders. Reprint edition (1985). New York: Garland Publishing, Inc.

Collier, J.(1947). *The Indians of the Americas.* New York: W.W. Norton and Co.

Collier, J.(1963). *From every zenith.* Denver: Sage Books.

Comandini, A (Ed.). (1936). *I saw them die: Diary and recollections of Shirley Millard.* New York: Harcourt, Brace and Company.

Cushing, H, (1936). *From a surgeon's journal.* Boston: Little, Brown and Company

Deloria, E. C. (1944). *Speaking of Indians*. New York: Friendship Press.

Dock, L.L., Pickett, S.H., Noyes, C.D., Clement, F. F., Fox, E.G., VanMeter, A.R. (Eds). (1922). *History of American Red Cross nursing*. New York: The MacMillan Company.

Fiske, A. (1985). *First fifty years of the Waltham Training School for Nurses*. New York: Garland Publishing, Inc.

Forster, E. (Edited by Sandweiss, M.) (1988). *Denizens of the desert* Albuquerque: UNM Press.

Friedan, B. (1963). *The feminine mystique*. New York: W.W. Norton and Co., Inc.

Gregg, E.D. (1965). *The Indians and the nurse*. Norman, OK: University of Oklahoma Press.

Hallstrom, L., & Kueter, M. (1987). *South Dakota country school days*. Dallas, TX: Taylor Publishing Company.

Hamilton, H.W., & Hamilton, J.T. (1971). *The Sioux of the Rosebud*. Norman, OK: University of Oklahoma Press.

Harrison, H.P. as told to Detzer, K. (1958). *Culture under canvas*. New York: Hastings House.

Hatch, J.P. (Editor-in-chief). (1920). *Concerning Base Hospital No. 5*. Boston: The Barta Press.

Kernodle, P. (1949). *The Red Cross nurse in action 1882-1948*. New York: Harper and Brothers, Publishers

Kvasnicka, R. and H. Viola (Eds) (1979). *The Commissioners of Indian Affairs, 1824–1977*. Lincoln, Nebraska, University of Nebraska Press.

Massachusetts General Hospital Memorial & Historical Volume. (1921). Boston: Griffith-Stillings Press. Used Ireland and Bock.

Meriam, L. (1928). *The problem of Indian administration*. Baltimore, MD: The Johns Hopkins Press.

Nichols, R. (Ed.) (1999). *The American Indian past and present* (5th edition). New York: McGraw-Hill College.

Ninety-eighth Annual Report of the Trustees of the Massachusetts General Hospital-1911. (1912). Boston: The Barta Press.

Parman, D. (1994). *Indians of the American West in the twentieth century*. Bloomington and Indianapolis: Indiana University Press.

Raup, R.(1959). *The Indian health program from 1800–1955*. Washington, D.C.: USDHEW.

Reutter, W. (1962). *Early Dakota days* (1-131), I of II, and (132-263) II of II. White River, SD: Paul and/or Winifred Reutter.

Schmeckebier, L.F. (1927). *The Office of Indian Affairs* (Service Monographs of the United States Government, No. 48). Baltimore, MD: The Johns Hopkins Press.

Sneve, V.D.H. (1993). *The Sioux*. New York: Holiday House.

Staff. (1995). *Through Indian eyes*. Pleasantville, NY: The Reader's Digest Association, Inc.

Sprague, M. R. (1987). *Newport in the Rockies-The life and good times of Colorado Springs*. Athens, OH: Swallow Press/Ohio University Press.

Tapia, J.E. (1997). *Circuit chautauqua*. Jefferson, NC: McFarland & Company, Inc.

Washburn, F.D. (1939). *The Massachusetts General Hospital, Its development, 1900–1935*. Boston: Houghton Mifflin Company.

Worcester, A. (1927). *Nurses and nursing*. Cambridge, MA: Harvard University Press.

Zeiger, S. (1999). *In Uncle Sam's service-Women workers with the American Expeditionary Forces, 1917–1919*. Ithaca, NY: Cornell University Press.

Dissertations

Emmerich. L. (1987). *To respect and love and seek the ways of white women: Field matrons, the Office of Indian Affairs, and civilization policy, 1890-1938*. Doctoral dissertation, University of Maryland.

Pflaum, J, (1996). *Helper woman: A biography of Elinor D. Gregg*. Doctoral dissertation, University of San Diego.

Interviews

All interviews were conducted by Edwina A. McConnell unless otherwise noted.

Harlow Beene, January 27, 1998 Glorieta, NM
F. Gregg Bemis, February 1, 1998 Santa Fe, NM
Margot Bemis Chase, July 9, 1998 Staunton, VA
Kay Chiba, February 4, 1998 Tesuque, NM
Michael Cooke, January 10, 1998 Stoke-on-Trent, England.
Stuart Cooke, January 11, 1998 Stratford-upon-Avon, England.
Lynette Heminway Emery, August 6, 1998 Denver, CO
Alice Ewing, January 30, 1998 Santa Fe, NM
T. Ray Faulkner, June 12, 1999 Steamboat Springs, CO
Joan T. Gilmour, July 17, 1998
Elinor Delight Gregg by John and Margaret (Peg) Rose, 1963, England.
Michael Gregg, March 24, 1998 South Gilford, VT
Peter and Sophie Gregg, March 23, 1999 Vancouver, BC, Canada
Richard (Sandy) Gregg, June 22, 1998
William Hudgeons, nd
Larry Lunt, January 10, 2000
Judy, Bridget and Liz Matthews, March 18, 1998 Bath, England (interview includes a letter delivered at that interview from Gill Bowron)
Barbara Meem, January 29, 1998 Santa Fe, NM
Deborah T. Meem, June 23, 1998 Cincinnati, OH
Mary Gregg Misch, 1998, Arlington, Virginia.
Victoria Thompson Murphy, January 30, 1998 Santa Fe, NM
Lorraine Wood Nichols, March 16, 1998 London, England
George O'Bryan, January 11, 1998 Santa Fe, NM
Pam O'Bryan, March 18, 1998 Bath, England
Annette Richards Parret, August 12, 1998 Silver City, NM
Arthur Perry, Sr., July 17, 1998
Arthur Perry, Jr. July 17, 1998
Catherine Rayne, January 21, 1999 (by phone) Santa Fe, NM
Bruce H. Rolstad, February 2, 1998 Santa Fe, NM
Ford Ruthling February 3, 1998 Santa Fe, NM
Verda Sloman, March 3, 1998 Hudson, FL
Rebekah Taft, January 29, 1999 Colorado Springs, CO
Kate Thompson, March 30, 1998 South Tamworth, NH
Ted Thompson, March 30, 1998 South Tamworth, NH
Judge Jack Watson, February 3, 1998 Santa Fe, NM

Fred Wilson, April 6, 1998 Brookville, PA
Nancy Meem Wirth, January 28-29, 1998 Santa Fe, NM
Helen Wood, March 13, 1999 San Jose, CA
Rachel Wood, March 22, 1998 Olympia, WA

Journal Articles

Allison, G. (1919). Some experiences in active service-France (Part III). *AJN* 19(6) p. 430–434.

Allison, G. (1919). Some experiences in active service-France (Part IV) *AJN* 19(7) 513–517.

Allison, G, (1919). what the war has taught us about nursing education. *AJN* 19(11) p. 834–839.

Anderson, I. (1920). Mobile Hospital No. 1 in France. *AJN* 20(2) p. 124–126.

Babb, S. (1931). Public health nursing in the Indian Service. *Public Health Nurse* Vol. 23, p. 539–541.

Becker, L. (1990). To be one of the boys: Aftershocks of the World War I nursing experience. *Advances in Nursing Science* 12(4) p. 32–43.

Butler, R. (1963, February). The life review: An interpretation of reminiscence in the aged. *Psychiatry* 26, p. 65–76.

Faddis, H. (1937). Experiments in solving the staffing problem. *AJN* 37(9) p. 991–993.

Gregg, E. (1925). The nursing service of the Indian Bureau. *AJN* 25(8) p. 643–645.

Gregg, E. (1926). Public health nursing in the Indian Service. *Public Health Nurse* Vol. 18 p. 11–14.

Gregg, E. (1928). Work of the US Indian Bureau. *Public Health Nurse* Vol. 20 p. 17.

Gregg, E. (1929). Review of *The Problem of Indian Administration. Public Health Nurse* Vol. 21 p. 57.

Gregg, E. (1936). A federal nursing service above the Arctic Circle. *AJN* 36(2) p. 128–134.

Gregg, E. (1939). The government hires a nurse. *AJN* 39(5) p. 524–528.

Haight, B. (1991). Reminiscing: the state of the art as a basis for practice. *International Journal of Aging and Human Development.* 33(1) 1-32.

McMahon, A. & Rhudick, P.J. (1964). Reminiscing: adaptational significance in the aged. *Archives of General Psychiatry* 10 (May, 1964) p 292–298

Molinari, V and R. Reichlin (1985). Life review reminiscence in the elderly: A review of the literature. *International Journal of Aging and Human Development.* 20(2) p. 81–92.

Staff (1936). Study program for board and committee members. *Public Health Nurse* 28 p. 814–819.

Staff (1937). Carrying on for Jane Delano. *AJN* 37(7) p. 737–740.

Staff (1937). The federal government nursing services. *AJN* 37(11) p. 1239–1242.

Staff (1939). News about nursing: Miss Gregg resigns from the Indian Service. *AJN* 39(1) p. 84.

Staff (1970). Obituary: Elinor D. Gregg. *AJN* 70(6) p. 1327.

Stewart, I. (1917). Testing the nursing spirit. *AJN* 17(8) p. 707–711.

Letters

Charles H. Burke to W. Frank Persons, March 25, 1922. National Archives, College Park, MD. Record Group 200 American National Red Cross. File 500.003. Central Files 1917-1934 (Group 2). Box 556.

Charles H. Burke to James H. McGregor, August 21, 1922, National Archives, Washington, DC. Record Group 75, Central Classified Files 1907-1939 Rosebud, 130826-1912-721 to 48327-1935-722.1. File 78771-22 Rosebud 721. Box 564.

Charles H. Burke to J. H. McGregor, October 5, 1922, National Archives, Washington, DC. Record Group 75, Central Classified Files 1907-1939 Rosebud, 130826-1912-721 to 48327-1935-722.1. File 78771-22 Rosebud 721. Box 564.

Elizabeth G. Fox to Florence Patterson, July 19, 1922. National Archives, College Park, MD. American Red Cross Historical and W W I Nurse Files 1918-1950. Box 70. NN3-ARC-93-001.

E. D. Gregg letter to Alice Bemis, November 15, 1922. From the Alice Bemis Thompson letter collection. K. Thompson, South Tamworth, NH

Elinor D. Gregg to Miss Clara D. Noyes, Red Cross Headquarters, April 2, 1919. Hazel Braugh Records Center, American Red Cross, Falls Church, VA. Elinor Delight Gregg File.

James H. McGregor to Charles H. Burke, September 16, 1922, National Archives, Washington, DC. Record Group 75, Central Classified Files 1907-1939 Rosebud, 130826-1912-721 to 48327-1935-722.1. File 78771-22 Rosebud 721. Box 564.

James H. McGregor to Commissioner of Indian Affairs. November 4, 1922. National Archives Central Plains Region, Kansas City, MO. Record Group 75, Rosebud Indian Agency, Rosebud, South Dakota, Commissioner's Chronological File 1921-1928, 10-1-1921 to 12-31-1922 Folder 11-1-1922 to 12-31-1922, Box 548.

James H. McGregor to All Field Matrons, November 8, 1922, National Archives Central Plains Region, Kansas City, MO. Record Group 75, Rosebud Indian Agency, Rosebud, South Dakota, Chronological File 1921-1929, 10-16-1922 to 1-15-1922, Folder 11-1-1922 to 11-15-1922, 1 of 2, Box A-502.

James H. McGregor to the Farmers, November 8, 1922, National Archives Central Plains Region, Kansas City, MO. Record Group 75, Rosebud Indian Agency, Rosebud, South Dakota, Chronological File 1921-1929, 10-16-1922 to 12-15-1922, Folder 11-1-1922 to 11-15-1922, 1 of 2, Box A-502.

James H. McGregor to James R. Holsclaw, November 8, 1922. National Archives Central Plains Region, Kansas City, MO. Record Group 75, Rosebud Indian Agency, Rosebud, South Dakota, Chronological File 1921-1929, 10-16-1922 to 12-15-1922, Folder 11-1-1922 to 11-15-1922, 1 of 2, Box A-502.

James H. McGregor to W.E. Wingfield. November 14, 1922. National Archives Central Plains Region, Kansas City, MO. Record Group 75, Rosebud Indian Agency, Rosebud, South Dakota, Chronological File 1921-1929, 10-16-1922 to 12-15-1922, Folder 11-1-1922 to 11-15-1922, 1 of 2, Box A-502.

James H. McGregor to James A. Sturdevant. November 14, 1922. National Archives Central Plains Region, Kansas City, MO. Record Group 75, Rosebud Indian Agency, Rosebud, South Dakota, Chronological File 1921-1929, Folder 11-1-1922 to 11-15-1922, 1 of 2, Box A-502.

James H. McGregor to Commissioner of Indian Affairs, November 16, 1922, National Archives Central Plains Region, Kansas City, MO. Record Group 75, Rosebud Indian Agency, Rosebud, South Dakota, Commissioner's Chronological File 1921-1928, 10-1-1921 to 12-31-1922 Folder 11-1-1922 to 12-31-1922, Box 548.

James H. McGregor to Commissioner of Indian Affairs, November 25, 1922, National Archives Central Plains Region, Kansas City, MO. Record Group 75, Rosebud Indian Agency, Rosebud, South Dakota, Commissioner's Chronological File 1921-1928, 10-1-1921 to 12-31-1922 Folder 11-1-1921 to 12-31-1922, Box 548.

James H. McGregor to the Commissioner of Indian Affairs, November 27, 1922. National Archives Central Plains Region, Kansas City, Mo. Record Group 75, Rosebud Indian Agency, Rosebud, South Dakota, Commissioner's Chronological File 1921-1928, 10-1-1921 to 12-31-1922, Folder 11-1-1922 to 12-31-1922, Box 548.

James H. McGregor to William P. Marshall, November 27, 1922, National Archives Central Plains Region, Kansas City, MO. Record Group 75, Rosebud Indian Agency, Rosebud, South Dakota, Chronological File 1921-1929, 10-16-1922 to 12-15-1922. Folder 11-16-1922 to 11-30-1922, 1 of 2, Box A-502.

James H. McGregor to all district farmers, November 27, 1922, National Archives Central Plains Region, Kansas City, MO. Record Group 75, Rosebud Indian Agency, Rosebud, South Dakota, Chronological File 1921-1929, 10-16-1922 to 12-15-1922, Folder 11-16-1922 to 11-30-1922, 1 of 2, Box A-502.

James H. McGregor to Commissioner of Indian Affairs, November 28, 1922, National Archives, Washington, DC. Record Group 75, Central Classified Files 1907-1939 Rosebud, 130826-1912-721 to 48327-1935-722.1. File 95352-22 Rosebud 721. Box 564.

James H. McGregor to Charles H. Burke, December 7, 1922, National Archives Central Plains Region, Kansas City, MO. Record Group 75, Rosebud Indian Agency, Rosebud, South Dakota, Commissioner's Chronological File 1921-1928, 10-1-1921 to 12-31-1922, Folder 11-1-1922 to 12-31-1922, Box 548.

James H. McGregor to Mr. William Spotted Tail, February 17, 1923, National Archives Central Plains Region, Kansas City, MO. Record Group 75, Rosebud Indian Agency, Rosebud, South Dakota, Chronological File 1921-1929, 2-16-1923 to 4-15-1923, Folder 2-16-1923 to 2-28-1923, 2 of 2, Box A-504.

James H. McGregor to Charles H. Burke, April 23, 1924, National Archives Central Plains Region, Kansas City, MO. Record Group 75, Commissioner's Chronological File 1921-1928, 1-1-1924 to 2-28-1924 Folder 3-1-1924 to 4-30-1924, Box 550.

James H. McGregor to Charles H. Burke, May 28, 1923, National Archives Central Plains Region, Kansas City, MO. Record Group 75, Rosebud Indian Agency, Rosebud, South Dakota, Commissioner's Chronological File 1921-1928, 1-31-1923 to 12-31-1923, Folder 5-1-1923 to 6-30-1923, Box 549.

James H. McGregor to Charles H. Burke, August 6, 1923, National Archives Central Plains Region, Kansas City, MO. Record Group 75, Commissioner's Chronological File 1921-1928, 1-31-1923 to 12-31-1923 Folder 7-1-1923 to 8-31-1923, Box 549.

James H. McGregor to Charles H. Burke, September 7, 1923, National Archives Central Plains Region, Kansas City, MO. Record Group 75, Rosebud Indian Agency, Rosebud, South Dakota, Commissioner's Chronological File 1921-1928, 1-31-1923 to 12-31-1923, Folder 9-1-1923 to 10-31-1923, Box 549.

E.B. Meritt to James H. McGregor, October 17, 1922, National Archives, Washington, DC. Record Group 75, Central Classified Files 1907-1939 Rosebud, 130826-1912-721 to 48327-1935-722.1. File 00-22 Rosebud 721. Box 564.

Robert U. Patterson to Chief Surgeon, A.E.F., Paris, France, September 9, 1917, National Archives, College Park, MD. Record Group 120, Records of the American Expeditionary Forces-World War I, Base Hospital #4 continued, Base Hospital #5. File Air Raid of September 4, 1917, Base Hospital 5, Box 210.

James L. Rieser to Walter Davidson, June 28, 1922. National Archives, College Park, MD. Record Group 200 American National Red Cross. File 500.003. Central Files 1917-1934 (Group 2). Box 556.

Magazines

Corey, H. (1923). He carries the white man's burden. *Colliers* 71 : May 12, 1923.

Gladwell, M. (1997). The dead zone. *The New Yorker,*73 (29): 52-65.

Miller, M.H. (1963). Chautauqua and the Wisconsin idea. *Wisconsin Academy of Sciences, Arts and Letters*, 52, 159-168.

Noyes, C.D. (1919). Trailing our troubadours of health. *The Red Cross Bulletin,* III(31), p. 5.

Staff. (1919). Chautauqua nurses hold preliminary conference at headquarters. *The Red Cross Bulletin*, III(22), p. 5.

Staff (1922). Indian health survey a unique service plan. *The Red Cross Courier* 1(31) p. 1.

Staff. (1922). Editors say: Survey of Indians. *The Red Cross Courier* 1(36) p. 4.

Staff. (1922). Health works among Indians expanding. *The Red Cross Courier* 1(49) p. 2.

Staff. (1923). Prepare S.D. Indians for nursing service. *The Red Cross Courier* 2(2) p. 11.

Staff. (1923). Indians 50 per cent over last roll call. *The Red Cross Courier* 1(3) p. 10.

Staff. (1923). Indian "sitters" the problem in reservation work. *The Red Cross Courier*. 2(5) p. 8.

Staff. (1923). Blackfeet Indian children acclaim Juniors' project. *The Red Cross Courier* 2(9) p. 2.

Staff. (1923). Health conditions among Indians now improving. *The Red Cross Courier* 2(9) p. 8.

Staff. (1923). Handy summary of 1923 programs of the Red Cross. *The Red Cross Courier* 2(12) p. 6.

Staff. (1923). Plan step for solution of American Indian problem. *The Red Cross Courier* 2(19) p. 5.

Staff. (1923). Delano nurses carry light to dark places; Heads of Red Cross and Federal nursing services. *The Red Cross Courier* 2(26) p. 12.

Staff. (1923). Red Cross nurses consolidate public health work. *The Red Cross Courier* 2(30) p. 8.

Staff (1923). Photograph—An Indian motherhood class. *The Red Cross Courier* 2(33) p.1.

Staff (1923). Heads Indian Bureau public health nursing. *The Red Cross Courier* 13(36) p. 1,3,8.

Staff (1927). Rosebud reveals the responsiveness of the Indians. *The Red Cross Courier* 6(5) p. 16.

Upjohn, A. (1925). Intimate views among the Indians of Rosebud. *The Red Cross Courier* 4(24) p. 12.

Work, H. (1924). Our American Indians. *Saturday Evening Post* 196: May 31, 1924.

Miscellaneous

Buechel Memorial Lakota Museum 2000 Calendar. St. Francis Indian Mission, St. Francis, South Dakota.

College of Nursing. (Accessed 2 June 2003) Introduction http://www.consg/Prospective_Splash.html.

Constitution and by-laws of the motherhood league of the Rosebud Reservation, Boston University Special Collections. Elinor D. Gregg Papers N25, Box 7, Folder 30. Mugar Memorial Library, Boston University, Boston, MA.

Gregg family biosketches from Michael Gregg and other Gregg family members.

Keohane, S. (Accessed 17 May 2002). The reservation boarding school system in the United States, 1870–1928. http://www.twofrog.com/rezsch.html.

Marr, C.J. (Accessed 17 May 2002). Assimilation through education: Indian boarding schools in the Pacific Northwest. http://content.lib.washington.edu/aipnwand.

Schultz. S. (Accessed 8 June 2003) American History Lecture 18 http://www.wisc.edu/hist102/lecture/Lecture18.html.

Surviving the Dustbowl. (Accessed 3 September 2003) http://www.pbs.org/WGBH/amex/dustbowl/peopleevents/PandeAMEX05.html.

Newspapers

Burke speech continued. (1922, 16 November). *Todd County Tribune,* pp. 2–3.

County correspondence by our steady writers. (1921, 26 May). *Todd County Tribune,* p.1.

County correspondence by our steady writers. (1921, 23 June). *Todd County Tribune,* p.1.

County correspondence by our steady writers. (1921, 25 August). *Todd County Tribune,* p.1.

County correspondence by our steady writers. (1922, 22 June). *Todd County Tribune,* p.1.

County correspondence by our steady writers. (1922, 21 September). *Todd County Tribune*, p.1.

County correspondence by our steady writers. (1922, 9 November). *Todd County Tribune,* p.1.

County correspondence by our steady writers. (1922, 16 November). *Todd County Tribune,* p.1.

County correspondence by our steady writers. (1922, 23 November). *Todd County Tribune,* p.1.

County correspondence by our steady writers. (1922, December 7). *Tribune Todd County*, p. 1.

County correspondence by our steady writers. (1922, 21 December). *Todd County Tribune*, p. 1.

County correspondence by our steady writers. (1923, 11 January). *Todd County Tribune*, p.1.

County correspondence by our steady writers. (1923, 18 January). *Todd County Tribune*, p.1.

County correspondence by our steady writers. (1923, 1 February). *Todd County Tribune*, p.1.

County correspondence by our steady writers. (1923, 22 February). *Todd County Tribune*, p. 1.

County correspondence by our steady writers. (1923, 11 March). *Todd County Tribune*, p.1.

County correspondence by our steady writers. (1923, 12 April). *Todd County Tribune*, p.1.

County correspondence by our steady writers. (1923, 24 May). *Todd County Tribune*, p.1.

County correspondence by our steady writers. (1923, 18 October). *Todd County Tribune*, p.1.

County correspondence by our steady writers. (1923, 15 November). *Todd County Tribune*, p.1.

Government spending $100,000 at Indian school. (1921, 26 May). *Todd County Tribune,* p.1.

Gregg, E. (1930, 14 March). Combating Indian practices in caring for ailing. *The United States Daily*. p. 14 Boston University Department of Special Collections E.D. Gregg Papers N25 Box 5 Folder 23.

Indian health survey a unique service plan. (1922 August). *Red Cross Courier*, pp. 1-2.

James H. McGregor to quit Rosebud Agency for Oregon post. (1926, 11 February). *Todd County Tribune,* p. 1.

Miller, H. (1934, 18 June). Nurse supervisor hopes to see Indians plan own health work. *The Washington Post.*

Staff. (1919, 12 June). Chautauqua is very popular. *The Goodland [Kansas] Republic, 33*(46), p. 1.

Staff. (1919, 13 June). Red Cross nurse is coming here. *Kiowa County* [Colorado] *Press*, pp. 5.

Staff. (1919, 19 June). A very successful Chautauqua. *Cheyenne County [Colorado] News*, p. 1.

Staff. (1919, 20 June). Chautauqua will end this evening. *Bent County [Colorado] Democrat*, p. 1.

Staff. (1919, 20 June). Eads Chautauqua is a huge success and well attended. *Kiowa County [Colorado] Press*, p.1.

Staff. (1919, 15 August). Red Cross nurse is coming here. *Gresham* [Nebraska] *Gazette, (25)*18, pp. 8.

Staff. (1919, 17 August). New England girls start on tour of the nation. *Boston Sunday Herald,(*48). p. D10.

Staff. (1919, 21 August). The Chautauqua. *Crofton* [Nebraska] *Journal*, p 7.

Staff. (1919, 21 August). Chautauqua closed Sunday. *Winside Tribune*, p. 1.

Staff. (1919, 28 August). Chautauqua is past. *Fillmore County News*, p.1.

Staff. (1919, 13 June). Red Cross nurse is coming here. *Kiowa County* [Colorado] *Press*, pp. 5.

Staff. (1932, 28 January). US begins survey to guard health of Seminole Indians. *The Florida Times* [Jacksonville] Boston University Department of Special Collections E.D. Gregg Papers N25 Box 5 folder 23.

Pamphlets

An account of the dedicatory ceremonies in connection with the Base Hospital No. 5 Memorial. (1928). Boston: D.B. Updike, The Merryound Press.

Personal Communication

The Reverend Webster Two Hawk. Pierre, SD, November 2000.

Reports

Annual Narrative and Statistical Reports from Field Jurisdictions of the Bureau of Indian Affairs, 1907-1938. (1922). National Archives, Washington, DC. Record Group 75, Superintendents' Microfilm Publication M1011, Roll 118.

Annual Narrative and Statistical Reports from Field Jurisdictions of the Bureau of Indian Affairs, 1907-1938. (1923). National Archives, Washington, DC. Record Group 75, Superintendents' Microfilm Publication M1011, Roll 118.

Board of Indian Commissioners. (1921). Fifty-second annual report of the Board of Indian Commissioners to the Secretary of the Interior. Washington, DC: Government Printing Office.

Board of Indian Commissioners. (1922). Fifty-third annual report of the Board of Indian Commissioners to the Secretary of the Interior. Washington, DC: Government Printing Office.

Board of Indian Commissioners. (1928). Report of the Board of Indian Commissioners to the Secretary of the Interior. Washington, DC: Government Printing Office.

Commissioner of Indian Affairs. (1919). Report of the Commissioner of Indian Affairs to the Secretary of the Interior. Washington, DC: Government Printing Office.

Commissioner of Indian Affairs. (1922). Report of the Commissioner of Indian Affairs to the Secretary of the Interior. Washington, DC: Government Printing Office.

Conference on possible cooperation of Red Cross with the government Bureau of Indian Affairs in providing public health nurses for Indian reservations—April 11, 1922. Present: Commission Burke and two assistants, Miss Fox and Miss Holmes. National Archives, College Park, MD. Record Group 200 American National Red Cross. File 500.003. Central Files 1917-1934 (Group 2). Box 556.

Gregg, E.D. (1922). Report for November 15th-30th, National Archives, College Park, MD. Record Group 200, American National Red Cross, 1917-1934. File 509.21 South Dakota Public Health Nursing, Rosebud Indian Reservation, Box 571.

Gregg, E.D. (1922). Report for December 1922, National Archives, College Park, MD. Record Group 200, American National Red Cross, 1917-1934. File 509.21 South Dakota Public Health Nursing, Rosebud Indian Reservation, Box 571.

Gregg, E.D.(1923). An analysis of first year of work to establish a public health nursing service on Rosebud Reservation, National Archives, College Park, MD. Record Group 200, American National Red Cross, 1917-1934. File 509.21 South Dakota Public Health Nursing, Rosebud Indian Reservation, Box 571.

Gregg, E.D.(1923). Report for January 1923. Rosebud Reservation. Record Group 200, American National Red Cross, 1917-1934. File 509.21 South Dakota Public Health Nursing, Rosebud Indian Reservation, Box 571.

Gregg, E.D (1923). Report for February 1923. Record Group 200, American National Red Cross, 1917-1934. File 509.21 South Dakota Public Health Nursing, Rosebud Indian Reservation, Box 571.

Gregg, E.D (1923). Report for March 1923. Boston University Special Collections. Mugar Memorial Library, Boston University, Boston, MA. Elinor D. Gregg Papers N25, Box 1, Folder 1.

McArdle, E.C. (1922). Report on Rosebud Reservation, South Dakota, National Archives, College Park, MD. Record Group 200, American National Red Cross, 1917-1934. File 509.21 South Dakota Public Health Nursing, Rosebud Indian Reservation, Box 571.

No author and no title. Positions and salaries 1924. National Archives Central Plains Region, Kansas City, MO. Record Group 75, Rosebud Indian Agency, Rosebud, South Dakota, Commissioner's Chronological File 1921-1928, 1-1-1924 to 2-28-1925 Folder 3-1-1924 to 4-30-1924, Box 550.

Survey of conditions of the Indians in the United States- Hearings before a subcommittee of the committee on Indian affairs United States Senate, Seventieth Congress (1929). Washington, DC: U.S. government Printing Office.

The Indian problem-resolution of the Committee of One Hundred appointed by the Secretary of the Interior and a review of the Indian problem. (1924). 68th Congress, 1st Session. House of Representatives. Document No. 149. Presented by Mr. Snyder. Washington, DC: Government Printing Office.

The Waltham Training School for Nurses. (1912). Twenty-seventh annual report. Waltham, MA: E.L. Barry.

Unpublished Manuscript

Gregg, J.B. (1920). *A happy life-time.* Colliston Road, Brookline, MA. From the Alan Gregg Paper, MS C 190, in the History of Medicine Division, National Library of Medicine, Bethesda, MD., Box 4.

ABOUT THE AUTHORS

Edwina McConnell, a nurse consultant and nurse educator, maintained a career-long interest in the life of Elinor D. Gregg, R.N., the figure about whose life this book revolves. McConnell first studied Gregg as a figure in nursing history during her undergraduate education. Fascinated by the spirit and character of this pioneering nurse, she collected primary and secondary research materials toward a biography for many years. The biography of Elinor Gregg was the focus of her work at the time of her death in 2002.

Teddy Jones is a nurse practitioner and nurse educator whose initial collaboration in this project was limited to critical reading of the developing manuscript and encouragement for her friend and colleague, McConnell. She also made a promise to complete the work should anything happen to prevent McConnell from doing so. Jones' participation as co-author began when McConnell bequeathed her the research material and the partial manuscript. Or perhaps it began when she made that promise.

© Kippra Hopper, 2004

Both McConnell (BSN, MSN, Ph.D.) and Jones (BSN, MSN, Ph.D.) have numerous publications in nursing and health care. This is their first work of biographical fiction.